Family Finance

Preparing for

the upturn

Colm Rapple

With many thanks to the efficient and informed sub-editors Nuala and Simone and to all who have helped over the years with information and advice.

ISBN: 978-0-9553982-3-0

Published by Squirrel Press

Cover designed by Karen Doyle

Cartoon by John Brennan

Printed in Ireland by
Brunswick Press, Dublin

Contents

1. Preparing for the upturn 5
2. Managing your cash flows 13
   Flexible friends if used sensibly 20
   Managing holiday finances 32
3. Maximising the return on your savings 40
   Secure investments 47
   Direct stock market investment 54
   Investment funds 57
   Investing a lump sum — some of the options . . 63
4. Life insurance — buying peace of mind 74
5. Borrowing — the benefits often outweigh the costs . . . 93
   Tackling debt problems. 108
6. Putting a roof over your head 111
   State housing grants 126
   Mortgage tax relief. 130
7. Inheritance, probate and making a will 133
8. Enforcing your rights as a worker and citizen. 142
9. Insuring yourself against the loss of home/possessions . 160
10. Planning for financial security in retirement 171
11. Using your rights as a consumer 188
12. Social Welfare benefits, who qualifies for what?. . . . 207
13. Money saving guide to the tax system 225
    Budget changes 2010 226
    PAYE guide 229
    Self-employed income 258
    Rental income. 263
    Motor vehicles. 265
    Working outside Ireland 266
    Capital Gains Tax 269
    Inheritance and gift taxes. 273
14. Some ways to reduce your tax liability 278
    Employing your spouse and/or child 279
    Tax and marriage. 283
    Share incentives 288
    Tax breaks for relatives and carers 298
Your guide to a quick and easy money makeover 301
    Worksheets for your makeover. 318
Appendix 1. Summary of tax rates. 330
Appendix 2. Civil service mileage rates 338
Appendix 3. Social welfare benefits 340
Index   342

1 Planning for the recovery

*Wealth consists not in having great possessions
but in having few wants — Epicurus*

Recessions were supposed to be a thing of the past, a spectre with which to to frighten young children but which would never again be a real threat to people's wealth or welfare. That was what business and financial power brokers liked to claim. But they were wrong. We may have learnt enough about managing economies to help lessen the impact of economic downturns but not enough to prevent them. That has been very clear over the last year or two. There is much still to be learnt about economic management. There will be other recessions, but the current one will end. Indeed the economic upturn has already started in some of the major economies and the Irish economy is expected to start growing again during the second half of 2010. It's time to start preparing for the upturn.

Economic output during 2010 is likely to be almost back to 2005 levels but we didn't consider ourselves particularly poor back then. Average incomes might be back to 2005 levels but, of course, national income isn't divided in the same way as it was then. The division is less equitable if only

■ There is no single way to balance a household budget. It depends on the individual as much as it depends on circumstances. Some can get by with penny-pinching over a wide range of spending items. Others feel happier zoning in on a few big items of spending and targeting those. The following are a few ideas.

■ **Reduce your mortgage repayments**

Mortgage repayments have to be met but there are ways of reducing the burden. It may be possible to extend the term of the loan, switch to an interest-only mortgage or, in exceptional cases, it may be possible to postpone repayments entirely and have the interest rolled up and added to the loan. Borrowers who find it difficult to meet mortgage repayments or rent may qualify for State assistance provided they are in receipt of a social welfare or HSE benefit. Application for this supplementary benefit is made to the Community Welfare Officer at the local HSE office.

If you are still in a job and your mortgage is well covered by the value of your property, you are the kind of borrower that many lenders are looking for. You may be able to negotiate a cut in your interest rate or switch to a cheaper option. See page 113.

■ **Family Income Supplement**

Family Income Supplement is a social welfare benefit payable to people on low incomes. To be eligible, you need to work at least 19 hours a week and have dependent children. So it can be of interest to those on short-time or who are considering whether some part-time work is a worthwhile option. See page 215 for full details.

■ **Get a tax rebate**

Claiming a tax rebate can provide a once-off income boost. See page 249.

■ **Shop around for house and car insurance**

Increased competition has made it essential to shop around for the best deal. Substantial savings can be made without suffering any loss of cover. It's best to do the legwork yourself on the internet or telephone. Don't assume that a renewal quote is the best deal available from your insurer. You're likely to be offered a better deal by pretending to be a new customer.

■ **Cancel unnecessary and bad value policies**

You need house insurance. The impact of losing your home, however small the risk of it actually happening, is too great to take even when money is tight. But you could survive losing your mobile phone or your credit card. So do you need insurance? See page 166.

■ **Cancel your cable TV**

All the BBC and ITV channels are free if you set up your own satellite dish. You'll also get Channel 4, Sky News, CNN, Film 4 and hundreds of other channels. You'll need a traditional aerial to get Irish programmes but a set-top one may well do. So do you need your cable TV? Yes, for sports and a wide range of film channels but otherwise, possibly not.

■ **Switch credit cards**

If you are not able to clear off your credit card debt, you can certainly save money by making use of the introductory offers available from other card providers. You have to qualify for the new card by being viewed as a good credit risk so it's not an option for the unemployed. But if you do qualify, you can save up to six months interest on your debt. But don't fall for a short-term gain at the expense of a longer term cost in the form of higher rates. Recognise it as only a quick fix, with a need for a more lasting repair as soon as possible.

■ **Maximise your credit**

Businesses are very good at delaying the payment of bills as long as possible and it makes sense for individuals faced with financial difficulties to do likewise. Even if you have the cash to pay the bill, it's better in your bank than in someone elses. It improves your cash flow. It's like getting a once-off boost to income. Even if you do not want to be permanently a month in arrears with your bills, by abolishing all your standing order and direct debits you gain more control over your finances and provide yourself with the ability to delay the payment of a bill when money is tight. But unless you are well organised you could run into trouble. So take care.

■ **Reduce your motoring costs**

The average household spends 13% of its income on personal transport and many families spend much more than the average. So even relatively small cutbacks can yield significant cash savings. Motoring offers the most scope. The biggest saving can be achieved by buying second hand and/or holding onto your car for another year or two. But you can also save money by driving sensibly. Fuel consumption is very high on short runs so avoid them if you can. Walking is good for you.

■ **Cut your heating costs**

Significant savings are possible in home heating bills without any noticeable deterioration in comfort levels. Heating and light account for about 4% of the average household budget, far more than that for many of low incomes, so the savings from even a small cut back can be significant. You should be able to claw back the impact of the Carbon Tax by improving the insulation of your home and lowering your central heating thermostat by a degree or two. There are grants available.

because there are now far more people out of work - over 400,000 either fully or partially unemployed. Among these are the people who have suffered most from the recession.

But the impact of the recession hasn't been confined to incomes. There has also been a sharp fall in asset values. The value of what we own has gone down: property, shares and pension funds. For many, that fall is reflected solely in figures on a sheet of paper and will only be translated into actual cash losses if, and when, the asset is sold. The losses are real enough. If your house has fallen in value, you certainly feel less wealthy. The feelings will be even more acute if your savings and investments have fallen in value and even more acute still if it's your pension fund.

Financial objectives are likely to be the same at any time in the financial cycle. Most people want to maximise both their income and the value of their assets. The objectives may remain the same but not the best ways of pursuing them. Attitudes to risk also change as confidence ebbs and flows.

So how best to prepare for the upturn while surviving the downturn? It's all a matter of planning. There are no single correct answers that apply to all people in all circumstances. But you stand a better chance of making the best decisions if you first take the time to set objectives and gather as much information as you can. You need to review your personal finances in as much detail as you can.

The Money Makeover section starting on page 301 outlines how you should go about setting goals, assessing where you are and how best to set a route to where you want to be. It's worth going through in some detail and repeating the exercise as frequently as possible as the financial climate and your circumstances changes.

Short-term objectives, in particular, may change.

- You may want to keep more money easily accessible in emergency funds during the downturn but less as the upturn takes hold.

- It may be sensible to postpone funding your pension when money is short.

- There may be scope to freeze or even dispense with some life insurance policies. Care is obviously needed but it's worthwhile reviewing your needs and cover.

Budgeting

Knowing exactly where your money is coming from and how it is spent is essential to your decision making whether or not you have taken a drop in income. It's good business practice to use recessions to cut out the fat that has accumulated during good years to create a slimmer, more efficient organisation. A similar approach can be taken with your personal finances. It can ease the problem of surviving the downturn and/or create additional savings that can be used to capitalise on investment or buy opportunities that arise during the upturn. You'll find suggestions on how to save or make money throughout the book.

Managing your assets

Asset values have fallen sharply during the recession and most will rise in value during the upturn. Money can be made by selling and buying at the right time. Bank of Ireland shares were selling at over €18 before the downturn. They fell to a low of 12c during the financial crisis, then recovered to €3.50, before falling again. That was a thirtyfold increase on that low. Fortunes could have been made on those swings. Maybe they were but nobody can get it right all of the time. Indeed, getting it right at any time is more a matter of luck than expertise. As a result many are content to hold onto their assets.

The best approach, of course, lies somewhere in between wheeling and dealing of the speculator and the "do nothing" approach of the conservative. Doing nothing may be the right approach is some circumstances. It may be the only thing to do with regard to your home. But it's very wrong to hold onto an asset simply, or mainly, because you don't want to crystallise a loss.

If you like your home and have no inclination to move, then its market value is of little concern, even if it has fallen to less than you actually paid for it or is worth less than the outstanding mortgage. Difficulties might arise if you have to sell, or if, because of a drop in income you find it hard to meet the repayments. But if you are not in that position, then there is little point in worrying about it.

Okay, so it's annoying to realise that your new neighbour has now bought an identical house to yours at a lower price than you paid. But there is nothing you can do about it. It happens, and on the basis of past trends, house prices will eventually rise again, maybe sooner rather than later, and you'll be sitting on paper profits again.

If you have to, or want to, sell to move to another house, don't get hung up on the fact that you may be taking a capital loss on the sale. The price you paid for the house is immaterial. It only exists in your mind. It's the current value that counts and the price you paid for the house has no bearing on that. It should not enter the decision making process at all. That may be easier said than done.

The price you paid for an asset has no bearing on its current value or on whether or not you should sell it

Nobody likes incurring a capital loss. But the price you paid for any asset has no bearing at all on its current value. That's true for all assets although it is all too often not recognised by those who invest in shares. What's important is not the past but the future prospects. The question to ask is whether your money is better invested where it currently is, or alternatively invested somewhere else. At any point in time your investment is worth whatever it will sell for. If you had the money would you invest it back in that share, or is there another investment outlet offering better future prospects? That's the question that investors should constantly be asking themselves.

Shares have an objective underlying value. It's the net present value of the future flow of earnings. But, of course, there are different views of what that earnings flow will be. Some investors will base their decisions simply on the prospects for future earnings. But others will base their decision on how they believe other investors will react, not to the actual reality but rather to market sentiment i.e. what other people think. They are not interested in the future flow of earnings because they are only gambling on making a capital gain by buying cheap and selling dear in the very short-term. Market sentiment can be very fickle reflecting mainly emotion and a herd instinct, all of which adds to the volatility of stock market values.

All of those factors have to be taken into account when buying or selling shares. They are just as relevant during a boom as they are during a downturn. The one factor that shouldn't be taken into account is the price at which shares were originally bought. But at the same time, there is no harm in being aware that other people may be inclined, rather illogically, to take original purchase prices into account. It can result in people holding onto shares in the vain hope of an upturn, long after they should have sold.

Maximising your income

Most people generate the bulk of their income from work. Nothing reduces income quite so sharply and significantly as having one's job made redundant. The inevitable drop in income creates financial difficulties that can only be solved by cutting back on spending. Balancing the budget involves all of the actions outlined above. The financial review and budgeting process applies equally whether you are in a job or unemployed, have suffered a drop in income or not. But maximising your income crucially involves keeping your job, preparing yourself for a better job as the opportunities arise during the upturn, and/or getting yourself back into the labour force after a job loss.

Of those the most urgent is obviously getting yourself back into a job when the old one has been made redundant. An important first step is to recognise that it is not you who is redundant, but rather the old job that has outlived its usefulness. So do not go around saying, or even thinking, that you have been made redundant - put it the other way, my job was made redundant. That should put you in the right frame of mind for the difficult tasks that lie ahead.

Much of what needs to be done to get back into a job can also usefully be employed by those in jobs to enhance their future employment prospects. Redundancy can be seen as an opportunity. For many it has been the spur to shake off inertia, recognise their potential and put that potential to use.

Employment growth will lag behind the upturn in economic output. But some businesses — they tend to be the better ones — start hiring in advance of their needs while they have the widest choice of applicant. The upturn brings with it opportunities to get, and to switch, jobs. To achieve your ambitions on the jobs' front, however, you need to work at it, look on it as a job in itself. Just as in the Money Makeover outlined above you need to:

- Establish your goals — what job do you ideally want?

- Set out the skills that you have. Not just the ones that you are currently using but all of the skills you have acquired. There is no need to be modest.

- Outline your strengths and weaknesses. Once again there is no need to be modest but be realistic.

- Discover what attributes are needed for that ideal job. It may be your current job as it evolves to meet changes or it may be a new job. What are the relevant employers looking for? Do some research. Talk to someone who is in or close to your ideal job.

- Get qualified for the job. Upgrade your skills. Get training. Get relevant work experience by taking casual, freelance or even voluntary work.

- Start applying for jobs.

- Keep your CV short and concise.

- List what you are doing, what you have achieved, what you can offer and what you are looking for.

- Summarise all important information on a single page and keep the whole CV to no more than 3 or 4 pages.

- Tailor the CV for each job.

- Do your homework on the potential employer.

- Put yourself in the interviewer's shoes. What is he or she looking for? Don't be afraid to ask.

- Be specific. Not "I'm well capable of doing that" but rather "I did that in my last job" or "I have had training in that".

2 Managing your cash flows

After the government takes enough to balance the budget,
the citizen has the job of budgeting the balance — Anon

Most of the money that we earn gets spent before the next pay day. But during those few days or weeks that it is yours, it needs to be kept safe, easily accessible and in a form that enables bills to be paid with the minimum of cost and inconvenience. We still have a preference for cash in Ireland but that's waning and increasingly money is being transferred electronically from one account to another. It's a trend that the Government has sought to accelerate by imposing an extra stamp duty on cheques. In addition to any transaction charges imposed by the bank, there is an additional stamp duty of 50c on each cheque or other bill of exchange.

The majority of people need a place to lodge money and/or to have their wages paid into. They need to be able to withdraw it when needed and to pay bills with the minimum of fuss and inconvenience. For most people the ideal arrangement is to have income paid directly into a bank that provides them with ready access to a good network of ATMs and the facility to make electronic payments directly from that account.

Choose your bank on the basis of convenience, cost and the quality and range of service provided

This type of money transfer service is best provided by what is known as a current account. That used to be synonymous with a cheque book account but that's no longer the case. The cheque book is being slowly, but inevitably, superseded by debit cards and electronic transfers. Most banks offer a similar range of services and there may be little difference in terms of convenience given that most ATMs accept all cards and you may seldom have to visit your bank branch.

But there can be significant differences in cost and quality of service, so it pays to shop around when opening a new account or when reviewing your existing account, as you should do from time to time. There have been a lot of changes in recent years as a result of competition from new entrants. But some of the new cheaper and better accounts are being marketed solely at new customers. Unless you ask to be switched you don't get the benefit even through you are a long-standing customer.

You should be able to get an account that:

- imposes no transaction charges,

- offers access to low cost loans and/or overdrafts, and

- pays interest on credit balances in some circumstances.

Mind you, you may not want all those features. Transaction charges won't break you although they can be as high as 34c a time and are best avoided. You may never want to borrow and you should always shop around even if your existing bank claims to offer the best rates.

If you never have much money in your current account, then any interest payments are bound to be small. And if you are into electronic banking, it's very easy to switch spare money out of your current account and into a high interest deposit account with another bank or with your existing bank.

The following are some of the packages available to new customers in December 2009. Existing customers may be on different, often more costly, accounts that are no longer being marketed.

- **AIB** has a "High Interest" account that pays 1% interest on credit balances provided at least €1,500 is lodged to the account each month. The rate is only 0.25% on its standard "Personal Bank Account Plus". There are no transaction charges on either account for those who make at least one purchase using their debit cards each quarter and also use either the online or phone services once, but there is a flat fee of €4.50 a quarter.

- **Bank of Ireland** offers two alternative current accounts. You can opt to pay a flat quarterly fee of €11.40 and have up to 90 transactions free or you can opt to pay as you go and be charged 28c per transaction. Fees can be totally avoided by keeping a minimum of €500 in your account or by making at least three transactions a quarter by phone or internet. Interest of 4% is credited to balances up to €1,500 provided you register and make three phone or internet transactions a quarter. Provided you register and meet some conditions you get 0.75% on cleared credit balances up to a maximum of €1,500.

- **Halifax** imposes no transaction charges and no fee for setting up an overdraft facility. Having such a facility can be useful if only to avoid penalties for getting an overdraft without permission. Provided you lodge at least €1,500 a month to your account – that can be your salary cheque – you earn interest of 5.12% on credit balances up to €1,500. You also qualify for a special overdraft rate of 12.93%.

- **National Irish Bank** has a range of current accounts offering no transaction charges, if kept in credit, but charges of up to 34c per transaction are applied if they are not. Quarterly fees are charged on two of their accounts, either €18.75 or €31.25 a quarter. Both provide extra benefits such as commission-free foreign exchange and special credit card facilities.

- **Permanent TSB** pays 2% interest on credit balances of up to €1,500, provided €1,500 is lodged each month and the customer has registered for this facility. There are no transaction charges.

- **Postbank** which is operated by An Post offers a full service current account including an ATM/debit card, access to overdrafts and internet banking. There are no transaction charges.

Joint accounts and inheritance

■ There are many reasons for opening a joint bank, building society or post office account. People sharing living expenses may find it the easiest way to operate. Elderly people sometimes open joint accounts with a relative or friend to ease access to their money. They can give the other person the right to withdraw money but they can also retain that right themselves. It may be intended that the money will automatically pass to the survivor but that is not always the case.

Indeed a court case, back in 1932, decreed that the money in such an account should pass into the estate of the deceased person to be divided up in accordance with the terms of any will or, where there was no will, the division laid down by the courts or the Succession Act. It was considered that this was necessary to curtail fraud and that it was an attempt to avoid inheritance taxes.

The precedent created by this judgment was effectively overturned by a later Supreme Court in a ruling on a new case. It concerned an elderly woman who opened a joint account with a niece. She clearly wanted her niece to inherit the money after her death but also wished to retain sole access to the account during her own lifetime. Both aunt and niece were in the bank when the account was opened. Both signed the documentation. The account was made payable to the aunt or to the 'survivor'. In other words only the aunt could withdraw money during her lifetime but it was her clear intention that after her death her niece should have access to the money.

After her death other claimants to her estate took a case against both the niece and the bank and a lower court found in their favour citing the 1932 case. That decision was appealed to the Supreme Court which found in favour of the niece. But the judgment does not give an automatic right of ownership to the survivor. There should be no problem, of course, where account holders have each contributed to the account but where only one has contributed, the other, or others, will gain ownership only where there was a clear indication that this was the deceased person's intention.

So the advice in a case like this is to make the intention clear in writing. Whatever about the actual ownership of the account, money in a joint account may be liable to Capital Acquisitions Tax in the hands of the survivor — see page 273 for more details of inheritance tax and the transfer of assets on death. Ownership, of course, is different to access. A surviving spouse doesn't require tax clearance to access an account held jointly with the deceased partner. In other cases, formal tax clearance from the Revenue is required if the account has more than €31,750 in it.

- **Ulster Bank** imposes no transaction charges on accounts nor any fee for arranging an overdraft permission.

It's not too difficult to switch banks if you think it worthwhile, but first check if your existing bank can offer you something better than the account you have. The banks have adopted a voluntary code under which customers or potential customers are provided with "switching packs" that outline, in simple language, the process of switching, who is responsible for what, how long it will take and what the customer has to do. There is a commitment to have the new account up and running within 10 days and all standing orders etc transferred from the old account within seven days after that.

If you are liable for charges on your existing account and can't be bothered switching, there are other things that you can do to reduce your costs. Paying a bill by credit card costs nothing, for instance, provided the balance is paid off in full each month. That is the only sensible way to use a credit card. Paying the same bill by cheque can cost almost €1.40 made up of as much as 34c to the bank, 50c in stamp duty and 55c in postage. Even without bank charges it costs over a euro, a cost that can be avoided by paying electronically. Many utility bills can be paid without charge at Post Offices or at PostPoint facilities in retail outlets. An Post's BillPay is also available on the internet at BillPay.ie.

> **Use online banking to speedily switch spare money out of current accounts into high interest accounts**

In all these examples, the savings are small enough but you may be able to save significant amounts by ensuring that you don't keep too much money in your current account. It makes sense to transfer any spare money out to a deposit account. Internet and telephone banking have made it easy to switch money between accounts. If you have the facility of operating your current account online, it only takes a few key strokes to organise an electronic transfer of funds out of your account into another either with your own bank or with another financial institution. You usually have to set up the account details in advance but that's a once-off chore that shouldn't take more than a few minutes. Inertia is the enemy. But don't simply complain about the banks. Do something to reduce their profits. Shift any spare money you have to where it can make the best possible return. There may be no interest paid on money left in your current account and over 5% on the same money transferred into a deposit account.

Credit Unions

Credit unions are co-operative non-profit making ventures established within a community covering perhaps a locality or a workplace. Through that community, all the members enjoy what is known as a "common bond". Their basic role is to encourage saving and provide loans but they are greatly expanding the range of financial services they provide. In addition to being a home for savings and a source of loans, many credit unions operate budget accounts which provide for the payment of regular bills. Members may also have access to group rate medical health insurance premiums which can offer a 10% discount on individual rates and increasingly credit unions are providing a wider range of financial services.

Credit unions are self-help non-profit making organisations

The dividends paid on share accounts vary from credit union to credit union. Members have the option of having DIRT deducted at source, or of declaring their own interest for tax purposes. Credit unions, in common with other deposit takers, can offer all of their deposit accounts on a DIRT-free basis to eligible savers who are over 65 or permanently incapacitated and not liable for tax.

A major benefit, of course, is the access to loans at reasonable rates of interest compared particularly to the more expensive finance houses — see chapter 5. The maximum rate of interest that credit unions can charge is 12.6% APR but many charge significantly less. Some also give subsequent rebates out of whatever surplus is generated. Loan protection insurance providing for the repayment of the loan in the event of death or permanent disability is included. Limits may apply to the size of the loan and the cover is curtailed for the over 60s and not available for the over 70s.

Another built-in insurance provides for the payment of a benefit to a member's estate in the event of death. In the case of a member aged under 55, the benefit is equal to the amount on deposit or in shares at the time of death. The benefit is lower for those over 55 and in the case of the over

70s, limited to savings made before reaching that age.

Security also varies from one credit union to another. Depositors are insured against loss resulting from fraud on the part of officials, and the credit unions are included in the Government's guarantee scheme covering deposits up to €100,000. Even without that Government guarantee there is a savings protection scheme with cover of up to €12,700 for each individual. The Irish League of Credit Unions also provides back-up funds and assistance to member credit unions should they run into difficulties.

Flexible friends, if used sensibly

Plastic money is steadily replacing cash as the premier method of payment. It has a lot going for it. For many purposes, plastic money is safer and more convenient than cash and it comes in a wide range of different forms. There are credit cards, charge cards, debit cards, ATM cards and cheque guarantee cards. And that doesn't exhaust the possibilities. There is a range of variants within most of those categories. The definition of plastic money can even be extended to include prepaid phone cards.

As the range of options has extended, so too has the competition and the need for the consumer to understand the pros and cons, the costs and benefits. The options can be confusing by times. All forms of plastic money can be used to advantage but, without care, most can prove costly in one way or another. The first step towards avoiding the pitfalls is to understand how the types of card differ. You can save money by knowing what you need and by shopping around.

Plastic money

The more popular forms of plastic money include:

- **Credit cards** such as Mastercard and Visa give you instant access to credit. You can make a purchase or pay a bill and not have to part with any cash for almost two months. You get a statement each month and can either pay it off in full to avoid interest charges or spread the payments over a period, effectively taking a loan.

- **Charge cards** issued by American Express and Diners Club as well as by Mastercard and Visa, offer the same facilities as credit cards — usually with a wider range of extra benefits — but you are expected to pay the bill in full each month.

- **Debit cards** such as Laser card and the Visa debit card offered by Halifax operate like an electronic chequebook. They allow the holder to make payments from their own bank or building society account. The card is used to make payments just as a cheque would.

| | Interest rate | | Cash | Extra charges | |
	purchases	cash withdrawals	withdrawal fee [1]	Late payment (L) Over limit (O)	
AIB Platinum	11.5%	23.4%	1.5%(€1.90)	€7(L)	€7(O)
AIB Click	8.5%	23.4%	1.5%(€1.90)[2]	€7(L)	€7(O)
B of I Clear	9.5%	19.9%	1.5%(€2.54)	€7.50(L)	€6.25(O)
B of I (2in1)[4]	13.9%	17.4%	1.5%(€2.54)	€7.50(L)	€7.50(O)
EBS Members	10.9%	16.7%	1.5%(€1.90)[2-3]	€15.24(L)	€12.70(O)
Halifax	13.4%	21.6%	1.5%(€1.90)[2]	€7(L)	€7(O)
MBNA	16.9%	19.9%	1.5%(€1.90)[2-3]	€15.24(L)	€12.70(O)
MBNA Platinum	14.9%	19.9%	1.5%(€1.90)[2-3]	€15.24(L)	€12.70(O)
National Irish[4]	11.6%	11.6%	1.5%(€2)[2]	€8.50(L)	
National Irish Gold[4]	10.7%	10.7%	1.5% (€2)[2]	€8.50(L)	
Postbank	14.9%	19.9%	1.5%(€1.90)[2-3]	€15.24 (L)	€12.70 (O)
Permanent TSB	13.5%	16.9%	1.5%(€2.00)[2]	€7.50(L)	€7.50(O)
Ulster Bank	17.9%	22.9%	1.5%(€2.54)[2]	€8.50 (L)	€8.50 (O)
Ulster Bank Zinc	15.9%	22.9%	1.5%(€2.54)[2]	€8.50 (L)	€8.50 (O)

Note: 1. Minimum charge in brackets. EBS, Halifax, MBNA, National Irish, and Postbank, charge interest on cash withdrawals from date of withdrawal.
2. Charged even when the account is in credit.
3. €31.74 maximum.
4. Higher rates may apply on existing cards no longer on offer to new customers.

■ **Cheque guarantee cards and ATM or cash dispenser cards** are often lumped in on a Laser card and provide the holders with cash withdrawal and cheque guarantee facilities linked to their bank or building society accounts. Those are the basic forms of plastic money.

Within each type there can be a wide variation. So let's have a look at each option in some more detail.

Credit cards

A credit card can be a true flexible friend if used sensibly. It need cost you no more than the annual €30 stamp duty if you pay in full each month and only use the card to make purchases. For that you can get up to 56 days free credit between the time you make a purchase and actually pay the bill. Your card provides a free and flexible way of paying bills by phone, post or over the internet and saves you having to carry around too much cash. But if you don't pay in full each month, run over your credit limit, miss payments, or use your card to withdraw cash, the costs can mount up and your flexible friend can become expensive.

At the end of 2009, personal card holders owed about €3 billion on their credit cards. During 2009, there were some months when repayments slightly exceeded the amount spent on the cards but there was little change in the overall level of debt over the year as a whole.

Low interest rates should be seen for what they are – marketing ploys. They shouldn't encourage you to run into debt or to switch to a card that's going to prove more expensive in the long run

The interest rate charged on that debt can be as high as 23.4%. That's what AIB charges on cash withdrawals. At the other end of the scale, some of the debt is interest free. There are generally no interest charges if the amount owing is paid in full each month before the interest free period runs out. In some cases, no interest is charged for a short period on balances tranferred from one card issuer to another.

Apart from using your card sensibly, you can also reduce the potential costs by shopping around for the best card. In choosing a card you need to consider:

- the rate of interest,
- charges for late payment or going over your credit limit,
- charges for using your card outside the Eurozone,
- introductory offers, and
- other benefits.

Buying on
the internet without
a credit card

■ It is possible to buy on the internet without using a credit card. If you don't have a credit card or if you are simply fearful of sending your card details over the web you can instead make use of a prepaid virtual card. One such card is offered by Permanent TSB in association with 3V. Blank cards are available at participating local convenience stores showing a Payzone logo or at Permanent TSB branches. You can also order one online. At that stage you pay nothing. The next step is to register your card and personal details with the bank. Once the card has been registered you can load it with up to €350 at one of the participating stores. You get a voucher with a 16-digit number which can then be used in the same way as a credit card number. Security details including a PIN and expiry date are emailed to you or can be obtained over the phone. A flat charge is levied for each top-up of more than €20. It's €2.50 for amounts between €30 and €100 and €5 for amount over €100. Funds left on the card can be redeemed for a flat charge of €5. A commission of 1.75% is charged on non-euro transactions.

Entropay is a preloaded card which can act as a Visa Electron card, a card which Ryanair is accepting for a limited period without imposing the €5 charge normally applied to credit card bookings. That's one possible use but its main attraction is that it can be used for online or telephone shopping without putting any more money at risk than you have pre-loaded onto the card. You can sign up for free at Entropay.com. If you want it to act like a Visa Electron Card you need to open a sterling account. But you can open a euro or US dollar account. You upload funds from your own credit card to the Entropay virtual card at which time a charge of 4.95% is applied. In other words, it costs you €5 for every €100 you spend. And there is a €4.50 flat fee for putting money back onto your credit card.

The weight that you give to each of those factors depends on how you intend to use the card. If you are never going to run into debt, for instance, you don't have to worry about the rate of interest. Unfortunately no single card ranks number one on all of those criteria but some cards rank very well on most of them.

You can get details of credit card interest rates and charges on the Financial Regulator's website itsyourmoney.ie. It's kept up to date but unfortunately isn't available in print, isn't interactive and much of the comparative data is only available on individual screens relating to the particular card. That makes comparisons difficult. A bigger failing is that it doesn't contain details of existing cards issued by Bank of Ireland and National Irish Bank which are not currently being marketed. Yet most of these banks' credit card customers have these older cards. Having details of them in the Financial Regulator's survey data would help customers in making a decision to switch. So it's difficult to shop around. The following is a brief overview of the cards that rank best and worst on those critera listed above.

RATE OF INTEREST

- Most card issuers charge a higher rate of interest on cash withdrawals than on purchases. Using credit cards for cash withdrawals is best avoided except in dire emergencies.

- Both AIB and Bank of Ireland has cards with low rates on purchases. On AIB's "Click" card the rate is 8.5% but a whopping 23.4% is charged on cash withdrawals. Bank of Ireland's "Clear" card charges 9.5% on purchases and 19.9% on cash withdrawals.

- EBS charges 10.9% on purchases and 16.7% on cash advances but you have to be a member to get a card.

- National Irish Bank's charges 11.6% on its standard card and 10.7% on its gold card. Those rates apply equally to purchases and cash withdrawals. But many of its customers are paying far higher rates on older cards. The same is true for many AIB and Bank of Ireland customers.

- Halifax charges 13.4% on purchases but a hefty 21.6% on cash withdrawals.

- Permanent TSB charges 13.5% on purchases and 16.9% on cash withdrawals.

- MBNA charges interest from the date that purchases are debited to the credit card account if there is any money owing on it or if the last two payments have not been made on time.

OVER LIMIT AND LATE PAYMENT CHARGES

- It's very easy to miss a payment and even go over your credit limit. It can be costly, up to €15.24 for a late payment and €12.70 for going over your limit. Those particularly high charges are imposed on MBNA, EBS and Postbank cards.

- MBNA imposes particular onerous charges on those who miss or are late with a payment. In addition to the high late payment charges, they are also charged interest on new purchases and cash withdrawals from the date they are debited to the account.

CHARGES FOR NON-EURO TRANSACTIONS

All cards impose extra charges for non-euro transactions. Among the best are:

- Permanent TSB, Halifax and National Irish Bank who charge an extra 1.75% of the transaction value whether it be a purchase or a cash withdrawal.

- Some of the others charge only 1.75% on purchases but impose extra charges for non-euro cash withdrawals

INTRODUCTORY OFFERS

A number of card issuers offer low rates of interest for new customers transferring balances from their existing cards. The low rates only last for a limited time, of course, but can provide a significant saving. It may get clawed back in the long run, of course, if you transfer into an account with a higher interest rate.

- Bank of Ireland charges no interest for six months either in transferred balances or new purchases - the choice is up to the new customer.

- PermanentTSB charges no interest on transferred balances for six months.

- Postbank gives a 10 month holiday on transferred balances if the new card is applied for online. Otherwise a rate of 1.9% APR for 6 months is applied.

- MBNA offers a similar 10 month interest rate holiday for transferred balances on its "platinum" account while charging a rate of 19% for six months on its Standard card.

> **It is well worth having at least one credit card. It can be worthwhile getting both a Mastercard and Visa card alternating their use to get the longest possible period of free credit. This simply means using the card whose bill you received last**

Credit cards can be usefully employed as a means of sending money to family members abroad or vice versa. The parents of a child studying away from home, for instance, can get an extra card on their Visa or Mastercard account and give it to the child. The parents can lodge money into the account and the child can draw it out through a local bank cash machine. It is completely secure although the cash withdrawal will usually be subject to a fee of 1.5%.

Do not be tempted to make a habit of postponing payment of the accounts beyond the due date. If you find yourself permanently in debt to the credit card company, you could save money by getting a bank or credit union loan at a lower rate of interest and paying off the credit card. If you have built up a credit card debt already, or intend making a big purchase, shop around for the cheapest personal loan. It's a far cheaper option than borrowing on the credit card.

If you just tend to forget to pay off your credit card bill, you should consider signing a direct debit form. That allows the credit card company to take either the full payment or a minimum payment from your account. So the payment is made automatically. It's a good idea if you intend making the full payment each time. Opting to make partial payments is, in effect, accepting that you are going to remain constantly in debt to the credit card company. And given the interest rates charged, that's not a good idea.

Charge cards

The front runners in this area are American Express and Diners Club although both Mastercard and Visa also issue charge cards. Charge cards have particular attractions for individuals who are high spenders or who do a fair amount of travel. Mastercard and Visa can be used at a far greater number of outlets worldwide but, if the quantity of outlets accepting charge cards is smaller, the quality is better and the big spender will possibly find a charge card accepted in most of the outlets he or she will want to frequent.

Charge cards have another advantage. It is possible to use them as super cheque guarantee cards to get cash from one's own account incurring no interest if there is a credit balance in your account and only the relevant bank rate if there is not.

Like credit cards, the charge cards offer some free insurance cover when you buy your travel tickets with the card — a point sometimes forgotten by the holders. Indeed the charge cards are more generous in this regard. Charge cards are, however, not free. In addition to the €30 stamp duty there is an annual subscription — it depends on the card. An American Epress standard card is €47 a year while a gold card costs €100. Diners Club charges €48 a year. Both American Express and Diners Club provide cash withdrawal facilities too. In addition to its cheque guarantee facility, American Express cards can be used at cash dispensers worldwide.

For those who travel a lot, the cost of getting a charge card or two is relatively small given the flexibility and security provided

Debit cards

A debit card is, in essence, an electronic cheque book with an endless number of cheques. They are issued by banks and building societies. The most common debit card in Ireland is Laser but Halifax and Ulster Bank issue a Visa debit card which is accepted worldwide where ever Visa credit cards are accepted, while Postbank issues a Maestro debit card that is similarly accepted worldwide. Unlike a credit card, the transactions on a debit card are charged directly to the holder's own bank account. Some banks issue debit cards in addition to a chequebook, others issue them instead of a chequebook.

Laser Card is an Irish-owned debit card scheme. They are held by almost three million people nationwide. The card is accepted in more than 40,000 retail outlets. In 2008 they were used for 181 million transactions worth €11.5 billion. There is an annual €2.50 annual stamp duty on debit cards. The same duty applies to single purpose ATM cards while the duty is €5 on combined Laser/ATM card.

You use a debit card as you would a chequebook. Payments made with a debit card are debited to the holder's account in exactly the same way as a payment made by cheque or a withdrawal from an ATM. The money may come out of

• Do not draw money on your Visa or Mastercard Card except in an emergency or unless you have already lodged money to the account so that it is in credit. The charges can be high and interest may start accruing immediately.

• The accounts of charge cards like American Express and Diners Club must be paid in full each month. Otherwise penal charges are imposed.

• Store cards are best avoided since they discourage shopping around, encourage overspending, and some charge hefty rates of interest.

• Do not keep constantly in debt to the credit card company. The interest rates are too high. There are much cheaper ways of borrowing.

• If you are still signing rather than using a PIN take care of your receipts. Remember they contain both your credit card number and a copy of your signature and could be useful to a fraudster.

• Never reveal your PIN to anyone. Never leave your cards in your car. And don't leave them in a coat on the back of a chair in a restaurant or even at work.

• Be careful when keying your PIN into a cash machine that you are not been watched either by someone close by or by a camera.

• Keep a couple of separate notes of your card numbers and the phone numbers of the relevant companies so that you can act quickly if they are lost or stolen.

• If you want to be sure of paying off your monthly statement in full and on time arrange to do it by direct debit.

• Ideally don't let your card out of your sight. Cards can be duplicated after being swiped through high-tech scanners. It takes only seconds to scan a card.

• Do not forget that most cards provide extra benefits such as travel insurance. Read the leaflets carefully and know what you are entitled to.

• If you are making a large purchase and have the cash, see what sort of a discount you can get by offering it as an alternative to a credit card. Remember that the shop has to pay the card company a commission of up to 6%.

• When buying over the phone, or on the internet, be careful to deal only with reputable firms.

• Always check your bills.

your account a bit quicker but transaction charges are lower — there's no stamp duty compared with the 50c applied to each cheque. In general, the same sort of rules apply to the use of debit cards as to the use of a cheque-book. You should have the money in your account or an overdraft permission. If you run up an unapproved overdraft you'll be liable for heavy charges. They were outlined in the previous section.

The shops accepting the card are charged about 20c per transaction by the operators of the system — that amount varies from shop to shop and from issuer to issuer but it is paid by the retailer not the consumer. With most of the banks the charge for a debit card transaction is similar to that imposed on a transaction at an ATM. Where charges are applicable they are added to the customer's current account in the normal way. But they are also waived in the normal way if the customer qualifies for 'free banking'. In any case it is cheaper to use a debit card than pay by cheque.

The main advantage of having a debit card is that you don't have to carry cash around. For those liable for bank charges a debit card is cheaper than writing a cheque for single trans-actions. But someone out on a mini spending spree could save money by withdrawing cash from an ATM. An ATM withdrawal only attracts a single charge while there would be a separate charge for each debit card transaction. In some outlets, shoppers are able to draw out up to €100 in cash in addition to paying for their purchases. The mechanics of using a debit card are similar to using a credit card. You have it swiped and key in your pin. The charge is then made to your bank account, a process that may take a couple of days but don't rely on it.

There's an annual stamp duty of €2.50 a year on ATM and debit cards

Store cards

Some of these are operated by the stores themselves but most are now operated for them by finance houses. There are a number of different types of account. There are monthly accounts which are like charge cards. The amount due has to be paid each month and no interest is charged. It is obviously a worthwhile facility to have if you do a lot of shopping in one store or with the one group.

Then there are budget accounts. The store generally sets a maximum credit limit calculated as a multiple of the minimum monthly payment. It may be 20 times so that if you are prepared to pay €100 a month, the limit is set at €2,000. The interest rate is usually quite high — about the same as on a credit card. The credit limit remains set so that the customer can continue to buy more goods as the amount due goes down.

There are other accounts which are like a Mastercard or Visa account. They are known as option accounts and allow the customer to pay off in full at the end of each month — incurring no interest — or else make a minimum repayment and incur the interest. There is usually no charge for getting a card — other than the interest. Store cards encourage you to shop in that particular store or group and not to shop around for the best price.

A budget account may be worthwhile to cover the cost of a major purchase but not if the money could be borrowed from one of the larger banks instead. An overdraft or term loan would cost far less in interest charged. In general, the advice must be to steer clear of store cards. Mastercard or Visa provide similar benefits in most cases without the need to confine your shopping in one store.

There are exceptions. Monthly cards are cost free and you can benefit from promotions which stores sometimes put on for card holders — special sales and pre-Christmas openings for instance. Both Clerys and the Brown Thomas Group issue cards that are true credit cards and can be used anywhere that credit cards are accepted.

ATM cards

All the major banks and the building societies have their own ATM cards and they all use different names. With AIB it is Banklink while Bank of Ireland has PASS; Ulster Bank has ServiceTill and NIB has Autobank. All of the bank systems are interlinked so it is possible to use most, but not all, bank cards in any of the other banks' machines. On the basis of the queue, it seems that many people don't realise this. It is, of course, necessary to have an account with one of the institutions concerned and to either have some money in it or else have permission to overdraw. The machine is simply an automated teller and the transactions are just computerised versions of what was, and still is, done at the bank counter. Most of the machines operate on a round-the-clock basis providing the most flexible way of getting ready access to cash.

Cheque guarantee cards

To make full use of a cheque book account, you need a cheque guarantee card that guarantees your cheques up to a value of €130 each. The bank will charge you up to €4 for such a card in addition to a stamp duty of €2.50. Without the card you may find it very hard to cash cheques except where you are well known and they are being phased out. The banks are intent on reducing the use of cheques and in pursue of this objective they are going to refuse cheque guarantee cards to new customers. Anyway, cheques are an expensive way of paying bills. It is far cheaper to pay by credit card provided you don't run up interest charges. If you need cash it is cheaper to draw money out of a bank machine. The charges for automated transactions are generally much lower and there is no stamp duty.

Managing your holiday money

The broadening range and sophistication of debit, credit and charge cards has greatly eased the problems of managing your finances while abroad. Within the single currency eurozone it's almost as easy as being at home. The currency is exactly the same and under EU regulations, bank charges for credit card or ATM transactions can't be any higher than they are on similar transactions at home. There may be restrictions on the use of some cards and there's a need to watch out for extra ATM charges that some independent ATM providers charge in other countries, but for the most part the money transactions are exactly the same as at home.

Outside the eurozone, however, the charges can mount up. There are currency exchange rates that can vary from day to day and from one bank or bureau de change to another. This applies not only to the purchase of currency or travellers cheques but also to credit or debit card transactions and withdrawals from ATMs. A commission of 1% to 1.5% is usually charged on currency purchase, while a fee of up to 3.5% may apply to card transactions. Such fees may be subject to a minimum so that small transactions can be particularly expensive. By taking a little care you can save yourself a lot of money.

The eurozone comprises 16 countries: Austria, Belgium, Cyprus, Finland, France, Germany, Greece, Ireland, Italy, Luxembourg, Malta, Netherlands, Portugal, Slovakia, Slovenia and Spain. The euro is also readily accepted in many eastern European countries and is the currency of choice in Monaco, San Marino and the Vatican. The EU countries remaining outside the eurozone are Bulgaria, Czech Republic, Denmark, Estonia, Hungary, Latvia, Lithuania, Poland, Romania, Sweden and Britain.

So what's the best way to carry money abroad? Like most money problems there is no single correct answer. There are three basic options: cash, travellers' cheques and plastic. The best solution usually contains elements of all three with an ever increasing emphasis on plastic cards for all areas except the particularly financially underdeveloped. In making your choice you have to consider convenience, security and cost. Let's have a look at the options in some more detail.

Cash

Cash is the most readily acceptable form of money. Local cash is always acceptable but some other currencies, such as the US dollar, sterling and euro, are also widely accepted in many popular holiday resorts. The euro has become acceptable in many non-eurozone holiday destinations. In some developing countries there may be advantages in having a recognisable currency like dollars or euro. But be careful of carrying high value notes, particularly US dollars, which have a bad reputation in some countries as potential forgeries.

The simplest thing, of course, if you are holidaying outside the eurozone is to change all your holiday money into local cash before you leave Ireland. You can shop around for the best exchange rate and incur only one set of commission charges. The only drawback is the risk — and it is a major one. Cash is too easily lost. But it is advisable to have some local cash to take with you — if only for incidental expenses when you arrive and maybe to carry you though a weekend if you arrive on a Friday night or Saturday morning.

Travellers' cheques

Travellers' cheques are much less popular than they once were. They are relatively expensive and can be inconvenient although they still have their uses. They can be bought in a wide range of currencies and there is some advantage in buying cheques denominated in the local currency of wherever you are going. Usually a commission, of 1% or 2%, is charged when the cheques are bought and a further commission may be charged when they are cashed. The commissions vary from place to place. If your cheques are not in the local currency, it is better to cash them in a bank — shops and hotels often give bad exchange rates particularly those that don't charge a commission. There should be no commission on cashing local currency cheques, at least in banks, but that is not always the case. Sometimes those cashing travellers' cheques charge a fixed commission on each transaction, so using them for small purchases can be very expensive. It is better to change them in bulk every now and then in a bank — weighing the risk of holding the extra cash against the cost of a multitude of transactions.

Credit cards

Credit cards such as Mastercard and Visa and charge cards such as American Express and Diners can all be used abroad. Not all outlets accept them, of course. So in some countries - and particularly in the more remote areas - they cannot be relied upon. But they are, at the very least, a very useful standby and in the more popular holiday resorts they may cover most requirements, although they would always need to be supplemented with some local cash. If you have put your credit card account into credit, most issuers charge nothing for euro cash withdrawals from ATMs. The exceptions are MBNA, Postbank, Ulster Bank and EBS on its members' card.

The cost of purchases outside the eurozone is translated into euro at the exchange rate on the day the item is debited to the credit card account. The exchange rate may include some hidden charges but may be no worse than you would get from buying foreign currency. Most banks also charge a transaction fee of 1.75% but Ulster Bank charges 2% while Postbank, MBNA and EBS, on its members' card, charge 2.65%.

If you need to withdraw cash outside the eurozone, use your bank or Laser card in preference to a credit card and if possible make one large withdrawal rather than many small ones

These charges also apply to cash withdrawals from ATMs outside the eurozone and are in addition to the standard cash advance fees detailed in the table on page 21. That can push the cost to over 4% with some cards while 3.25% is fairly typical. So using your credit card to withdraw cash is best avoided except in emergencies particularly outside the eurozone.

Debit cards

Debit cards are convenient and cheap to use in the euro-zone. They include Laser, the Visa card issued by Halifax and the Maestro card issued by Postbank. Not all Laser cards can be used abroad but those issued by AIB, Bank of Ireland and National Irish Bank which carry the Maestro,

Cirrus, or LINK logo on them can. Within the eurozone debit cards are used in exactly the same way as at home in outlets or ATM machines. The charges are the same as if you were using them in Ireland.

Outside of the eurozone extra charges apply. There's a hidden charge within the foreign exchange rate that you get and some banks apply transaction charges up to 1.75%. Minimum charges generally apply and are higher for cash withdrawals.

Bank ATM cards

Very often your Laser card is combined with a bank ATM card but there are stand-alone ATM cards that can be used to make cash withdrawals from ATM machines abroad if they carry the Cirrus, Maestro, Visa Plus or LINK logos. LINK is a British network and it is usually cheaper to withdraw money from one of its machines than other independent ones.

As with the other cards, there are no extra charges for withdrawing money within the eurozone. The same charges apply that would apply in Ireland. Depending on the card, the charge can vary from nothing to as much as 34c. Outside the eurozone the usual foreign exchange costs are incurred together with transaction fees of up to 3.5%. Some ATM providers abroad also add their own charges and while these should be outlined on the screen before you withdraw your cash the notice is easily missed.

Travel Insurance

Travel insurance can provide a real benefit in the form of peace of mind even if you never have to make a claim. But be sure to read the fine print and know exactly what you are covered for and what you have to do to make a claim. It's usually necessary to report any loss to the local police, for instance, and to make the claim within a fixed time period. There are a wide range of policies available and the cover varies greatly, as does the cost. Travel agents normally offer insurance with their holidays and may charge an extra fee — perhaps €10 — if it is not taken out. But it can still

Your holiday financial checklist

■ A bit of advance planning can help you avoid some unpleasant financial surprises while on holiday. The following are some pointers:

■ Increase your credit limit just in case you need it — unless, of course, that might prove too much of a temptation to overspend.

■ Check that the magnetic strip is in good order.

■ Get additional cards for your partner.

■ Get a PIN number to use for withdrawing cash if you don't already have it. If you haven't lodged money to your account in advance, it can be an expensive way of getting cash but useful in an emergency.

■ Check out the Cirrus, Visa Plus, or Maestro facilities that may be bundled with your bank card. Get the information on how to use them and where they can be used.

■ Make a note of all your card numbers and details of where you have to ring to report their loss. Keep a couple of copies so that you can report any loss quickly.

■ If you're going to an EU country, make sure to get a European Health Insurance Card from your local Health Board. This electronic card which is about the size of a credit card may eventually contain medical details such as blood type. It replaces the old form E111 and ensures that you get the same sort of free medical insurance as the locals in whatever EU country you go to. Once you get the card, it will last for years but it may take a few weeks to get, so apply to the local area Health Service Executive a few weeks before you first need it. You can get an application form from your local citizens' information or health centre.

■ If you have medical insurance, check what cover it provides when abroad and make a note of any special contact telephone numbers to be used. It's not an alternative to travel insurance but it is a very useful addition.

■ Don't forget to take out some form of travel insurance. The insurance offered by the travel agency may not be the cheapest or best. It can be worthwhile getting your insurance elsewhere even if the travel agent charges you a small fee for allowing you to do so. Read the section on page 35.

■ Cancel the milk and the newspaper deliveries, leave some washing on the line, turn off the water, ask a neighbour to keep an eye on the house and have a good holiday.

be worthwhile shopping around. It is not too difficult to save €10 on a holiday insurance premium and still get wider cover. Don't forget that you may already have insurance cover for some risks. You may have items like jewellery, cameras, etc. covered for 'all risks' both inside and outside your home on your existing household policy.

People who travel a lot should consider taking out an annual policy rather than one for each trip. There's certainly a saving to be made if you make three or more trips a year. You may want cover for the potential loss of having to cancel a holiday should a close relative die. This cover is usually fairly restrictive. You also need cover for medical expenses. Quinn Healthcare, VHI and Hibernian Aviva provide some cover but not enough. Some insurers give discounts to people with medical insurance. VHI has its own separate travel insurance product.

It's worth shopping around for travel insurance

You can save money on travel insurance by shopping around. If you have access to the internet you should check out Insureme.ie; Simplymortgages.ie; Quinnhealthcare.com; Getcover.com; Justcover.ie; Ryanair.com; Chill.ie, VHI.ie, Aerlingus.com, and AIB either in branch, or if you get it online you qualify for a 10% discount. It's also worth checking your union or staff association which may have negotiated a special group deal. There is a wide variation between the cheapest and the dearest but the choice shouldn't be made solely on price. The dearest is not necessarily the best. It may not provide the best cover and the rules and exemptions may not be the least onerous. So in making your choice don't simply look at the price. Price is, of course, important but you should look at the cover you are getting and read the fine print.

Having taken out a policy there may be very little you can do if you subsequently find out that a certain risk isn't covered. It's no wonder that disputes arise over whether or not the conditions outlined in the fine print have been met. Knowing what these conditions are and then complying with them can be of prime importance.

One case considered by the Insurance Ombudsman, before she was subsumed into the Financial Services Ombudsman service, concerned a traveller who, on arrival at Dublin Airport, discovered that two of his suitcases had been damaged. He was tired and naturally wanted to get home as quickly as possible. The damage didn't seem to be too great so he didn't report it to anyone at the airport. After he arrived home, however, he discovered that some items were missing from his luggage. Six weeks later, he submitted a claim form to his insurance company. It refused to meet the claim.

Don't expect insurance companies to automatically accept your word. You must substantiate a claim

The problem was that the policy document required claimants to have obtained a police report within 24 hours of discovering any loss relating to personal baggage and to have obtained a *'Property Irregularity Report'* from the airline involved. Neither of these conditions had been met. The Ombudsman ruled in favour of the insurance company.

She also found in favour of the insurance company in a dispute over whether a sum of money could be deemed to be "unattended" when left in the claimant's holiday apartment. An 'unattended clause' is common in travel insurance policies and its meaning is frequently being disputed. The Ombudsman referred to a British court judgement which suggested that an item was unattended if there was no-one in a position to observe any attempt to interfere with it and close enough to have a reasonable prospect of preventing any such interference.

3 Maximising the return on your savings

Foul cankering rust the hidden treasure frets.
But gold that's put to use more gold begets — Shakespeare

People save more during recessions. While some have to dip into their savings to survive or to maintain their living standards in the face of falling incomes, others adopt a precautionary approach, cut back on spending and save more in anticipation of worse to come. That's not just an economist's model. It is borne out by facts. The trend has been very evident in Ireland in recent years. In 2006, we saved just over 10% of our income. The savings rate is now fast approaching 20% and it's unlikely to diminish until there is a renewal of confidence in our economic future. That's down to many subjective factors. The expectation is that the economy will start growing during 2010 but how quickly that upturn translates into improved consumer confidence has more to do with appearances and expectations than it has to do with reality. The quicker confidence returns, the speedier the recovery. Each individual will have his or her own view but it's impossible to accurately forecast the timing or strength of the recovery.

Not only do people save more during recessions but they are also likely to prefer less risky options — cash and deposits rather than asset-backed investments such as shares and property. At this time, deposits have the added advantage of being Government guaranteed but at some stage the recovery will be firmly enough established to improve the attractions of the asset backed investments. To maximise returns coming out of a recession requires constant vigilance and a willingness to take some risk. That means a willingness to accept that asset values can go down as well as up and it's not for everyone.

There is no clear-cut boundary between savings and investments and no generally accepted definitions. But the term 'savings' is often taken to apply to assets such as bank accounts that can easily be converted into cash without risk of loss. Everything else that can be expected to yield a financial return, by way of income or capital gain, can be considered an investment. That includes property, shares, investment funds, pension funds, and business assets.

Investment decisions need to be geared to your own particular circumstances and attitude to risk

At its simplest, saving may only involve holding onto some money to meet the occasional expense that arises less regularly than pay days — a holiday, the car or house insurance, even the ESB or gas bills. But that type of saving has more to do with managing your cash flows— a topic dealt with in the last chapter. The sums involved are generally small and the money is only being kept for relatively short periods so the main considerations are convenience and ease of access. But when larger sums of money are being put away for longer periods, different factors come into play — most importantly the rate of return and the risk involved.

In general, the greater the expected rate of return, the greater the risk. The return on a bank deposit is more secure than an investment in shares which may fall in value. So where should you save or invest?

Your choice of investment outlet depends on a wide range of factors. First you have to decide:

- **YOUR OBJECTIVES:** What is the investment for? Is it to be a contingency fund providing security for the future or is it money earmarked for a specific purpose: to provide a regular income, to pay the deposit on a house, to fund the children's education, or for retirement. Some investments are particularly suited to specific objectives.

- **YOUR TIME FRAME:** When do you expect to realise the investment? Your objectives may dictate the answer. In general the longer the investment term, the greater the potential return.

- **YOUR NEED FOR ACCESS:** Is there a possibility that you'll need to convert some or all of your investment into cash at short notice? Most medium and longer term investments impose penalties on early encashments. Such penalties are not a worry if you definitely won't need access to your money. Otherwise you have to decide whether to keep some funds readily accessible in short-term outlets or take the chance of incurring the penalties.

- **YOUR RETURN/RISK BALANCE:** There is usually a trade-off between the two. Risk may be measured in terms of volatility i.e. the extent to which the value of an investment moves up and down. The greater the volatility of an equity fund, for instance, the greater the potential returns but also the greater the chance of loss. There is no objective measure of how much risk a person should take. It depends partly on personal make-up and partly on circumstances. Attitudes to risk vary greatly. There is nothing intrinsically wrong with being a risk-taker or with being risk-averse. The important thing is for the investor to recognise the degree of risk appropriate to his or her personality and to avoid overstepping the mark.

Circumstances may dictate an even tighter limit on the degree of risk to be taken. A pensioner investing his or her life savings, for instance, may need to keep a risk-taking personality in check. Equally, an overly risk-averse individual might benefit from a cool assessment of his or her fears. But in all cases, both personal make-up and circumstances need to be taken into account and potential returns balanced against possible personal anguish.

- **THE COSTS:** While it costs nothing to put money on deposit, most other investments involve some charges. Charges reduce your net return and need to be taken into account when deciding not only between alternative investments but also between advisers. Stockbrokers vary in their commission rates. Investment fund managers differ in their initial charges and annual management fees. There may also be a choice between indi-

■ Buying financial services is fraught with danger. Taking out the wrong insurance policy or making the wrong investment can prove very expensive and wrong does not necessarily mean bad. There are policies and investments which, while excellent in some circumstances, may be disastrous in others.

Professional advice can be well worthwhile but only if it is knowledgeable and soundly based. Advisers have to meet minimum competency requirements and a list of those who do can be assessed online at www.qfaboard.ie/register or phone (01) 4553018. But being 'competent' is no guarantee that the advice is always the best. It's all too easy for an adviser or a salesperson to err through ignorance or a lack of concern for a client's real needs or by not knowing enough about the range of products available.

That's true whether you pay by way of a fee or by way of commission. You need to check around before choosing an adviser and then compare the costs.

The Financial Regulator provides authorisation for three types of financial adviser.

AUTHORISED ADVISERS are independent of the banks, insurance companies and other financial institutions that supply investment and insurance products. They are expected to trawl the market to find the best option for you.

MULTI-AGENCY INTERMEDIARIES can only offer you products for which they hold agencies. They must hold agencies for at least two product providers.

SINGLE-AGENCY INTERMEDIARIES only hold an agency for one supplier. They are sometimes known as tied agents.

In all cases, your adviser should ask you a lot of questions. To give adequate advice, a financial adviser needs to know something of your other savings, income and responsibilities, tax situation, attitude to risk etc. You need to ask some questions too, making sure that you understand the answers.

■ What do I need?

■ How is the product going to supply that need?

■ Why that product rather than something else?

The answers to some of these questions should be evident from documentation that advisers are now required to give to clients. For instance they have to complete a 'fact find' outlining your financial situation, your objectives and your attitude to risk. They also have to supply you with a letter outlining their terms of business. ➡

But you should still keep those "what, how and why" questions firmly in mind. The "what" question is one that you have to ask yourself. Supermarkets and shops are very much into encouraging impulse buying. You can guard against it by making a shopping list and sticking to it. The same is true in the financial area. It's up to you to decide what you want. Don't let the adviser decide for you. He or she may make suggestions but make sure that you make the decisions.

Before you take any advice, decide what you want yourself — if only in very broad terms, such as "I need to save for the children's education" or "I need insurance cover". Then try to go a bit further than that. If the product is insurance what cover do you need? Do you need it on yourself or your spouse or both? Try to put broad figures on your needs.

Are you willing to take a risk with your savings? How much can you afford to save? Jot down your answers. Use it as a check list to see if the salesman or adviser has got you to deviate from your original objectives. If so, did he give adequate reasons why you should?

The other "how and why" questions are asked of the salesman or the adviser. How is that particular product going to satisfy your particular needs and most important, why that product rather than something else? And that includes the most important question of why one company's products rather than another's.

Do not be afraid to keep asking why or how and make sure you understand the answers. Ask about alternatives. You can be sure that there are alternatives even if you don't know what they are. The salesman or adviser should know what they are and be able to justify the alternative he has chosen for you. Has he or she taken all the alternatives into account? Do you need to do some shopping around yourself?

And remember that if you don't understand it, it is not your fault. A salesman or adviser who understands a product should be able to explain it in simple, easily understood, language. If he or she is calling to your home it can do no harm taking out a tape-recorder explaining that you are a bit muddle headed and would like to go over the detail later. That should at least stop excessive claims. Don't forget that your professional adviser is getting paid for his time and expertise either by way of fee or commission. There is no need to feel guilty about asking questions and getting answers before you make your decision.

See page 88 for details of the information that must be given with life insurance and investment products.

rectly paying a broker's commission or paying a fee to a fee-based adviser and getting the commission yourself. While tax cannot properly be regarded as a cost, it has much the same effect and should be taken into account particularly when comparing investments taxed in different ways.

Read the following sections for more details on these various investment options

There is no single option that is best for everyone. It all depends on individual circumstances and the factors outlined above. But there are some general rules of thumb that one can follow in making a decision. Even with a decline in the rate of inflation, the return on deposits and similar safe investments, such as the post office schemes, are still below the rate needed simply to ensure that a nest egg keeps pace with rising prices and retains its purchasing power.

Those willing to take some risk can hope for better returns and there is a range of options open to them. The amount of risk varies and is usually unpredictable as the stock market slide of recent years proves. There are investment products that guarantee at least a return of the initial investment — so that the worst that can happen is that you'll get your money back. But such guarantees come at a cost in terms of potential return. Others guarantee a minimum rate of return with the chance of something better. But most investment products offer no guarantees. There is the hope of a good return but also the risk of losing part, or even all, of the initial investment. The following are some of the options which are outlined in more detail in the sections that follow:

- <u>Paying off debt</u> yields a very high and certain return. Invest €1,000 at the best deposit rate available and you earn just over €40 a year after DIRT tax. Invest the same money in paying off a bank term loan — carrying an interest rate of 10% — and your gain is €100 a year. It makes sense to pay off the loan. Paying off the loan does reduce your flexibility but that's not a problem if you are in a job and are fairly sure of being able to borrow again if you need to. Mortgages are the exception. The interest rate is low and some of the interest may be eligible for tax relief. The true cost of a mortgage at 2.5% may be as low as 2% after tax relief at 20% or only 1.875% if you are a first time buyer entitled to tax relief at 25%. The cost is higher, of course, if all the interest doesn't qualify for tax relief. Taking the example above the gain from paying €1,000 off such a mortgage is €20 a year. That's less than the tax free €32 to be earned on €1,000 in An Post Saving Certs or the €26 that could be earned net on a good deposit account late in 2009. So from a financial point of view there is not a lot to be gained from paying off the mortgage.

If you once pay off the mortgage, it's not so easy to borrow again at such a favourable rate. It is, of course, possible to get a top-up mortgage but it may not be eligible for tax relief. And there'll be set up costs. Assuming a mortgage rate of 3%, a married couple who qualify as a first-time buyer can get tax relief on a mortgage of up to about €666,000 while a single borrower gets relief on a mortgage up to €333,000. There is no tax relief on the portions of the loans above those levels. The limits are lower for non first-time buyers. See page 130 for more details of mortgage tax relief.

Using spare money to pay off debt can yield a very high return although it may not always make sense to pay off a mortgage

- **Deposit accounts** with banks, building societies and credit unions — rates vary greatly depending on the institution, the amount involved and the period of notice required. **See page 47.**

- **Postbank,** the new An Post/Fortis bank offers a similar range of deposit accounts as other banks. Older investment schemes such as Saving Certs and Bonds are again very attractive for those who are liable for DIRT and can afford to leave their money untouched for a few years. Money can be withdrawn on demand but the money must be left for a few years to gain the best return. **See page 50.**

- **Investment funds** offer a wide range of options. Some guarantee a return of capital while others make no guarantees, the return depending solely on the performance of the underlying investments which can range from very high risk to very low risk. **See page 57.**

- **Direct stock exchange investment** carries a high degree of risk in the short term. As was very evident in recent years, share prices can be very volatile, even the shares of what may seem to be the most secure of companies. Those with a relatively small amount to invest can't spread the risk adequately over a number of shares and the cost of dealing in small lots of shares can be very high. **See page 54**.

■ <u>Investments under certain tax incentive schemes</u> such as the Business Expansion Scheme (BES), Film Relief and certain property investments, where still available, combine the chance of a good return, partly based on tax relief, with the risk of loss. It is important to understand the risk and not be mesmerised by the tax relief which can, in some cases, confer more benefit on the promoter or developer than on the investor. **See page 292**.

■ <u>Property investment</u> has tended to yield good returns over the longer term although not, it seems, for those who bought at inflated prices during the boom years. The drawbacks of direct property investment are the relatively high costs of entry and the difficulty of converting an investment speedily back into cash. One of the attractions is, or was, the fact that you can, or could, more easily gear up your own resources with borrowings. But that's a major drawback during a recession when property values fall.

Those are some of the options. The choice depends very much on the individual and on his or her particular needs. As stressed above, it depends on attitudes to risk and on what is required from the investment. There is no single best option. It all depends on individual circumstances and objectives. And, of course, the relative attractiveness of different options can change with time.

Secure investments

No investment is entirely secure but putting your money on deposit with a financial institution is almost risk free. There are other options where the loss of your capital is equally unlikely. Investors may look for two levels of security. The most basic is an assurance that the capital invested will be returned either on demand or at some specific time in the future. That is all some secure investments promise. The other level of security involves the rate of return. A fixed term bank deposit offers a fixed rate of interest so the investor can expect to get not only the capital back but also a specified return on that capital. With other investments, such as demand deposit accounts or tracker bonds, the rate of return may depend on circumstances.

There tends to be a trade off between security and rate of return. The more security built into an investment, the lower the potential return. In many cases the rate of return is too low to maintain the purchasing power of an investment when inflation is taken into account. But at least there is a floor under the potential losses and that security can be important for many investors if not on all of their assets, at least on some of them. The following are some of the options open to those who want to limit their risk.

Deposit accounts

Banks, building societies and credit unions all pay interest on deposits. The rates vary with the size of the deposit and with the length of notice required to withdraw the money. They also vary from institution to institution and, of course, over time. There are rates fixed for a set time and variable rates that can be changed from day-to-day without notice. It is important to shop around to get the best rate. The newspapers carry weekly lists of the rates available but it is as well to check by phone as well since rates can change frequently. That's also a good reason for regularly reviewing your deposits ensuring that you continue to get the best rate available. While competition for deposits is intense it hasn't resulted in a convergence of the rates on offer. There is a wide gap between the lowest and the highest rates

The interest rates on offer change frequently so you may need to switch your money regularly to ensure the best return

available, particularly on smaller amounts. It's important to shop around, not only when you are initially putting the money on deposit but regularly thereafter to ensure that you are still getting the best rate available.

Regular saver accounts

A number of banks offer higher rates on regular savings accounts than on standard variable rate deposits but there are limits to the amount that can be invested and usually restrictions on withdrawals. They have been used as a marketing ploy and since the rates are generally not fixed, it is important to occasionally check what the current rate is. It's all too easy to open an account offering a high rate and find that it has been significantly reduced. While rates of 7% were on offer during 2009, by the end of the year the best rate available was 5% offered by AIB but the maximum monthly saving is €200 and you have to have another AIB account. EBS has an account paying 4.85% on up to €1,000 a year while Anglo Irish was paying 4% also on a maximum of €1,000 a month.

Credit unions

While credit unions are more about community self-help than maximising returns, most do offer a good financial deal as well

Many credit unions offer good dividend rates on members' shares. They are not strictly deposit accounts and the rate is not fixed in advance. It depends on the dividend declared and agreed by members each year. That, in turn, of course, depends on the finances and management of the credit union. While they don't have to make a profit, credit unions have to be mindful of the margins between the rate they charge on borrowings and the return they provide for their saver/shareholders.

With interest rates generally low, most credit unions have reduced the interest rate they charge on borrowings from the standard 12.7% and, as a result, have had to reduce the rate they pay on savings. A significant proportion of any surplus goes into reserves. These are owned by the members although they don't show up in the immediate rate of return credited to savers.

■ Deposits with banks and other financial institutions operating in Ireland are covered by a number of guarantees. The most wide-ranging is the Government Guarantee Scheme which guaranteed depositors against loss on deposits without any upper limit. The current guarantee runs until October 2010 but the Government has indicated that it will be extended. Some foreign-based institutions are covered by guarantees operating in their home countries.

■ The Irish Government Guarantee

All deposits in the following institutions are covered by this guarantee.

AIB,
An Post,
EBS Building Society,
Irish Nationwide Building Society,
Postbank Ireland Limited.

Anglo Irish Bank,
Bank of Ireland,
ICS Building Society,
PermanentTSB,

■ Irish Deposit Guarantee Scheme

All the institutions listed above are also covered by this guarantee which protects 100% of deposits up to a maximum of €100,000. The following institutions are also covered in addition to many other financial institutions registered with the Financial Regulator.

ACC Bank,
Halifax (Bank of Scotland),
IIB Bank plc (KBC Bank Ireland),
Ulster Bank,

Credit Unions,
First Active,
Pfizer International Europe,
National Irish Bank.

■ British Compensation Scheme

This provides full cover for deposits of up to £50,000 sterling per person. The following banks operating in Ireland are covered.

Investec Bank plc,
Nationwide Building Society,

Leeds Building Society,
Northern Rock.

■ Dutch Guarantee Scheme

This provides full cover for deposits of up €100,000 per person. It covers

Rabodirect.

■ Danish Guarantee Scheme

Cover of up to €50,000 per person is currently provided. It is to be increased to €100,000 by October 2010. It covers

Danske Bank (trading as National Irish Bank).

DIRT

DIRT is levied at the standard income tax rate — 20% up to January 1, 2009, 23% to April 8, 2009 and 25% thereafter — on most deposit interest. No further tax is due on deposit interest even if the recipient is liable to pay a higher rate of income tax. People who are not liable for income tax and who are either over 65 years of age or permanently incapacitated can claim back the tax or alternatively, since 2007, they can have the interest paid or credited to their accounts tax free once they verify to the deposit taker that they are over 65 or permanently incapacitated and not liable for tax. In the case of a married couple, it is sufficient for either partner to be over 65 years of age. This facility is available on any deposit account. Get in touch with the deposit taker and make the necessary declaration.

A claim for repayment of DIRT is made on a simple form that you can get in any tax office, at larger post offices or from wherever you have your savings. You also need a certificate from the bank or building society giving details of the DIRT stopped. Fill out the form, attach the certificate, and send it off to the tax office — the address is on the form. You can make back claims going back four years — in 2009 you can still make a claim for 2005 but in 2010 you can only go back to and including 2006.

An Post investments

Postbank, the joint venture between An Post and Fortis Bank launched a wide range of new products during 2008 including current and deposit accounts. An Post itself still offers its long established range of medium to long term investment products. These include Instalment Savings, Saving Certificates, and Savings Bonds.

- **Savings bonds** are a three year investment with guaranteed returns each year. It is possible to withdraw money at any time without penalty other than the fact that no interest is payable if the money is withdrawn during the first year. The rates of return are as follows: money left in for one year – 2.2%; two years – 5.2% (which is 2.6% a year); three years – 10% (3.23% a year). That three year return is equivalent to a gross return, before DIRT (at 25%), of 4.3% a year.

- **Saving certificates** offer a tax free return of 3.53% a year if held for five years and six months. That's equivalent to 4.7% gross. An initial investment of €1,000 grows to be €1,210 over that period. With the interest only added in every six months, it is important — if you have to cash in — to do it as soon as possible after a six-monthly anniversary. That way you lose the least amount of interest. But ideally you should stay the course because the best returns come in the latter years.

- **Instalment savings** are primarily aimed at those savers who can save a fixed amount each month for a year. As a scheme for encouraging savings it's great and the returns are not bad considering that only relatively small sums are being deposited. The saver — who must be over seven years of age — agrees to save a stated amount each month for 12 consecutive months. The minimum monthly saving is €25 and the maximum €500. At the end of the 12 month period, the total amount saved is left on deposit. If the savings are left for five years after the initial year's saving period you are guaranteed your money back plus 20% — that works out at only 3.37% a year. But that is tax free and equivalent to a 4.49% return that would be liable for DIRT at 25% – better than on some of the regular saver accounts mentioned above.

The Instalment Savings Scheme is an option for those wanting to save a fixed amount regularly each month

Tracker bonds

Tracker bonds are now less attractive than they were

Tracker bonds are fixed term investments generally over five or six years. There is a range of different options. Most offer a guarantee that the investor will at least get his or her money back at the end of the agreed period. Some offer a minimum return on top of that basic guarantee. The maximum return possible is usually based on the performance of some stock exchange index or mix of indices. For instance the return may be linked to the performance of the FTSE100 index of British stock market prices. So, for example, a person making an investment of €2,000 might be guaranteed the return of that money at the end of six years. That's the worst outcome. There may also be a guarantee that the value of the bond will rise by half of any increase in the FTSE100 index. So if the index happened to go up by 60% over the period then the return would be 30% of €2,000. The investor would get back €2,600 less tax at 28%. In most cases, there is a cap on the maximum return just as there is a floor under the potential loss. Bonds are opened for investment from time to time. There is usually a range to choose from, at any one time, but with the guarantees reduced as a result of declining interest rates the interest in them has waned somewhat. They should be viewed as a fixed term investment. There can be heavy penalties for withdrawing money too soon.

Guaranteed bonds

Guaranteed bonds are much the same as term deposits i.e. deposits for a fixed period of time. The fixed term is seldom less than a year and is more often three to five years although it can be longer. The rate of return is normally fixed at the outset and is guaranteed. Early encashment penalties can be heavy so it is essential to be reasonably sure that you won't require access to your money during the set term of the bond. Some bonds provide a facility for taking a regular income. It may even be possible to take an income larger than the interest being accumulated. In which case, of course, you are eating into your capital. Riskier investment funds are dealt with in more detail on page 57.

Income from annuities

Annuity rates can vary. It is important to shop around for the best rate

An annuity is a way of using a lump sum to provide an income for life. It was the traditional way of providing an income during retirement mainly because it was the only option open to those with personal pension money to invest. But that is no longer the case for the self-employed, directors of family firms, and those not in company pension schemes. But while individuals with personal pension funds to invest are no longer required to purchase an annuity, they are still there as an option – an option that may be attractive to some. Annuities may have an appeal to anyone with limited capital that they want to spread out as income over the post-retirement years. The basic idea behind an annuity is that in return for a lump sum investment it provides a guaranteed income until death. There are also annuities suitable for couples. Known as **'joint survivor annuities'** they are taken out on the joint lives of the couple. On the death of one, the income continues at a reduced rate until the death of the other. The rate of return on joint survivor annuities is, of course, lower than on a single life annuity — about 20% less in the case of a husband aged 65 whose wife is 61 when the annuity is taken out. This 20% reduction also assumes that the income is halved on the death of one partner.

Around that central idea there are a fair number of options. In all cases the income is guaranteed for an uncertain period. The assurance companies that sell annuities do not know when the person is going to die. But they have an idea of the average life expectancy of annuity purchasers. In money terms those who live longer get a very good return while those who die younger do not. But in all cases there is the security of knowing that the income will continue until death.

When interest rates are low, annuity rates are also low. In 2009 one company was quoting that a man aged 65 would require about €100,000 to buy an income of €5,507 a year for life with half that income carrying on to his widow, assuming she was aged five years younger than he. But annuity rates can change from day to day and from company to company so it is important to shop around. You can do it very easily by phone. The initial payment would be smaller if the income is to subsequently rise with inflation. The standard annuity usually provides for the first income payment to be made six months after the annuity is purchased. Thereafter the payments are made at six monthly intervals. It is usual to guarantee that the annuity will be paid for at least five years even if the purchaser dies during that time.

> It may be possible for those in bad health to get better annuity rates

People with medical conditions that are likely to shorten their life span can, in some cases, get higher returns than those in good health. Most companies, however, refuse to take medical history into account even though they would make sure to do so when quoting life insurance premiums. Some companies may, however, offer what is known as **'impaired life annuities'.** If appropriate, it is worth searching them out. The annuity rates can be significantly higher.

Direct stock market investment

The Irish stock market peaked on February 2, 2007 ending a long upward trend that started early in 2003. The ISEQ index of share values closed at 10041 on that day with the shares quoted valued at a total of €150.8 billion. After that, the trend was downwards although there were some small recoveries. The ups and downs of stock market trends don't come in straight lines. The ISEQ hit bottom on March 3, 2009 closing at 1880. Shares at that stage were worth €28.2 billion, down €122.6 billion or 83% on the peak. Since then there has been some recovery but it has by no means been constant or marked. At the end of 2009, the Index was still well below the 4000 level at which it stood late in 2002 when the last upswing started.

The small investor may be better spreading the risk by investing in shares indirectly through a managed fund

Investors have lost heavily. Most of them own their shares indirectly though pension and other investment funds. The fund managers will have been selling and buying, making money and losing in the process. Even in a recession, it is possible to make significant returns on investments by buying in the troughs and selling on the peaks. But it needs a large degree of luck. Bank of Ireland shares, for instance, were selling at over €18 at the peak. At the bottom they could be bought for as little as 12c. They recovered to over €3.40 a share during 2009 before slipping back again. No-one can now doubt the truth of the old adage that share values can go down as well as up. The message has been brought home with a vengeance. The impact has been traumatic for many, although some are gambling on the up and down swings and others still are simply waiting to buy in when the inevitable upswing is more firmly established.

It is hard to believe at the moment but shares tend to outperform other investments over the longer term. But in the short-term, the downturns can be very sharp. The shorter the term of any investment the greater the risk of incurring losses rather than making gains. There can be no certainty. Even when the market is tending upwards there will always be some shares moving in the opposite direction and the general upward trend can always be punctuated with sharp downturns of uncertain duration.

Irish investors are not, of course, restricted to investing on the Irish stock exchange but few markets have escaped the recent downturn. There is no additional foreign exchange risk when investing within the eurozone. But non-euro shares have to be bought in foreign currency and there is always the risk that the euro will devalue against that currency. Whatever the prospects, small investors must always be particularly wary of investing in shares. They cannot spread their money over a wide range of shares in order to spread the risk and they must realise that share values can go down as well as up. But for those willing to take a gamble, there may be money to be made providing they realise and accept that there can be no certainty.

It can be argued that the small investor is better advised to invest indirectly through an investment fund. These are considered in the next section. By investing in a fund rather than directly in individual shares, the investor gets the benefit of skilled management and also gets to spread the risk to a far greater degree than would be feasible by investing in individual shares. A knowledgeable, or lucky, individual can always hope to do better than a fund manager, of course, and he or she might be able to do just that. But it does require time and knowledge, not only of how the stock market works – that's the easy bit – but also an insight into how economic trends are going to impact on sectors and individual companies. You'll need to be able to pick the winners and the losers or, at least, some of them.

Investing in a company on the Stock Exchange gives you a part ownership in the company concerned. The return on this part ownership depends on the performance of the company, so together with the prospect of a high return, goes the risk of no return. The degree of risk varies with the type of share and with the company.

There are debentures and preference shares which carry a fixed rate of interest and have first claim on a company's profits, and then there are ordinary shares, which are the real ownership shares, and carry with them full risks of ownership and the full prospects. If the company makes no profits, they get no dividend; if it prospers, they get all the cream.

Investing on the stock exchange requires time and a bit of dedication. If you don't have both and still want to invest on the stock market then indirect investment through an investment fund is possibly the best option. An alternative is an investment club where a small number of individuals share their expertise and money to invest

How to buy shares

Given the costs involved it doesn't make sense to invest very small amounts. Brokers who don't offer any advice and simply execute your order charge the lowest commission. One such broker, Fexco, charges a commission of 1.25% on euro deals up to €9,000 and 0.35% above that with a minimum commission of €25 plus a fixed administrative charge of €7.50. Somewhat similar rates apply to sterling and dollar transactions.

Brokers who offer advice typically charge up to 1.65% on deals up to €15,000 with a minimum of between €60 and €70. There is also a Government stamp duty of 1% on all purchases of Irish shares, 0.5% on British shares.

Transaction costs can be kept to the minimum by dealing in shares online through the internet. Both AIB and its stock-broking wing Goodbodys offer such services. In both cases, you have to register and keep a minimum amount of money in either a special account with Goodbodys or, in the case of AIB, your ordinary bank account. A commission of 1.25% is charged on the first €25,000 and 0.5% on anything above that. There is a minimum commission of €32 per trade. There is also a €26 annual registration charge and a charge of €13 if you withdraw a share holding from the service and a final charge of €40 if and when you close the account. Davy Stockbrokers also offers an online service. There is a twice yearly account maintenance charge of €40 while commission is charged at the rate of 0.75% on the first €25,000 and at 0.5% above that.

Online services include access to information and research but not individual advice. Even brokers who offer advice don't keep a permanent eye on your investments, unless you pay them to. They issue regular newsletters with buy and sell recommendations and prepare detailed reports on selected companies but it's not a personalised service. It's up to the investor to keep an eye on the market and his or her own portfolio of shares.

A list of stockbrokers may be obtained from The General Manager, Irish Stock Exchange, Anglesea Street, Dublin 2. Phone (01) 6174200.

Investment funds

Not everyone has the time, knowledge or skill to manage direct investments on the stock market or in property. Yet there is no doubt that in the long run both stock market and property investments have outperformed the return on deposit accounts. But that is an average over a long period during which values have fluctuated up and down. Some investments fell far short of the average and the total market in shares or property can sometimes fall significantly. Those risks of direct investment can be reduced, but not entirely eliminated by investing indirectly through an investment fund. And there is a wide range of funds to choose from. Most allow for lump sum investments and some accept regular savings.

All investment funds have one thing in common. They are pooled investments. Each individual investor's money is pooled with that of other investors and professional managers manage the whole fund on their behalf. They have to be paid, of course, and the companies they work for have to make a profit, so there are charges involved. There is always an annual management charge usually imposed as a percentage of the fund. In addition there is often an initial set-up charge.

In all cases, the investor should be looking to the medium or long-term in order to achieve a sufficient return to offset the costs and ensure some levelling out of the ups and downs. Investors should be prepared to leave their lump sum investments for at least five years while regular savers should be thinking in terms of at least 10 years. There are various different types of investment funds and within each type there is a wide range of funds offering varying degrees of risk. So what are the basic options? Funds can be categorised within the following types:

- Unit funds including unit trusts

- With-profit funds

- Tracker bonds

Unit funds

The term "unit funds" covers a multitude. They are operated by banks, insurance companies, building societies, and other financial institutions. Investors' money is pooled and managed on their behalf by professional fund managers. There is every conceivable type of fund. You can choose to have your money invested in almost any category of shares in a range of markets. So you can have all your money invested on the Japanese or Australian stock exchange or you can choose a wider option.

There are also funds invested entirely in property and others invested solely in government funds. You take your pick and usually you can switch to a different fund operated by the same company if and when you like. There may be some cost involved but usually some switching is allowed without any charge.

Each investor is allocated so many units in the total fund. Their value changes daily or weekly as the value of the underlying investments change. With most funds the movement can be down as well as up but some funds put a floor under your potential losses by guaranteeing a minimum return.

The returns are liable to a 28% income tax stopped at source similar to the way DIRT is stopped on deposit interest. The various types of unit funds are called different names by different companies and the same name may, in some cases, mean different things. The following are some of the terms with a brief explanation of what they usually mean.

■ Unit-linked funds: These are insurance-linked unit investments. The life insurance element is usually very small but it allows for the fund to be set up under life insurance legislation. If it's included, you pay for it so if you don't need it choose a non-insurance linked option. Different companies call their funds by different names.

■ Unit trusts: These are unit funds set up under a trust deed. From the point of view of the investor there is little difference between unit trusts and unit-linked funds.

The differences have more to do with how they are set up and administered.

- Managed funds: These are unit funds with a mix of investments. The term is usually applied to funds carrying a medium degree of risk because they have a wide spread of investments but there is no strict definition and the term could equally apply to a fund invested in a mix of riskier investments.

- Specialised funds: While a managed fund usually offers a spread of investments over a range of sectors, the specialised fund targets a particular sector, country or investment area. The investor is putting all of his or her eggs into the one basket. If the chosen investment area does well, then the returns will reflect that.

- Indexed funds: A fund managed in such a way that its performance matches the ups and downs of a stock market index or group of indices. It doesn't have to be as actively managed as other funds so management charges are sometimes lower. The managers don't try to outperform general stock market trends but they shouldn't underperform either.

- Consensus funds: A variant of indexed funds which are managed to at least match the average performance of other funds.

- Tracker bonds: These are a form of guaranteed investment fund. There is usually a commitment to return at least the initial investment at the end of a specified period, often five or six years. In addition, they provide a return based on the performance of some stock market index or group of indices. For example, a bond might guarantee to refund at least the initial capital at the end of five years and 11 months and to give a return equal to 70% of any rise in the FTSE index. Tracker bonds are dealt with in greater detail on page 51.

Investment funds must be viewed as medium to long-term options

Investment costs vary from fund to fund. Upfront charges range from nothing up to as much as 5% applied in the form of a spread between the offer price at which you buy the units in the fund and the bid price at which the fund managers will buy back the units if you wanted to immediately cash them in. Some of that cost may be covered by a greater

■ There are four factors to consider in choosing a fund.

● **What is the money invested in and how risky are those underlying investments?** A wide spread provides some protection against major or rapid downturn in value but greater returns may be obtainable from specialised investments in a single sector if it happens to do well. Your best choice depends on your attitude to risk and your personal circumstances.

● **What does it cost you to invest?** There may be a 5% upfront charge in the form of a spread between the offer price at which you buy the units in the fund and the bid price at which the fund managers will buy back the units if you wanted to immediately cash them in. Some of that cost may be covered by a greater allocation of units given to larger investors or by way of special inducement. But some fund managers impose no upfront charges — the bid and offer prices are the same. All funds will charge an annual management charge, usually at least 1% but sometimes significantly higher.

● **Are there any guarantees?** Most investment funds simply rise or fall in line with the underlying investments but some funds do provide guarantees to investors. Such guarantees will always lower the potential rate of return but for those adverse to risk they may offer the certainty of at least getting the initial capital back at a fixed time in the future. You should be very clear about what guarantee you are getting.

● **Can you switch funds without cost?** Most fund managers allow you to switch between different funds at least once a year without cost.

allocation of units given to larger investors or may be negotiated from an adviser willing to forego some of his or her commission. A growing number of fund managers impose no upfront charges — the bid and offer prices are the same but all funds will charge an annual management charge, usually at least 1% but sometimes significantly higher.

With-profit funds

With-profit funds are offered by insurance companies. In many respects they are the same as a managed fund with some exposure to the stock market but they differ from other funds in that the returns are averaged out over time by balancing the good times with the bad. How that balance between the good and bad years is achieved is determined internally by the company's actuary. The return comes by way of annual bonuses declared each year and a 'terminal' bonus at the end of the agreed term of the investment. That final bonus can be significant if the fund has done well but there is no certainty. Returns have been disappointing in recent years and these funds are now rarely actively marketed.

Some bonds offer a guarantee that if you cash them in at fixed dates in the future — for instance after five, seven or 10 years — you'll get at least your capital back. Others guarantee both your initial capital plus any bonuses already declared. But in all cases the guarantees operate at fixed times. Early encashment may involve fixed penalties and companies reserve the right to impose additional penalties known as "market value adjustments" in the event of a significant market downturn. That can impact on final payouts as well as early encashments. Entry charges, allocation rates, management charges and early encashment penalties vary from company to company. It's hard to make overall comparisons since the company that's good on one of those elements may be bad on another.

The set penalties for early encashment also vary greatly. Very often there is a penalty of 5% on encashment during the first year phasing out in later years with no penalty after the fifth year. Companies operating a 5% bid/offer generally impose no early encashment penalty since it is already built into the initial charge. With most companies, it is possible to take an income from the bond by way of regular withdrawals on a monthly, quarterly, six-monthly or annual basis. The withdrawals, of course, should not exceed the likely annual bonus rate otherwise the initial investment is been eaten into.

> **Returns on with-profit funds have been disappointing in recent years and these funds are now rarely actively marketed**

Which is best for you?

The type of investment you choose depends very much on your own circumstances and attitude to risk. Specialised unit-linked investments offer the best chance of high return, but there is a risk that it will not materialise. If, for instance, the fund is invested in equities, the amount eventually paid out will depend on the state of the stock market at the time of the payment. And who is to say what market conditions will be like in 10 years time. With-profit policies offer a chance of participating in the insurance company's own profit and usually once bonuses are declared, they can't be taken back. The risk is less than with unit-linked funds but the returns can be very disappointing and have been in recent years. Past performance is not a good guide to future prospects. The sophisticated investor will also want to look at the mix of investments within each fund. This can vary greatly from one fund to another.

With all of these investments it is important to take a medium to long-term outlook. It can be costly to withdraw too early. The cost of switching from one fund to another depends on the set-up costs involved. Most companies allow investors to switch without cost from one fund to another within their own stable – usually at least once a year. The switching option doesn't arise with tracker bonds or with-profit funds.

Normally with the unit funds, any income earned on the fund is reinvested to the benefit of the investors – although there are provisions in some plans for the investor to get a regular income. This is arranged, however, by the sale of units and there is no guarantee that the remaining units will continue to be worth as much as the initial investment. In other words, the income could, in some cases, be paid out of capital. There is no single answer to the question 'which is best?' It all depends on the individual, his or her personal circumstances and attitude to risk. Before seeking advice or making a decision, ask yourself what you are investing for, how much risk are you willing to take, and what are the chances of you needing speedy access to your money. Having the answers to those questions in your head will help you to make the right decision.

Investing a lump sum

You may come into a lump sum by way of an inheritance, a maturing investment, the sale of some assets, a redundancy, or a lucky win. Alternatively you may have accumulated a lump sum over time. It may be spread over a range of saving outlets but combined, it makes up a lump sum. Whether it's a new lump sum or one that you have had for a long time, you should be continuously examining your options. That's the ideal but at the very least you should do so occasionally. The following options are not listed in any particular order of preference, risk or likely return. The mechanics of some of them such as stock market investment, bank deposits and pensions are dealt with in more detail elsewhere in the book. Here they are listed in brief with an outline of the pros and cons.

Clear your credit card debt

Credit cards are truly flexible friends if used sensibly and that means totally avoiding interest charges by paying the full amount due each month. If that ideal can be achieved it doesn't matter what rate of interest is charged on the card. The banks claim that about 50% of accounts are paid in full each month but, of course, it may not be the same 50% each month. Most people with cards pay interest at some time or other. So it is well worthwhile shopping around for the card with the lowest interest rate – see page 21.

You could be paying over 20% on your credit card debt. Use spare money to clear a loan that's costing you 20% a year is the same as investing the money at 20% or indeed a little more. You'd need to be getting 26.6% before DIRT tax to end up with 20% net. So paying off the loan, that is costing you 25%, provides you with the same financial gain as investing money at 20%. That's not a bad return.

Pros

☐ **The financial return is many times better than putting the money on deposit.**

Cons

☐ **Having cleared off the credit card debt, you may be tempted to run it up again but that's only a drawback if you give into the temptation.**

Pay off a personal loan

The same sort of argument applies to personal loans as to credit card debt. The interest rate is likely to be lower so the saving is that much less. But if you're paying 8% on a bank loan and can clear it off, it's the same as investing the money at 10.6%, the rate which after DIRT would leave you with a net 8%. Make sure, of course, that there are no penalties for early repayment. Such penalties may apply to loans issued at a fixed rate of interest or to some finance company or hire purchase loans. But they are not very common now. With most personal loans, interest is only charged on the outstanding amount each day. The interest charges stop clocking up as soon as you make your payment.

Pros
- ☐ **Paying off debt provides a very good financial return.**

Cons
- ☐ **Make sure that there are no penalties for early repayments.**

Reduce your mortgage

The benefits of paying off a mortgage are not as clear cut as paying off credit card debt or personal loans mainly because the interest rate is lower and may even qualify for tax relief. Let's suppose you have a mortgage at 2.5%. If you reduce it by €10,000 your interest charges will be reduced by €250 a year. Assuming you are getting tax relief on that at the standard rate your net saving is €200. If alternatively you put the €10,000 on deposit you could earn about as much, or more, even after paying DIRT tax.

So you save little or nothing by paying off the mortgage but will have lost some financial flexibility as a result. Pay off the mortgage and the money is gone. You could always borrow it again, of course, but the new loan may not qualify for tax relief and there may be additional charges in setting up the top-up mortgage. If you keep the money on deposit, it's always available if an opportunity arises or you simply need it. A couple of euro a week may be a small price to pay for that additional financial flexibility.

Pros
- ☐ **There's a great psychological satisfaction in paying off or even reducing a mortgage. It's hard to put a money value on that but it can be worth a lot.**

Cons

☐ If, having used spare money to reduce your mortgage, you find your-self in a position of having to borrow again, the new loan is likely to be more expensive. Depending on your circumstances you may have to take out a new mortgage and bear the set-up costs and not get the benefit of tax relief or at worse have to rely on a much more expensive personal loan.

Buy an overseas property

You would need to have a sizeable lump sum to completely finance the purchase of a property abroad but you might have enough for the deposit. Before making any decision you need to be clear what you want from your investment. The decision making is fairly clear cut if you are simply aiming to make a monetary return on a property. You consider the price, calculate the likely rental income, take account of maintenance costs, taxes, local charges etc. and come up with a potential rate of return. Then you do a risk analysis. How certain is the rental income? Could changing trends, new developments or simply bad man-agement reduce rents or occupancy rates? What factors could affect the value of the prop-erty, up or down? Although, during the boom, we were lulled into believing that property always goes up in value, we now know that it's not true.

If you intend using the property yourself the calculations are more difficult. It's not too hard to put a value on your own use of the accommodation. It's worth at least what it would cost you to rent a similar house or apartment. There is, however, the intangible worth of owning a property, knowing that it's there, enjoying the flexibility to use it as you want. It may not be possible to put a monetary value on that. But it is worth thinking about.

Buying property abroad is a riskier venture than buying at home. Within the eurozone, there is no exchange risk and in countries, like France or Spain, the legal system is protective so long as you take the same sort of reasonable precautions that you would at home. But it is a lot more difficult to value a property in an area you don't know. You don't know enough about current valuations nor are you likely to be sufficiently *au fait* with likely future devel-opments that could affect the value of the property.

Pros

☐ Buy well and the rental income could fund your mortgage repayments while the property rises in value.

☐ If you are buying for your own use, the free accommodation for your-self and friends can provide a good return.

Cons

- ☐ There is no certainty that property values will rise.

- ☐ Many local factors can affect the value of your property and they are harder to evaluate in an area you don't know well.

- ☐ Rental income can be uncertain.

- ☐ Local taxes can prove a significant charge.

Spend the money on education

Many studies have shown that investing in education yields a very high return both to the individual and to the community. The return to the individual can come by way of extra earning power over a lifetime and increased job security. That return can be measured very easily in cash terms. But education can also provide less tangible returns. It can give you a greater degree of choice in picking a career and allow you to enjoy a broader and more satisfying lifestyle. Learning to appreciate art, literature or music may not put any money in your pocket but it can nonetheless yield a very rich return.

There is a very wide range of educational courses to choose from. You need to be clear in your objectives. If you want to increase your earning power you need to acquire knowledge and skills that are in demand and will remain so. But pick a course that suits your ability and will retain your interest. It can be costly in terms of wasted money and time to drop out of a course.

Pros

- ☐ Education can yield a very good return in terms of money and satisfaction.

- ☐ The benefits can last a lifetime.

Cons

- ☐ Money only buys you the teaching. The learning you have to do yourself and it takes time and effort.

- ☐ You generally need to pay up front and you may have wasted both time and money if you drop out.

Buy a new car

A significant proportion of the wealth generated by the Celtic Tiger was spent on buying cars. They satisfy two distinct needs. A car provides transport but it can also satisfy some less tangible needs to show off and boost the owner's status. If you are thinking of buying a car to gratify those latter needs then only you can judge whether or not you are getting good value. You'll possibly get most satisfaction from a new car, big or sporty. But if you simply need the car to get you from one place to another, then it makes a lot more financial sense to buy second-hand. The greatest single cost of motoring is depreciation. A car can drop in value by 25% in the first year and by a further 15% the following year. Even the €1,500 scappage grant doesn't cover that although it obviously helps. After the first couple of years the car depreciates at a somewhat slower pace, possibly about 10% a year. You can avoid the heavy initial depreciation cost by buying second-hand. If you take a little care, the gain is unlikely to be offset by additional repair costs.

Pros

☐ **There's an opportunity to show off, turn heads and maybe boost your status among some. If the existing car is getting past its best, you may actually save some money by cutting down on maintenance costs.**

Cons

☐ **The benefits may not justify the heavy costs involved particularly if 'new' means a really new car and not a second-hand one.**

Spend it on home improvements

A conservatory, an extension or an attic conversion can greatly improve your quality of life if they satisfy your needs. Only you can put a value on the enjoyment you may get from summer days spent in a conservatory and likewise with regard to the extra living space provided by say a kitchen extension or an extra room in the attic. If you are going to remain living in your home, that's what you should be considering and it's a very personal decision. But if you think of yourself as being on a property ladder moving ever onwards and upwards you'll need to be more concerned with whether or not the home "improvement" actually adds value to your home in the eyes of a potential buyer. Even if you are staying in the home, that is of some importance but it's a lot more so if you are planning to sell in the not too distant future. So what adds value to a home? Estate agents will tell you that a conservatory won't add much, if any, value to a property if it is poorly built or obviously only of use during a few warm days in summer. They are keener on extensions which if well designed, they say, can add significantly to the value of a property. But you need to see your house through the eyes of potential buyers. Families with young children might prefer a garden to an extension.

Pros

- ☐ Could greatly improve your quality of life if you need and will enjoy the extra space.

- ☐ May add value to your property but the emphasis is on "may".

- ☐ Building costs are currently at a low if you shop around.

Cons

- ☐ A badly designed or badly built extension won't increase the value of your property. It could even reduce it.

- ☐ There is no direct financial return until you sell the house and, even then, the actual value added by home improvements is uncertain.

Put it on deposit

Deposit accounts are about the safest place to keep your money. But you can't always expect to get a good return. At the end of 2009, it was possible to get a reasonably good real return since consumer prices were falling and some banks were very anxious to get deposits. But at other times, the purchasing power of your lump sum may be steadily eroded as a result of price inflation. There is always a wide difference between the best and worse rates on offer. It pays to shop around and to regularly review the rates available.

Pros

- ☐ Your investment is about as safe as it can be thanks to Government guarantees.

- ☐ You can get a return that will maintain the purchasing power of your nest egg.

- ☐ If you need it, demand accounts give you ready access to your money.

Cons

- ☐ Those willing to take some risk can hope for better returns.

- ☐ Getting the best rate requires some care and a willingness to shop around.

Invest in a pension fund

The attractiveness of this option depends greatly on your liability to income tax. If you are not liable for income tax, it's not really an attractive option at all. Since you can't get the benefit of the tax relief on pension contributions you'd be just as well saving the money in an ordinary investment fund where you could have access to it unlike a pension fund which is subject to access and other restrictions. By the beginning of 2010 it's not a particularly attractive option for standard rate tax payers either, because there is every indication that the tax relief will be standardised in the not-too-distant future at a rate somewhere between the top and the standard rate.

If you are liable for income tax at 20%

Take €100 in pay and you'll end up with €80 after tax. That's not taking account of PRSI and the Health Levy which can eat up a further €8. Alternatively if you put the €100 into a pension scheme it all goes in, less charges of perhaps €5. So the choice is between about €95 going into your pension fund or as little as €72 in your back pocket after tax and PRSI. So even for those paying tax at the standard rate, putting money into a pension fund must be seen as a good investment for anyone who wants to save for retirement. But personal consideration must determine when it is best to save. Despite the exhortations to start early, it doesn't really make a lot of financial sense to be putting money into a pension fund if it means having to skimp on other more pressing needs such as buying a house or rearing the children.

The current crazy and inequitable tax regime means that for someone on a rising career path, there's a great incentive to leave pension funding until tax relief on contributions can be claimed at 41%. That is going to change. It's likely that the tax relief for those paying tax at the standard rate will be improved. So while saving for retirement is good, at this stage it may be worth waiting for improved tax relief. Have a read of Chapter 9 on page 171 before making any decisions.

Pros

☐ **Tax relief and savings on PRSI and the Health Levy can add up to €28 to every €72 you save. That's better than the top up that was available on SSIAs.**

☐ **Provided you want to save for retirement, the inability to access your money can be seen as a plus.**

Cons

☐ **Your money can't be accessed until retirement.**

- ☐ You may be able to get a better top up on your money in the not-too-distant future when the tax relief regime is made fairer.

If you are a top rate tax payer

Since you are liable for tax at the top rate, you are entitled to far more generous tax relief than a standard rate tax payer. It can add almost €52 to every €48 that you put into a pension fund. That makes pension funds irresistible. But, of course, great care must be taken in your choice of fund, if you have a choice, and in the costs involved. If you are in an occupational fund these matters may be outside your control although check that your representatives on the board of trustees are keeping an eye on such matters.

If you have or intend to open your own personal pension plan, use Personal Retirement Savings Accounts (PRSAs) as a benchmark. The maximum charges on a standard PRSA are 5% of each contribution plus a 1% annual management fee. Be sure that any charges above those norms are well justified.

Pros

- ☐ **The State will add at least €50 for every €50 you contribute. That level of relief may not be available in the future when the tax relief regime is changed.**

- ☐ **A quarter of your fund can be taken as a tax-free lump sum on retirement.**

Cons

- ☐ **Your money can't be accessed until you retire and there may, in some cases, be limitation on your access after that.**

Put your lump sum into an investment fund

This is an option for those who want to invest their money for the medium to long term. It's an alternative to putting money into a pension fund where it would have to stay until retirement or of using the money to invest directly in property or on the stock market. Investment funds provide professional management and a better spread of risk.

All investment funds have one thing in common. They are pooled investments. Each individual investor's money is pooled with that of other investors and professionals manage the whole fund on their behalf. To pay for those services, there is always an annual management charge and there may also be a set up charge. With some sums, an immediate 5% of your investment goes in set-up charges and then up to 2% is taken off each year as a management charge. But there are funds which impose no initial charge and levy only 1% a year management fee and that's what you should be looking for.

There are also guaranteed bonds and tracker bonds giving guarantees of at least getting your money back after perhaps five years while offering the chance of some return linked to stock market performance. But in return for the guarantee you have to accept some limitation on the return you can hope for. Make sure that you know exactly what you are being guaranteed and how any return is to be calculated. With most funds the value of your stake depends on the performance of the underlying investments. Values can fall just as easily as they rise. So in choosing a fund you need to consider, not only the set-up and ongoing management charges, but also how the money is to be invested and the outlook for those particular investments. You may also consider the past performance of the fund managers involved but don't forget that past performance is not necessarily a good guide to future prospects.

In summary — look on investment funds as at least a medium term investment. Try not to pay any set-up charges and no more than 1% annual management charge. Make sure you know what the fund invests in and be aware of the risks involved.

Pros

☐ **Investment funds give you an opportunity to spread your risks and get professional management.**

☐ **There's the potential to get a better return than you would by keeping the money on deposit.**

Cons

☐ **Set-up and management charges can be high if you don't shop around for the best deals.**

☐ **With most funds, values can move down as well as up so you can lose and lose significantly.**

Buy shares through the Stock Exchange

Direct stock market investment is one of the options open to those who have no immediate need for a lump sum, don't want to spend it and would prefer to put it aside earning them a return. It's also an option for someone who wants to gamble on the ups and downs of the market. It's not, of course, a risk-free option. Trends over the past couple of years amply confirm that. Share prices can be very volatile although, in the long run, the potential is good. Shares tend to outperform other investments over the longer term, but there can be no certainty, and losses can be substantial in the short term.

Even when the market is tending upwards, there will always be some shares moving in the opposite direction and the general upward trend can always be punctuated with sharp downturns of uncertain duration. All share markets experience the same sort of swings and some shares, of course, experience a greater degree of volatility than others. Investments outside the eurozone carry an additional foreign exchange risk. The shares have to be bought in foreign currency and there is always the risk that the euro will devalue against that currency.

To invest directly in shares you need some knowledge, some luck and a willingness to maintain an active interest in your investments. Investing small sums can be expensive because of minimum dealing charges but you could split €20,000 between a few different shares without incurring unduly onerous charges particularly if you make your own choices and don't look for any advice from the broker. The choice is endless. At one end of the scale you can go for a high dividend income with limited potential for major capital gain. At the other end there are speculative shares offering no dividends but the chance of a sharp increase in value, if all goes well. See page 54.

Pros

☐ **Shares in general have tended to provide good returns over the longer term. But like all averages that doesn't necessarily hold true for specific shares at specific times.**

☐ **By investing directly you are in control. You pick the shares and can buy and sell as you see fit.**

Cons

☐ **Share prices can just as easily move down as up. The movements can be quite sharp at times.**

☐ **Dealing charges can make small transactions quite expensive and can be a disincentive to spreading the risk over a number of shares.**

Use your lump sum to start a business

A small lump sum may not be sufficient to finance the start up of a business but it could be a start. There are other sources of finance available including grants and tax rebates. Those on PAYE who leave their jobs to start up a business on their own can (subject to terms and conditions) claim a rebate of all the income tax they paid over the previous six years. Only certain categories of business qualify. Very high earners can claim rebates of over €250,000. The rebate is limited, of course, by the amount of tax you actually paid over the six years.

Businesses that can qualify include manufacturing projects, tourism projects approved by Fáilte Éireann, fish farming and processing, the cultivation of mushrooms, micro-propagation of plants, horticultural cultivation in greenhouses and the production, publication, marketing and promotion of musical recordings. See page 292.

If you meet the requirements you can make a back-claim for tax relief extending over the past six years on up to a maximum of €600,000 invested in the new business. At 41%, that gives you a maximum rebate of €246,000. In essence that means that you can get back all of the tax you paid on up to €100,000 of income in each of those years. If you've paid tax on that amount each year at the top rate of 41% you are eligible for a rebate of €41,000 (41% of €100,000) for each year. The basic requirement is that the would-be entrepreneur is setting up a new business and leaving a PAYE job. The incentive isn't available to an existing businessman moving into a new venture and each claimant must own at least 15% of the shares in the venture. See page 292.

But apart from the finance, starting and running a business requires skills, creativity and determination which not everyone has.

Pros

☐ **Being your own boss can be very satisfying even if you have to work harder.**

☐ **Few people manage to become really wealthy on their wages.**

Cons

☐ **Starting a business is hard work and there can be no certainty of success.**

☐ **A worker in a larger firm can be more secure than the owner/manager of a small firm.**

4 Life insurance buying peace of mind

I detest life insurance agents; they always argue that
I shall some day die, which is not so — Stephen Leacock

Life insurance is primarily about providing financial cover for dependants in the event of premature death although the general term may also be applied to products providing benefits in the event of illness or disability. The need for life insurance varies from individual to individual and it changes over time. Obviously the more cover you have the better, but there is a cost involved. Choices have to be made and they usually involve large sums of money.

Insurance products are sometimes made unduly complicated. Policies are often composed of different elements in a unique package that is impossible to compare from a cost point of view with even a broadly similar product from another insurance company. It is not uncommon for companies to combine insurance policies with savings plans but it is important for the buyer to separate the twin objectives of protection for dependants and saving for the future. Be sure of what you need and what you are buying.

Apart from death, suffering an illness, accident or disability can also have a major financial impact in terms of lost income and expense. Hopefully you'll avoid all three but you can never be sure. Insurance can provide the peace of mind of knowing that if the worse does happen the impact will, at least, be eased by some financial benefits.

Such peace of mind comes at a price in terms of premiums and only you can decide if the benefit is worth the cost.

- **Assess your needs, ideally within the context of a general financial review,**

- **prioritise them,**

- **take into account any cover you have,**

- **make decisions on what additional cover you want,**

- **take advice.**

It is important to assess the cover you already have. In particular you should take into account any cover you have as a member of a pension scheme. Most occupational pension schemes provide benefits for your dependants should you die before retiring and many include insurance that guarantees a continuing income should you be unable to work because of an illness, accident or disability.

The provision of protection for family and other dependants is the first and primary role of life assurance. An essential part of any family finance plan must be the protection of one's dependants against the financial loss which inevitably results from the death of a bread winner.

One thinks usually of the death of the husband in this regard, and the loss of income which will result. But the early death of a wife, even if she is not an income earner, can also impose a financial burden on a widower trying to keep a family together. Life assurance offers a way of easing these financial burdens caused by death. But many life assurance policies involve more than basic life insurance. They combine cover for dependants in the event of death with a

Even a small monthly premium represents a significant cost when payable over a long period. So it makes sense to take your time considering exactly what you need and how best to satisfy those needs at the lowest possible cost

way of saving for the future — for retirement, educating the children, or even marriage. Most assurance policies satisfy both needs to some extent. Some are aimed more at protection while others are aimed more at saving. Some only offer protection with no monetary return if the insured person lives beyond a certain age.

It is important for people taking out the insurance to be clear on what they need from the policy and to keep the distinction between protection and saving in mind. The insurance industry is pledged to emphasise the differences, in response to the complaints over a lack of clarity in the past, but it is no harm to keep it uppermost in one's mind. Let's first have a look at the type of policies generally available, and then examine how they can be used to satisfy the average family's needs.

> **It is important when buying life insurance to distinguish between protection and saving for the future**

There are four basic types of life assurance:

- term or temporary insurance,
- whole of life assurance,
- endowment assurance, and
- disability and illness insurance.

Term insurance

A man aged 30 can ensure that his dependants receive €200,000 if he dies within the next 10 years at a premium cost of about €14 a month. Taking a similar policy out at age 50 would cost about €47 a month. But quotes can vary greatly from one company to another so it's important to shop around. You can get an independent broker to do it for you but he or she may not always offer the cheapest option. Some insurance companies don't deal through brokers. It's as well to supplement a broker's efforts by shopping around yourself.

This type of insurance is called term insurance and all too little of it is sold. In Ireland, we tend to spend a lot on life insurance compared to our counterparts in other countries but we favour savings-type policies which are really geared towards saving for the future and which only pay out a relatively small amount in the event of early death.

Term insurance pays out nothing if the insured person lives for the set term of years. Suppose like our example above, you are 30 years of age and take out a 10 year policy. If you live until you are 40, the policy ends and you get nothing back. But it is not a complete loss. Indeed it is no loss. What you have bought during the 10 years is peace of mind: the knowledge that should you die your dependants will be provided with some financial resources.

That peace of mind is worth buying. Not everyone needs term insurance. But there are a lot of people who need it and do not have it. If you are in a company pension scheme, you are possibly fairly well covered for life insurance within the scheme. But it is worth checking out how high the cover is and considering whether or not you should take out a little more.

> **Pure life assurance which pays out only if death occurs during a fixed period of years is relatively cheap**

Then what about insurance on the stay-at-home spouse. The financial cost of keeping a family together following the death of a wife and mother can be substantial. A lump sum would certainly make living more bearable. A survey, conducted for Ark Life Assurance, indicated that full time house parents spend an average of 86 hours a week on household tasks including childcare, preparation of meals, general cleaning duties etc. If the minimum wage was applied, the weekly cost would be over €740 a week without building in any provision for overtime rates.

Term insurance may also be important for people who lose their jobs. The loss of the job may also mean the loss of the insurance cover provided within a pension scheme. In some cases, employers will keep the insurance cover in place for a short time, or it may be possible for the redundant worker to keep up the payments himself. There are a wide range of term insurance options to choose from.

You can pick the number of years and the size of the cover. The older the person is when the policy is taken out, the higher the premiums. Term insurance is the cheapest way of providing real financial protection for dependants and it is the first type of policy young parents on slender means should consider. Within this general category there are a number of different possibilities.

Level Term: In this case the sum insured remains fixed for the term of the policy. If the person insured survives the term no payment is made by the insurance company. If he or she dies during the term, then the sum insured is paid out. Even if there is no pay-out, and hopefully that will be the case, the policy offers value for money in the peace of mind it provides.

Convertible Term: This provides the same basic insurance cover as level term assurance, but there is an option to convert the policy into another type. Usually the assurance company allows conversion at any time during the life of the policy and agrees not to require any further medical test or proof of good health. The policy into which you convert will operate from the date of conversion and will be at the normal premium rates applied to such policies given the insured person's age at the time of conversion. A convertible term assurance policy need not cost much more than a level term policy — particularly if it is a relatively long term policy. Unless your means are very slender and unlikely to improve over time, convertible term assurance makes much more sense than level term. It provides flexibility in the future when life cover may be less important.

Decreasing Term: This type of policy is often referred to as a mortgage protection policy since they are often taken out for this purpose. The life cover gradually decreases over the term of the policy. For instance, a policy may provide initial cover of €100,000 declining over 20 years. If the insured person dies in the first year his family would get the full €100,000, but by year 10 it has reduced to €79,500 and in the last year the cover is only €12,000.

This, of course, is an ideal way of providing for the repayment of a house mortgage in the event of death. The sum owed to the bank or building society is decreasing year by year as repayments are made and the sum payable by the insurance company will more or less keep pace. Some decreasing term policies simply guarantee to pay off the mortgage in the event of death — less any arrears — provided interest rates remain within set limits.

Banks and building societies make it a condition of granting a mortgage that the borrower takes out a mortgage protection policy but you don't have to take out the policy with the lender's own insurance company. It is, however, often cheaper and easier to do so since the premium can be collected with the repayments and some lenders make it expensive to switch by imposing an additional fee on borrowers who take out the insurance elsewhere.

Family Income Benefits: This is another type of term insurance which provides, instead of a lump sum, a regular income for the family or dependants. For example, the policy on a married man might provide for the payment of €10,000 a year every year between his death and the end of a 20 year term. The payment made by the insurance company would not be liable to income tax.

Whole of life assurance

Term assurance is pure protection. There is no element of saving since no payments are made if the insured person survives the term. With whole of life assurance there is an element of saving, although it is saving for your dependants after your death. The insurance company undertakes to pay the agreed sum — plus bonuses if you go for a with-profits policy — whenever you die. So unlike term assurance, the payment is made at some time.

Obviously the premiums payable for a given life cover are higher in this case than on a similar term assurance. You can opt to pay premiums up to your death or else elect to stop paying premiums at a certain age. For most people, whose incomes fall after retirement at 65, it is a good idea to have premium payments stopping then. In some cases, the premiums are reviewed every so often, maybe every 10 years. Whole of life policies are often included in combined hybrid policies offered by insurance companies — see below. Special whole of life policies are used to provide for the payment of inheritance tax.

Endowment assurance

With endowment policies the saving element is uppermost. Pure life insurance is often kept to the minimum.

The actual sum payable on death is relatively small per premium euro compared with term or whole life assurance. They are best viewed as a method of saving or investing and for this reason have been dealt with in chapter 3 on investment.

Combined insurance plans

Most insurance companies offer life insurance plans which may have elements of all the above. They are difficult to understand and it's practically impossible to compare one plan with another. They usually include some life cover and some element of saving although the saving is often geared towards building up a fund out of which future premiums may be paid. As the insured person gets older, the cost of the life insurance portion of the plan rises so less of each premium is going into the investment fund.

At some stage the cost of the ongoing life insurance exceeds the premium and the accumulated savings start to be drawn down. If, and when, all of the savings are used up, the insured person has the options of paying more, accepting reduced cover or ending the policy. The advantage of these plans is that they are flexible and they may be less costly than other options over the longer term. But the premium for a set amount of life cover will be higher in the earlier years than an equivalent term policy. A typical policy works something like this.

Beware of insurance policies that mix cover with savings in a way that's not totally clear to you

The life cover is provided by way of a whole of life policy with premiums rising periodically as the insured person gets older. The cover is effectively renewed from time to time with a guarantee that the cost will not be affected by any medical condition that has arisen in the meanwhile. It will rise but only to the rate payable by a healthy person at that age. That guarantee continues for whatever term you pick. The longer the term, the higher the insurance cost.

In the initial years, the premium payable is higher than the cost of the insurance and the surplus after charges is put into a fund. In due course the cost of the insurance exceeds the premium that is being paid. At that stage the insurance company taps into the investment fund. How long the fund can continue to pay the ever-increasing cost of the life cover depends on the investment return. In addition to life cover, most plans will also allow you to add in other types of cover such as serious illness and income continuance. The one-stop-shop aspect of a plan can be appealing but each element of the plan should be assessed as to:

- whether you actually need it, and

- whether there are better stand-alone alternatives.

The comments made with regard to endowment policies also apply. Putting money into an investment fund to pay future life insurance premiums can make sense but it does involve two different decisions. It may not make sense to save for the future if you are in debt or saving to buy a house and what you really want is the maximum life cover at the lowest possible cost.

Income protection insurance

Disability benefits are often included in company pension schemes. About three-quarters of all private pension schemes provide for income continuance where a member is unable to continue working due to disability or long-term illness.

For those who are not covered through a company scheme there is always the option of providing the cover through what are known as Permanent Health, Income Continuance or Income Protection policies.

Self-employed people can be particularly vulnerable to loss of income in the event of illness or disability. As with all insurance, it is well worthwhile shopping around or getting a broker to do it for you. It is important to compare not only the price but also the extent of the cover and, most importantly, what is **not** covered.

As an example of the type of cost involved, one company is quoting a premium of €38 a month to insure a man aged 30 for €317 a week while he is unable, because of illness or disability, to work at his usual job. The premium goes up to €60 for a man aged 40. No benefits are paid for the first 13 weeks of illness unless the claimant is hospitalised.

While tax relief on life assurance policies has been abolished it is still allowed in full on the premiums paid for this type of policy up to a limit of 10% of income. So the true cost can be reduced by almost half for a top rate tax payer. Any benefits received, however, are taxable if the recipient is liable for tax.

Serious illness insurance

We usually think of disability arising as a result of an accident but, of course, it can also arise as a result of serious illness. And serious illness can put many strains on a family's finances. Over the past couple of years, the insurance companies have been vying with one another in devising ever more elaborate policies providing lump sums in the event of the insured person suffering a serious or critical illness. Payment is usually only made if the person survives for 14 days after being diagnosed as suffering from one of a stated list of illnesses. Not all illnesses are covered so it is important to read the fine print.

This type of policy should not be seen as an alternative to medical insurance, such as VHI, Quinn Healthcare or Hibernian Aviva insurance plans that are designed to cover the cost of medical care. Neither is it an alternative to permanent health insurance designed to pay an income if you are unable to work because of an illness or disability. It is not really an alternative to basic life assurance either.

Critical illness insurance is not really an alternative to medical insurance like VHI, Quinn Healthcare or Hibernian Health

But it does pay out a lump sum which may be used for any purpose. It may help to pay medical expenses or to supplement income. But there is no need to show that the medical expenses have been incurred or that you have lost income. The claim is allowed provided you have suffered one of the designated illnesses and survived for more than 14 days. The vast bulk of claims in Ireland are made in respect of people suffering from cancer followed by heart problems and multiple sclerosis.

With some policies, premium levels are fixed and guaranteed for the term of the policy. With others, the premium is reviewed from time to time and you may be called upon to increase the premium or else accept a reduction in the level of cover. With this second type of policy, part of each

■ Lenders often sell payment protection insurance alongside their loans but it is generally as much a protection for themselves as it is for the borrower. Indeed it is worth a lot more to the lender. If a sister company isn't providing the insurance, the lender is at least earning commission. Payment protection insurance is very profitable. It is designed to provide cover should you have difficulty in meeting the loan repayments as a result of illness, disability or simply losing your job.

Many people have benefited from such insurance in recent times as jobs were lost but this type of policy may be unnecessary for those in secure jobs with good sick pay schemes. Of course, no job is totally secure in the current climate but, in many instances, the worst outcome is likely to be redundancy with some lump sum compensation. It's nice to have insurance if you have to make a claim. But against that security you have to weigh the cost.

To take out the insurance all you have to do is tick a box on the application form or simply nod yes when asked by the salesman filling out the loan form on your behalf. It can sound attractive and worth having but unfortunately the cost is seldom fully explained. The information is, of course, all there somewhere in the fine print but even if you do get around to reading it you may still find it very difficult to work out the true cost in terms of euro and cent. Be assured that this type of insurance is not cheap.

For instance the payment protection cover offered by credit card companies typically costs about 60 cent a month for every €100 outstanding. At first glance that seems to be a very small amount. But 60 cent a month adds up to €7.20 a year. Since that is on every €100 outstanding it's the same as paying an additional 7.2% on your debt.

With the interest rate on some credit cards now below 10%, that's a significant addition to your costs particularly when you consider how little you are getting for your money. The benefit is usually no more than a phased reduction in the debt over 12 months if the cardholder is disabled or loses his or her job.

The cover might be nice to have if you did happen to fall ill or lose your job, but the benefit is very small when set against the cost. It's hard to get figures in Ireland because of the way the official statistics are compiled but in Britain it is estimated that only 15% to 20% of the premium income from such policies is paid out in claims.

The survey also found disturbingly high levels of commission being paid. This was particularly true in small and medium-sized retail outlets when about 40% of the firms visited were considered to be offering a level of incentive to sales staff that could encourage the mis-selling of policies. The commission payable was as high as 80%.

premium is invested and the policy may build up a surrender value. The level of future premiums, after an initial fixed period, depends on the performance of the investment fund.

There is heavy competition among the companies so it is well worthwhile shopping around for the widest cover at the cheapest price if you feel that you need this cover.

Products are changing. But by way of illustration, a man of 45 should be able to get cover for €64,000 in respect of serious illness or total permanent disability for a monthly premium of about €34 but some companies quote premiums as high as €60 a month.

Conditions vary from policy to policy so you can't compare on a strictly like-with-like basis. You can shop around, however, by yourself or through a broker. A good broker should be able to justify his or her recommendation. Just ask, why this product rather than another and make sure you get a credible answer.

You should also ask how many quotes the broker sought and for a list of the companies he approached. Most brokers only have agencies for a limited number of companies and may not seek quotes from others. It's always well worthwhile to do a little shopping around on your own behalf.

What to choose

No family should be without some form of life assurance. As mentioned in the introduction to this chapter the early death of husband or wife can impose severe financial burdens on the surviving spouse. And for a relatively small sum, life assurance can provide some protection and a certain amount of peace of mind.

Life assurance is primarily concerned with providing protection for your family and dependants in the event of early death

Remember, that even if you live to pay all the premiums on a term assurance, and therefore get no monetary gain, you have still got a return in the peace of mind you have enjoyed over the years knowing that your family had some protection against the financial loss they would have suffered through your early death. It is important, however, to get the right type of assurance geared to your own particular circumstances.

There can be no hard and fast rules. Every family's circumstances are different, but here are some guidelines to follow. Protection is obviously the first consideration. And a newly married couple on a tight budget can get this through term assurance. Unless their budget is extremely tight, convertible term assurance offers the best bet providing the flexibility to convert into other types of assurance as the family circumstances, and possibly budget, improve.

So the first policy should be a convertible term assurance providing a lump sum on the death of either spouse but particularly on the death of the principal earner or, alternatively, the guarantee of a regular income over a set number of years. This basic cover may well be provided as part of an occupational pension scheme. In that case, term insurance may not be needed.

First check if there is adequate cover through an occupational pension scheme. If not, then term assurance is the cheapest way to get protection. A 25 year old might take a policy over a 25 year term — by the end of which the need for cover may have declined as children mature. If money is really tight, a shorter term policy can provide similar cover at a lower premium.

If a house is being purchased on a mortgage the lender will undoubtedly require a mortgage protection policy. For a very low premium this will provide enough funds to pay off the mortgage should the breadwinner or, in most cases now, either spouse die within the set term. Basically it is a declining balance term assurance i.e. the amount paid out on death goes down each year in line with the reduced indebtedness to the provider of the mortgage. It is also possible to get a term assurance to cover the full value of the house without any decline in the amount payable on death, but this is more expensive.

Even if both spouses are not earning it is important to consider having insurance on both. A mortgage protection policy will usually be on the joint lives ensuring that the mortgage is paid off in the event of either dying. But even with the mortgage paid off, a surviving spouse with children can be burdened with a lot of additional expense while at the same time the family may have lost the earnings of the deceased spouse. Few people think of the costs imposed on a family by the untimely death of a parent even if he or she was not wage-earning. The surviving spouse who wishes to keep the family together might need to employ a housekeeper and will certainly face some extra expense in looking after the children.

A mortgage protection policy is normally taken out on joint lives ensuring that the mortgage is paid off if either spouse dies

One approach is to combine a mortgage protection policy on the joint lives of the spouses with a term insurance on the life of the principal earner and a 10 to 15 year endowment policy on the life of the lower earning or non-earning spouse. The endowment policy provides a lump sum in the event of death but if the spouse is still alive at the end of the 10 or 15 year term, as hopefully he or she will, then the policy will pay out a useful lump sum which can be put towards the children's education.

But you must never lose sight of the main aim of life insurance. The objective must be to provide financial cover in the event of premature death. While that can be combined with saving for the future through endowment policies there are many other ways of saving. It is important to separate the twin objectives of protection for dependants and saving for the future. Be sure of what you need and what you are buying. These are just some general guidelines for deciding what type of policy you need. So how do you go about buying insurance and what about the fine print? Let us look first at the usual conditions that apply to life insurance.

How to buy assurance

It has become a lot easier for consumers to pick the best life insurance products for their needs. It still requires a bit of work but consumer protection laws mean that at least the consumer can get access to most of the information needed to make informed choices. Sellers are required to provide standardised information on the purpose of the product, all the costs involved and details of any penalties for early encashment. But the information is no good if you don't make use of it.

Before buying life insurance it is as important as ever to assess your needs and prioritise them. It is also important to take into account any cover you already have through a company pension scheme, for instance. And since it's a complicated area, some expert advice can be well worthwhile. Some advisers are paid through the commission they receive on the products they sell. Others charge a fee, often on a per hour basis, and give the client the benefit of any commission. Either way you need to assess the advice given.

Buying life assurance can be a far bigger financial decision than many people realise. It is a long-term contract which can cost a lot over the years and can involve considerable loss if cancelled too soon. So it is essential to make the right decisions at the start. Don't be afraid to shop around, ask questions, and take your time. Take advice from more than one person before committing yourself. You should first be clear on the type of policy you think you need and have the reasons clear in your mind.

What insurance cover do you need? Do you only need it for a fixed term until the children are older? What type of cover have you got already? Don't forget the cover you may have through a company pension scheme.

All too often in the past, life insurance was confused with saving. The two are still often combined but it's important when shopping around to be very aware of the distinction and of your own particular needs. Basic life insurance cover is somewhat like car insurance. It pays out if the insured person dies within a fixed term. If the person is still alive at the end of the agreed term then the policy lapses and nothing is paid out. The premiums have bought peace of mind.

The disclosure requirements also apply, of course, to investment products

Saving for the future may be linked to an insurance policy but it doesn't have to be. Consider your needs in both areas separately and satisfy yourself that there is some advantage in linking them – usually there isn't.

It can be well worthwhile getting independent advice. Financial intermediaries or brokers are regulated by the Financial Regulator within the Central Bank. There are two basic categories. There are authorised financial advisers who can provide advice on the full range of options and there are restricted advisers who can only advise on the products of those companies for which they hold agencies.

Even if a restricted adviser has a large number of agencies, they cannot cover the whole range of options since some insurance companies, such as Quinn Life, do not sell through the broker network. See the section on financial advisers on page 42. But then there is no guarantee that an authorised adviser will actually look at all the options.

Advisers have to be paid, of course. Some take their remuneration by way of commission on the products that they sell while others charge a fee for their services giving the client the benefit of any commission that might be payable. There is a wide range of regulations aimed at ensuring that advisers do the best job possible for their clients. Before offering advice at all they are required to spend some time doing what is known as a *fact find* designed to get information on the customer's requirements and personal circumstances.

An adviser must perform a fact find to access your financial position; any other assurance cover you have; your prospects for the future; the size of your family; and your plans for them

Having obtained that information and having decided on a recommendation, the adviser is required to give the client a "statement of suitability" outlining why this particular product has been picked. The customer is also entitled to get a statement outlining details of the type of service provided by the adviser, the fees charged or commission collected, and an outline of the firm's complaints procedures. The statement also has to contain details of the compensation scheme that covers the transaction and be given a copy of the firm's Statement of Authorised Status as issued by the Financial Services Regulator.

Those requirements apply to the adviser. The insurance companies are also required to provide potential customers with a range of information on any life insurance products they intend to buy prior to the deal being concluded. The information includes:

- An outline of the main purpose of the product, is it primarily a savings or protection product and if there's insurance cover, is it for life or illness.

- Detailed information of all charges and of the commission that will be paid to brokers or salespeople.

- Examples of the expected return on savings and investment products together with details of any tax liability. A clear statement of any guarantees.

- Projected values if the product is surrendered early and details of the procedures for early encashment or cancellation.

- Information on the insurance company and the broker or other intermediary with whom the customer is dealing.

- The premiums payable with details of whether they can be reviewed.

There are systems for dealing with complaints — for details see chapter 11.

The fine print

An important point to bear in mind with all insurance policies is the condition of 'utmost good faith' implied in all contracts. This simply means that you are required to tell the assurance company all the facts relevant to its assessment of the risk it is undertaking in assuring your life. If you withhold a relevant fact then the policy can be declared null and void and no payment will be made.

Recent court judgements have made the law less certain on this matter and the insurance companies are taking more care in asking the right questions and stressing the need for full disclosure of relevant details. It is important to give full details of past illnesses etc but there is no need to get unduly worried if you forget to declare some minor illness.

A further point is that you can only take out a life assurance policy on someone whose death will clearly involve you in financial loss. You must have an insurable interest in the person's life. A husband or wife is considered to have an infinite insurable interest in the life of his or her spouse and a child, of course, has an insurable interest in its parents. But the insurable interest of parents in their children is considered to be very small. This last point was written into law many years ago to prevent unscrupulous parents from taking out large assurance policies on their children and then being tempted to murder them.

Only surrender assurance policies as a last resort. There are other options worth considering if you can't afford the premiums or need to get some money

With life assurance, the other sections of the policy are usually straightforward enough. They contain details of who is insured; conditions on the payment of premiums; how claims are to be made and paid. A point to bear in mind is that the name on the policy should coincide with the person's name on their birth certificate. Otherwise problems can sometimes arise. There will also be provisions on surrender values, conversion rights if applicable, and options available should you be unable to keep up your premium payments. Let's have a look at these in more detail as they can sometimes lead to difficulties and misunderstandings.

Surrender Values: On term assurance there is often no surrender value and certainly in the early years of a whole of life or endowment policy the surrender values are very small. So it is not something to be considered except as an absolute last resort.

Paid-Up Policy: If you find that you can no longer meet the premiums it may be possible to convert the policy into one that is 'fully-paid up'. Suppose you have a 20-year endowment policy on which you have paid premiums for 10 years and the life cover is €2,000. It is usually possible to stop paying premiums and continue to have a policy covering you for half (ten-twentieths) of the original sum assured.

> A policy with a surrender value is good security for a loan

Conversion Rights: If you have a policy carrying conversion rights — say a convertible term assurance — bear it in mind when you come to take out fresh assurance. You may have reached the stage where you can afford higher premiums so consider first whether it is better to convert an existing policy rather than take out a new one. If your health is failing, this option may be particularly valuable as you will not usually have to undergo a new medical test.

Selling a policy: If you have an endowment policy which you have to surrender it may be possible to sell it to an investor for rates up to 25% higher than the surrender value. It's better not to surrender a policy at all but if you have to, it can be well worthwhile shopping around and not simply surrendering it back to the insurance company. There are companies specialising in arranging this type of sale.

Medical Insurance

While every Irish citizen is entitled to basic hospital care free of charge it is sometimes, but not always, possible to get speedier treatment if you are able to pay your own way. You also have a wider choice of consultants and the type of hospital accommodation you get. Private medical care can, however, be very expensive and is beyond the reach of most people who don't have insurance cover.

The VHI (Voluntary Health Insurance) had a near monopoly of the provision of medical insurance up until January 1997 when the law was changed allowing for competition subject to an overall condition that while each company, while determining its own premium level, must provide cover at the same rate to all adults seeking it. This is known as "community rating".

Community rating still exists although it is currently being inforced by an artificial tax system that provides insurers with extra relief for older members. Unfortunately community rating has become less meaningful because of the wide range of different plans that are now available. There are over 30 basic medical insurance plans on offer from three providers and that's not counting add-ons and variations. All of the plans are designed to meet all or some of the cost of hospital treatment and accommodation and varying amounts of outpatient treatment. The amount of cover depends on the plan and the choice is wide and confusing.

Medical insurance premiums are allowed in full for tax relief at the standard rate but the relief now comes by way of lower premiums and is generally already built into the price you get quoted

The fact is that while there is obviously increased competition, consumers now have a near impossible job comparing products and choosing the one that provides the best value for their particular needs. A good starting point, however, is the guide "Selecting a private health insurance product" published by the Health Insurance Authority. It can be accessed on its website at www.hia.ie or requested by phone at (01) 4060080. It also publishes price comparisons between VHI, Quinn Healthcare (formerly BUPA) and Hibernian Aviva.

While community rating does still exists the varying rates charged for the many different plans on offer are undoubtedly contrary to its spirit. Companies are still not allowed to load premiums on the basis of age but there is nothing to prevent them from charging more for those products that are of particular interest to the elderly and that is what the insurers are doing. All of the companies also impose some restrictions in the form of waiting periods. At present, for instance, anyone joining VHI under 55 is not covered for pre-existing ailments for the first five years after joining and get no benefits for ailments arising in the first 26 weeks. Those aged between 55 and 59 on joining are not covered for existing ailments for seven years and get no benefits for ailments arising in the first 52 weeks. For those joining over the age of 60, there is no cover for pre-existing ailments for 10 years and no benefits for ailments arising in the first 52 weeks.

In a move that would further erode community rating there are proposals to allow insurers to charge higher premiums on those who join or upgrade their insurance cover after reaching age 35. It has been suggested that the loading could be as high as 80% for someone aged over 65 taking out medical insurance for the first time. Those aged between 55 and 64 on joining might incur a loading of 45% while a loading of 25% might apply to those aged between 45 and 54 and 10% on anyone aged between 35 and 44.

It is proposed that some credit be given for any previous period of cover. So someone taking out medical insurance at age 66, who had been insured for a period earlier in their lives, wouldn't incur the full 80% loading.

There are proposals to impose a loading on anyone over 35 taking out medical insurance for the first time

While such loadings would be viewed by many as fair, there is no certainty that the proposals will make it into law or that loadings will be imposed on those starting off over age 35. But if you are over 35 and thinking of taking out medical insurance it may be worthwhile taking it out before the law changes but there is no indication that the change is going to be introduced soon.

All three companies allow a 10% reduction in premiums for those in group schemes. One way of getting this if you are not in a job-based scheme is to join a credit union. Many operate group schemes. Not only do you get a 10% saving on the premium but the credit union may also provide you with a cost-free facility for paying the premium in monthly instalments.

5 Borrowing – benefits often outweigh the costs

It is lawful to borrow for usury from a man who is a usurer by profession; provided the borrower has a good end in view, such as the relief of his own or another's need
— Thomas Aquinas

Sensible borrowing can play an important and beneficial role in managing the family finances. The operative word is sensible. There is a cost involved in borrowing. The benefits can, however, very often outweigh the costs particularly when interest rates are low but it all depends on what you use the borrowed money for. Just as a business loan makes sense if the borrowed money yields a return greater than the interest paid on it, a personal loan is justified if the returns, both tangible and intangible, outweigh the costs.

Borrowing enables you to buy something now rather than having to wait until you have saved up the money. That's the main benefit. If delaying a purchase means that the price goes up, maybe simply because of inflation, then the savings you make, by buying now rather than later, helps to offset some of the costs involved. So when considering interest rates it is important to also take account of inflation.

A loan can easily cost three times as much from one borrower than from another. Always shop around

✳ In some circumstances, tax relief can also reduce the cost of loans but apart from business loans tax relief is only allowed when the borrowed money is used to buy, maintain or improve your principal residence, certain other residences that you provide for specific people rent free, or to buy shares in your own company. Mortgage tax relief is detailed in Chapter 6 on page 130.

Apart from the interest charged on the loan there is another cost involved in borrowing. It's not a cost that can be accurately quantified but it is a cost nonetheless. It's the reduction in financial flexibility that results from having to meet the repayments on the loan. The lender, of course, takes the risk of not being repaid. But the borrower is also taking a risk. If he is unable to meet the repayments he could be forced to sell assets to meet the debt or even be declared bankrupt. At the very least, the borrower is taking on an extra burden and that involves risk.

Each individual will exercise a different degree of caution, but there is no need to be cautious to the point of not borrowing at all. Most reputable lenders will allow a degree of flexibility to help a borrower over an unexpected bad patch. If having considered all that, you still want to borrow, the next step is to shop around for the cheapest possible loan.

Shopping around

There is a wide range of options open to the would-be borrower: bank loans, finance houses, credit sales, budget accounts, HP, etc. And the cost can vary greatly. Except in the most general of advertising, all those providing credit, either by way of loans or by way of credit sales, are required to show the true rate of interest being charged on their loans in ads, sales literature, loan agreements etc. So it is possible to shop around by just keeping your eyes open and comparing rates.

The difference between the dearest and cheapest loan can be significant. Getting the cheapest available can save you a lot of money and remember the borrower is currently in a buyer's market. Lenders want to lend money: that is how they make a profit. If nobody borrowed, they would go out of business.

Where the loan is arranged by the seller of a product or service you should also carefully check the price you are being charged. It's no good saving on the loan and ending up paying over the odds for whatever you are buying. Similar caution is necessary when buying goods or services on credit, perhaps paying by instalments. You may find that you are paying for so-called "free" credit in the price of the goods and services you are buying. So shop around not only for the cheapest loan but also for the cheapest goods and services.

Borrowing is a normal business transaction, the lender is selling a commodity to the borrower. The commodity in this case is money. It might be more correct to say that the borrower is hiring the use of the money for a period and will be paying a rental — the interest — for the use of it. The lender has one thought in mind — will he get the money back? This is the risk factor, and the higher the risk he considers he is taking, the higher the interest he will charge. The longer the period of the loan, the greater is the risk he foresees: so normally the longer the term of the loan, the higher the interest rate. The major exception to this rule are mortgage loans on which rates are relatively low because of the security provided.

Lenders, be they banks, finance companies or pawnbrokers, want to lend money. That is their business and that is how they make their profit. There is no need to go out with the begging bowl

Most lenders, of course, have their interest rates fixed at any particular time and, as a result, have a set idea about the risk they are willing to take, or, in other words, the type of person they will lend to. Lenders wants to lend the money — they just need convincing that you are a good risk.

Obviously, you want to pay the lowest interest rate possible, and as a rough guide the rates will go up as you move along the following list: mortgage lenders, the major banks, credit unions, finance houses, credit accounts, hire purchase, credit cards, money lenders. All lenders must declare the annual percentage rate (APR) charged on their loans. This can be defined as the true rate of interest and can be used to compare alternatives.

The APR shown on loan advertisements, shop notices and loan agreements has to be based on the global cost of the loan — interest and other charges. So it is ideal for compar-

Interest rate	3 years	5 years	7 years	10 years
8%	€31.27	€20.21	€15.52	€12.06
9%	€31.72	€20.68	€16.00	€12.58
10%	€32.17	€21.14	€16.49	€13.10
11%	€32.62	€21.62	€16.99	€13.63
12%	€33.07	€22.09	€17.49	€14.18
13%	€33.52	€22.57	€18.00	€14.73

ing one source of finance with another — the lower the APR, the cheaper the loan.

For the sake of comparison, it does not really matter how the rates of interest are actually calculated as long as they are all calculated in the same way. That's the advantage of using APRs. While they allow you to compare like with like, it is no harm having some understanding of what a true rate of interest is. Suppose you get €100 now and repay €110 this day next year — i.e., the initial €100 plus €10 interest — that is a true rate of interest of 10% — €10 on €100.

But suppose that instead of repaying in a lump sum, the re-payments are spread over the full year and you still repay a total of €110, that is nearer a 20% rate of interest, since you did not have the use of the €100 for the full year. Indeed, you only had, on average, the use of €50 for the full year, since you had more than €50 for the first six months, but progressively less than €50 for the second six months.

As mentioned above, the borrower has a wide range of options open to him and the cost difference between the cheapest and dearest loans can be considerable. So it pays to shop around.

To avail of an overdraft you need to have a current account i.e. an account that allows you ready access to your money by way of a chequebook, a Laser or ATM card. In effect you ask your bank manager if you can overdraw your account to a specified sum. If he agrees you can then spend that amount of money over and above the funds you have in your account. You only pay interest on the actual amount you have drawn and, as mentioned above, interest is calculated on a daily basis. If you don't make use of the overdraft permission you pay no interest.

Overdraft permissions, however, are only given to cover short-term borrowing requirements. There are no set repayments, but the account has to be back in credit at least within a year and the bank manager will want some assurance of that. So overdrafts generally have a limited use. They are particularly useful to cover the odd bad month when a number of large payments fall due. In other words it should be viewed like an advance, or a "sub" on your salary or wages which will have to be paid off on the next pay day or at least over a few pay periods. Of course, it is a loan that you have to pay interest on and the interest rates are set substantially above the rates on personal loans and on the better credit cards. If you have a relatively low interest credit card charging less than 10%, it would usually be cheaper to use it to get over a short-term bad financial patch. If you need finance over the longer term, shop around for a personal loan with set repayments.

In some cases the flexibility offered by an overdraft can offset the higher interest rate and possible set-up costs. But you need to do the sums. Running up an overdraft, even for a short period, may lose you your right to free banking and result in you having to pay bank charges for a full three months. Those charges must be considered as additional to the interest in working out the true cost of an overdraft. You may also have to pay an arrangement fee of as much as €35 a year. Once an overdraft has been approved, it can be drawn on at any time without fresh recourse to the bank. Every cent put into the account immediately reduces the amount

Overdrafts are the most flexible way of borrowing and they can be one of the cheapest

of the loan and, since interest is charged on the amount outstanding each day, there can be a significant saving.

Suppose, for instance, the borrower has his or her wages paid into the bank each month. Let's suppose that a net €3,000 is lodged. If that money is spent evenly over the month the customer has a net €1,500 on average in the account over the year — more than €1,500 early in the month and less than €1,500 later in the month but an average of €1,500. That's automatically reducing the size of the overdraft. At 10% a year the interest saving would be €150 to help offset the extra charges which might be incurred.

- **Budget Accounts:** Some banks and credit unions run budget type accounts where the customer sets out his spending requirements in advance. They are not unlike formalised overdrafts. The spending needs will not, of course, be spread evenly over the year but the bank allows for overdraft type loans to cover the lean periods while requiring fixed regular payments. It is simply a way of balancing out one's cash flow. But it is fixed and formalised — unlike the normal overdraft.

Term loans

Unlike overdrafts, term loans have fixed repayment commitments. Also, unlike an overdraft, the full amount of the loan is handed out to you or transferred into your current account and interest liability begins to accrue immediately. Interest rates can vary greatly depending on the lender, the borrower, the term of the loan, and even, in some cases, what the loan is for. It is up to the borrower to shop around and take care.

While lenders do have schedules of interest rates that apply in most cases, they can and do charge higher rates to some customers and for some purposes. It's important to check. In general the larger banks charge the same rate for normal term loans as they do for overdrafts but ignoring the impact of bank charges — as mentioned above — a term loan may prove more expensive for short term borrowing since you do not have the flexibility of drawing down only what you need. Repayments are normally set in monthly amounts extending over a fixed period.

Most term loans are given at variable rates of interest. The rate charged may change during the term of the loan in line with changes in wholesale interest rates. The rate may go up or down. If rates go up, some lenders will leave repayment levels unchanged and add some extra repayments at the end to cover the higher interest rate. Others may require an immediate increase in the repayments.

Fixed rate loans are also available but there are drawbacks. If variable rates are expected to rise, the fixed rate will be set higher than the initial variable rate. On average, fixed rate loans will be more expensive than variable rate ones. The borrower pays a premium for the security of knowing that the interest rate will not be increased during the term of the loan. If rates do go up it will have been worthwhile but if rates decline, a variable rate loan would have worked out cheaper. Remember you are doing the lender a favour by borrowing.

The major drawback with fixed rate loans is a lack of flexibility. There are usually penalties, sometimes quite heavy, for early repayment. Opting for a fixed rate loan can make sense where the borrower needs assurance that the repayments won't increase. That can often be the case with a mortgage loan where the repayments represent a large proportion of the borrower's income. But it's less likely to apply in the case of a smaller term loan. The extra flexibility and potential lower cost of a variable rate loan usually makes it the best option.

Term loans are available from a wide range of lenders, banks, building societies, credit unions and finance houses. Building societies, better known for their mortgage finance, can and do provide unsecured personal loans. Credit unions have been increasing their range of services. They are covered in more detail below. Finance houses often provide loans through car dealers or shops. Sometimes they are at special low rates subsidised by the retail outlet. It is important to be sure, however, that you are not paying for the cheaper loan by paying over the odds for the goods or services being bought.

Interest rates on term loans can vary greatly from lender to lender so it pays to shop around

In other cases it is cheaper to go directly to the finance house itself rather than take out the loan through the retailer, service provider or agent. The intermediary often takes a

> **Save money by switching your debt**

■ Financial decisions, once made, are all too seldom reviewed. This is particularly the case with personal borrowings. Built up over time for various different reasons, it is very easy to let each loan run its course. Yet personal circumstances change, interest rates vary, and the need for the debt may diminish as other assets become available.

So it's worth doing an occasional wealth check on your borrowings. It is possible to re-finance debt in order to alter repayment schedules or avail of lower interest rates. It may be worthwhile using savings to reduce or pay off a loan.

The biggest interest savings can be made by rolling up a number of loans into a mortgage top-up. The interest rates are the lowest available and the repayments can be spread over 20 or more years. It's an option which needs very careful consideration and it's not the only change which can produce savings.

Before you can make any decisions, of course, you need to take a little time to itemise your current loans and work out what they are costing you. Then you can start looking at the alternatives.

But first list your loans. They are likely to fall into three main categories.

Mortgage: You know how much you initially borrowed but how much do you owe now? If it was an endowment mortgage you still owe as much as you did on the day you took out the loan but your endowment policy should be worth something. Find out how much it is worth. It's seldom worth cashing in a policy on which you have already incurred heavy set-up charges but it's nice to know where you stand. How much equity do you have in your house? If it is worth significantly more than the outstanding loan you should be able to get a top up mortgage. ➡

commission — which you pay — and in any case you are in a stronger bargaining position when buying the goods if you arrange the loan yourself. As far as the seller is concerned, you are then a cash buyer.

Mortgages

Loans for house purchase are dealt with in Chapter 6, page 111 but there are other uses for loans secured with mortgages on the borrower's house or other property. Such loans are, of course, mainly used for house purchase but need not be. The interest rate is lower than on other loans

What rate of interest are you paying? Is it fixed or variable? How does it compare with the competition? It can be worth switching mortgages although it is a big step and likely to require a heavy up-front cost.

Bank Loans: We can include credit union and finance company loans in this category. You should check what rate of interest you are paying. There isn't a lot of variation at this time between one institution and the other but if you have a loan that's a few years old you may discover that you are still paying a fixed rate that's a little over the odds. If so, you need to find out if you can pay it off without penalty.

Also check your overdraft. An overdraft can be the cheapest form of bank borrowing since you only pay interest on the amount outstanding each day. So when your pay cheque is lodged to your account, your interest liability immediately goes down. A well-used overdraft can be cheaper than a term loan even though the interest rates are the same on both. But running up an occasional overdraft can be very expensive since it usually makes you immediately liable for bank charges during the relevant quarter and most banks impose a hefty arrangement fee.

Credit Cards: Credit cards should ideally only be used to secure free credit by paying the bill in full each month. Occasionally letting some of the bill run on for a month or two is not too costly but ongoing debt should definitely be avoided. The interest rates can be penal — over 18% on some cards.

It's easy to get into the habit of letting the credit card debt run on and on paying only the minimum requirement each month. The answer is to get a term loan to pay off the debt. If you then let the credit card debt run up again it may be time to bring out the scissors and cut the card in two.

but there are usually set-up costs involved in taking out the mortgage — they are detailed in Chapter 6. Those costs are lower, of course, in the case of a top-up mortgage.

Topping up a mortgage sometimes involves taking out a new increased mortgage and paying off the existing one. But it is possible to top up an existing mortgage. A bank or building society with an existing mortgage on the property should be able to provide the top-up at the lowest cost but it is important to check interest rates. Because of the cost of setting up a new mortgage, you need to be borrowing upwards of perhaps €3,000 or even €5,000 to ensure that the saving in interest payments covers the set-up costs. And

Care is the watchword with equity release

■ Many of those currently in retirement didn't have the opportunity or forethought to fund pension entitlements although they may have a lot of money tied up in a house. Trading down to a smaller house is one way of releasing some of that wealth although seldom attractive for the over 65s particularly if it means moving to a new area.

But there are other options available.

An ideal way is to have the children borrow against their own houses and advance the money to the parents in the expectation that the family home will be theirs in due course. But that doesn't suit every family situation. The alternative is to opt for what is known as an equity release scheme. These fall into two broad categories. There is a basic loan scheme type similar to any other mortgage secured on the house except that there are no regular repayments. The interest is rolled up and the loan is repaid when the borrower and his or her spouse eventually leave the house either on death or to move elsewhere.

The other type of equity release involves actually selling a share in the house for delivery when you and your spouse eventually move out of it. That's a more complicated option considered in more detail below. Neither option should be taken lightly. Long and careful thought should go into the decision making process. You should get independent advice.

Bank of Ireland was the first to offer a loan type product. It's known as Lifeloan. The amount that the Bank of Ireland will advance depends on the age of the youngest applicant who must, in every case, be over 65. It will lend 20% of the estimated value of the property to those aged 65 to 69 rising to 30% to those aged over 80. A sliding scale applies to those aged between 70 and 79. Other providers offer similar products but some set a lower age limit of 60.

Negotiating a value for the home is not of prime importance. The value does determine the maximum amount that can be borrowed but eventually the house will be sold on the open market. At that stage, the loan is repaid together with the accumulated interest and anything left goes to the borrower or his or her estate. In comparing loan products it is important to consider the interest rate. The Bank of Ireland rate is fixed for 15 years. Some lenders fix the rate for the duration of the loan while others charge a variable rate that can change at any time. Flexibility may or may not be a consideration. Bank of Ireland imposes penalties for early repayment, for instance.

The other type of equity release scheme is more complicated. It involves actually ➡

selling a share in the property. The decision making process is more involved. Valuing the property is, of course, crucial. It's easy if similar houses in the locality have been sold recently on the open market. But it is a lot more difficult with a unique house. Getting an independent valuation is important but that's only the first hurdle. Suppose you agree that the house is worth €500,000 and you want to sell half of it. That's currently worth €250,000 but because you and your spouse have the right to live in it for life you're not going to get €250,000.

The price you will get at this stage depends on age and gender. It should also, of course, depend on your health but it's unusual to take that into account although if you are in poor health it's well worth arguing for a higher pay out. In all cases you need to negotiate the best deal. An example based on buying a 50% share of a house currently worth €500,000 suggests that a man aged 70 could receive about €140,000.

Independent advice and careful consideration is essential.

Anyone considering equity release through the sale of a share in their home should steel themselves for hard and heavy negotiations. It's not like going into a shop or a bank and simply paying the asking price. Don't accept the first value put on your house. Be ready to bargain hard over the extent to which that price should then be reduced to take account of your lifetime right to live in it. If you are not up to hard negotiating, get someone to do it for you. The primary aim of the people offering these products is to make a profit for themselves. There's nothing wrong with that but you need to be very conscious of it.

With a loan you know exactly what you are getting. You'll incur interest on the loan only until it is repaid. If you and your spouse were to die after a year then only a year's interest would have been paid. But if you sell a share in your home, the price you'll get is irrespective of how long you'll live. If you and your spouse were to live only a short while or the house was to soar in value, you or the beneficiaries of your estate would have lost badly. One of the earlier companies in the market guarantees to give a rebate if the house is passed over within four years or rises significantly in value. But it is, of course, only a limited guarantee.

Another factor to consider in all cases is that the proceeds from loans or the sale of a share in your home could affect eligibility to means tested social welfare or health benefits. At present €190,460 of the proceeds from the sale of a house is ignored for social welfare means-test purposes where the recipient moves into more suitable alternative accommodation. But since you are not actually moving house this exemption doesn't apply.

Be very careful.

it is important to appreciate that the loan is secured on the property. The bank or building society has the right to sell the property to get its money back if the borrower defaults on payments.

It is that security which allows them to charge a lower interest rate. So in return for a cheaper loan the borrower is putting his home or other property on the line. Borrowing by way of a mortgage can make sense where the money is being spent on a house extension or other long term investment in real assets — that can include education. But despite the lower interest rate it may not be a good idea to borrow on a mortgage simply to pay off short-term debts or finance short-term purchases such as a car or a holiday.

People have been encouraged to extend their mortgages to pay off their bank and credit card debts. Their monthly re-payments may go down as a result but that is partly because the debt is being spread over a longer period. In two or three years time, they will still be facing many years of higher mortgage repayments while the bank and credit card debts may have again emerged. And they have put their homes up as security. So care needs to be taken.

It is usual for mortgage finance providers to charge the normal house purchase rate for personal loans related to the house. And many charge that basic rate on all secured loans. But some charge more where the loan is used for other purposes.

Used sensibly, a top-up mortgage can save the borrower a lot of money. The interest rate on an unsecured personal loan can be about twice as high so the potential saving is significant, even allowing for some set up costs. But those who have any doubts over their financial discipline need to consider carefully why the interest rates on these top-up mortgages are low. It's because the loan is secured on the borrower's home. If you default on a personal bank loan the worst that can happen is that you're taken to court and ordered to pay what the judge decides you can afford. Default on a mortgage and your home could be sold to repay the debt. It doesn't happen too often but it does happen — unfortunately with increasing frequency.

Of course lenders don't want to repossess homes and will do their best to ensure that borrowers are well able to meet whatever liabilities they take on. But they also want to lend as much money as they can. That's how they make their profits. Mortgage top ups are most suited for major spending needs such as home improvements or education and are best avoided by those who are easily tempted into running up debt — that obviously includes those who see it as a solution to an existing debt problem. It is, of course, possible to reduce monthly repayments by rolling up a number of debts into a single mortgage top-up and spreading the repayments over a longer period. But it is all too easy to let the debts mount up again and the second time around your home is being put at risk.

Store budget accounts

Most of the larger stores have their own budget account facilities and a growing number of smaller stores have budget accounts run for them by finance houses. The interest rate is much the same as charged by the finance houses. The best advice is to avoid them. While a budget account is handy, it can be relatively expensive to run — it is cheaper to try to get a term loan from your bank or, cheaper still, your credit union. Budget accounts are flexible, however, allowing you to spend up to the maximum credit level at any time. The worst part, however, is that you have to use it in the one store, or group of stores, so there is a disincentive to shop around. Indeed, borrowing on your credit card is likely to be as cheap while still leaving you the freedom to shop where you like.

But in either case, of course, you may be tempted to spend more than you should, or really want to. The advice is to try to get a bank or credit union loan for major shopping sprees. If you want to have a store card to avail of special offers or promotions try to keep it on the basis of a monthly card. That should cost you nothing. If you actually do a lot of shopping in the one store there can be some advantage in having a card, even for credit purposes, since the card is generally free and the interest rate can be lower than that charged on a bank or building society card.

Credit unions

Credit unions are among the cheapest providers of loans but they are, of course, only available to members. Membership is open to those who are part of a 'common bond' i.e. live in the locality or work in the particular firm covered by the union. To qualify for a loan, it is usually necessary to be a member of some standing having shown an ability to save. But that can be well worth the effort. There are credit unions now based in most localities and in many organisations and large firms. The standard interest rate is 1% a month — an annual percentage rate of 12.6%. But many credit unions now charge less than that and a few charge considerably less. They are non-profit making organisations. Any surplus made belongs to the members. Some credit unions use a portion of the surplus to give interest rate rebates to their borrowing members.

Limits may apply to the size of the loan and the cover is curtailed for the over 60s and not available for the over 70s. Another built-in insurance provides for the payment of a benefit to a member's estate in the event of death. In the case of a member aged under 55, the benefit is equal to the amount on deposit or in shares at the time of death. The benefit is lower for those over 55 and not applicable in the case of the over 70s.

Hire purchase

Hire purchase is generally an expensive way of buying on credit. Not only are interest rates high, but there are also high administrative charges built into the hire purchase price. Most people who buy on HP could borrow elsewhere. The best alternative for most people tempted to borrow on hire purchase is the local credit union.

Insurance

It is sometimes possible to borrow against the surrender value of with-profits endowment life assurance policies. Most insurance companies will provide such loans and the interest rates are usually relatively low. In some cases, there is no need to repay the loan, since the sum involved will be taken out of the final sum due on maturity of the policy. Indeed, the interest payments can also be rolled forward in this manner. But the policy does need to have a cash-in value higher than the size of the loan.

Credit cards

Credit cards are best seen as a means of getting short-term credit — they are a boon if used wisely in this way. They save you carrying cash; enable you to keep a record of your spending; and can provide you with a handy period of free credit. But used unwisely, they can be very expensive. If you exceed your permitted period of free credit you can end up paying a fairly high rate of interest on the outstanding amount — up to twice the rate you would pay on a bank or credit union loan. See the section on credit cards in chapter 2 on page 20.

Moneylenders

The best advice is not to borrow from moneylenders at all, whether legal or illegal. If there is no other alternative, pawnbrokers are not all that expensive provided you do not make a habit of using them.

Tackling debt problems

It is all too easy for debts to become a problem and when they do there is a strong temptation to bury your head in the sand and hope that the problem will go away. Of course, that just makes it worse. The only solution for those with debt problems — or heading that way — is to confront the difficulty head on. The quicker that is done, the quicker the problems can be solved.

There is no debtors prison today and contrary to some popular notions it is not possible to end up in prison simply for being in debt. But you can get locked up for failing to meet debt repayments decided on by a court. Initially when a person is brought before a court for debt it will do no more than decide on equitable repayments in the context of the person's ability to pay. It is only if those repayments are not met, that a person may face jail and then only for blatantly failing to pay. A court can always be asked to adjust a repayment order if circumstances change. But there should be no need for anyone to appear in court for debt. If creditors are kept informed of any financial difficulty, it is often possible to reschedule repayments and sometimes even have interest charges reduced. It is important to take action as early as possible.

Debt is not a bad thing, in itself. Borrowing, indeed, has an important role to play in most families' finances. But borrowing can get out of hand. Problems start to arise when a person's — or a family's — spending needs start to outstrip their income. Initially it may seem possible to handle the problem. But it is usually only being compounded. The balance on the credit card runs up. The gas bill is missed so that something else can be paid. There is a hope that something will turn up. But it doesn't. Postponed debts do not go away. With interest added on they only get worse.

Swopping a number of small loans for one big one can be a big mistake too. You can, of course, reduce your monthly repayments by replacing some short-term expensive loans with a cheaper home mortgage loan spread over a longer period. But you may be only storing up problems for the

In brief, if you have a debt problem you need to face your problem, come clean with your creditors and make them an offer based on a full disclosure of what you can afford. **Take it one step at a time.**

ONE: The first step is to work out exactly what your income is. Get out a copy book or a few sheets of paper and detail your income — what actually comes into the house from all sources each week or month.

TWO: Next list your total spending needs. Do not leave anything out. There are the obvious things like rent/mortgage repayments, food, fuel etc. But do not forget to include the irregular spending items — clothes, TV licence and cable, the ESB or gas bill which only comes in every two months, insurance bills which may only come once a year etc. Bring it all down to a monthly or weekly figure.

THREE: Then compare your first list with your second. If your income exceeds your spending needs then you do not have a problem in meeting your ongoing commitments. Check your figures again. If your outgoings do exceed your income an obvious approach is to cut your spending. Divide your spending into essentials and non essentials. Can you cut back? Is there anything you can sell to bring in money to reduce some debt — not goods that you have on HP, although if you do have goods on hire purchase and you have not paid a third of the price, the HP company may take them back.

FOUR: Examine possible ways of increasing your income. Are there any social welfare benefits you are entitled to — supplementary benefit or the family income supplement (see chapter 12). If you are on social welfare and have difficulty meeting your rent, you may be entitled to rent allowance under the supplementary benefit scheme administered by your local health board.

FIVE: List exactly how much you owe. Divide the loans into priority ones and others. The priorities would be rent/mortgage, ESB, other fuel bills. If you fall too far behind with these you could lose your house or have the electricity or gas turned off.

SIX: Lastly having gathered all that information, the final step is to talk with your creditors. Summarise the figures you have listed and let them see the details of your income and spending. That way they will realise how much or how little you can afford to pay. Make an offer.

future. If you do not meet the repayments on the mortgage you will be putting your home in jeopardy.

The quicker you face up to debt problems the quicker they can be solved

This is not the answer if you have major debt problems. If you see it as part of a solution you need to be absolutely sure that you will be able to meet the mortgage repayments and you also need to check that there are no heavy penalties involved in paying off your existing loans early. With many finance house loans there are such penalties. And there is no sense in replacing your loans with even more expensive ones. Overall there is no easy solution down this road.

Remember that you have to deal with the priority debts first. A building society will normally agree to reduce repayments as long as you are at least meeting the interest portion. In the early years this may, unfortunately, represent more than 90% of each repayment so that the possible reduction is not great. But if you are not meeting the interest, then the amount outstanding keeps going up. Banks, credit card companies, and finance houses will sometimes agree to reduce interest charges. Some of their rates are so high they can well afford to. If you feel unable to do the negotiating, your local St. Vincent de Paul Society or credit union is likely to know of someone who may be able to help.

The Department of Social Welfare supports a money advice and budgeting advice service (MABS) throughout most of the country. It's a free service of course. Ask about it at your local Social Welfare Office or public library. It has its own website www.mabs.ie which provides useful advice and the locations of its offices nationwide. Another scheme administered with help from the St. Vincent de Paul Society and credit unions, provides advice on budgeting and will negotiate with creditors on behalf of borrowers. It is not there to pay off loans but rather to help people budget their way out of difficulties. Arrangements may be made to pay off expensive loans and replace them with cheaper credit union loans.

The European Consumer Centre, 13A Upper O'Connell Street, Dublin, phone (01) 809 0600 can help you prepare for a district court appearance over debts of up to €6,300. The legal adviser will provide advice but will not actually represent you in court.

6 Putting a roof over your head

If all but myself were blind I would want neither fine clothes,
fine houses nor fine furniture — Benjamin Franklin

The sharp decline in house prices is beginning to put house purchase back within reach of those many young people who viewed home ownership as a vain aspiration during the boom days of upward spiralling prices. The financial crisis is, at least, having the beneficial effect of bringing house prices back down to more reasonable levels. The desire to owe a home is not surprising given the long tradition of home ownership in Ireland and the absence of an adequate rental market offering security of tenure. Even with the drop in prices, the purchase of a house is likely to require many times the average person's annual salary and represents the single largest financial commitment of a lifetime. And if the money is borrowed, the repayments will take a considerable part of the family budget.

Assuming that you do not pay an inflated price for the house, there is little doubt that it generally makes more sense to borrow and buy, rather than rent. But in the uncertain climate of late 2009 this conventional wisdom may not apply. With house prices falling, and rental properties readily available, there must be a temptation to delay a purchase until there is some sign of a market upturn. With the economic outlook remaining uncertain, there could be plenty of time.

There are, of course, exceptions. Few people can hope to get in at the absolute bottom of the market and fewer still can hope to get their ideal home at a rock bottom price. So it may not be a good idea to wait if that once-in-a-lifetime dream home happens to come onto the market. Even if you don't manage to buy at the lowest possible price, you can be fairly sure of gains over the longer term.

Buying a house does not simply add to household expenses. It is a major investment decision as well, and the return on the investment can be sizeable.

Apart from the pleasure of living in a home that you like, you can be fairly sure that in the longer term, property values will rise faster than the rate of inflation unless the economy collapses completely.

You need some money for the deposit and expenses and you also need to convince a lender that you will be able to meet the repayment on a loan. But there are plenty of lenders in the market. They may be a little more cautious than they were in the boom years but they still want to lend money. That's the business that they are in. It's important to remember, however that there are traps along the way and a lot of critical decisions to be made. Unfortunately, many of those decisions have to be taken on the basis of assumptions about the future rather than hard facts. So what are the options?

What are the options?

The main constraint on what you can buy is the availability of finance. For most people this simply means the amount they are able to borrow. The range of borrowing options open to the house buyer has widened significantly in recent years with most lenders actively seeking mortgage business. The banks and building societies want to lend money so there is plenty of scope for the borrower to shop around. The choice is wide and you can never be sure of making the right decision. It's impossible to predict what is going to happen over the next 20 years. What appears to be the cheapest and best option now may prove to be

■ If you have a fixed rate loan, the penalties for early repayment are likely to offset any potential saving from switching to a lower cost lender. But there are no penalties for paying off a variable rate loan. So is it worthwhile switching? Setting up a new mortgage can cost as much as €1,500. It depends on the size of the mortgage, the way it is registered and the legal costs. However, given the current competition in the market many lenders are willing to absorb some or all of the cost. Let's assume you can switch for €750. That's not cheap but what are the potential savings? Let's take the case of Tom and Mary who borrowed €200,000 two years ago with an annuity mortgage at a variable rate. They are currently paying 2.8% — higher than the 2.5% they see one lender advertising. The annual saving is simple enough to work out. It amounts to 0.3 of a percentage point. Tom and Mary still owe almost the full €200,000 so the saving works out at about €600 a year. If it costs €750 to set up the new mortgage Tom and Mary will be net winners after little more than a year. There is no certainty, but if the current differentials remain for that time they can't lose. Do your own sums and it may be sufficient just to warn your existing lender that you intend switching unless they lower their rate. That might produce the desired result without the need to switch. That, after all, is what competition is all about.

otherwise over the course of time. A little care can help to reduce the risks. There are a number of factors to consider:

Interest rates: It is easy enough to compare interest rates so it is not too difficult to pick the cheapest loan on the basis of current rates. That's where you have to start. Have a look at the stated interest rate first and then at the monthly repayments. The repayments may be as good a guide as any. While all lenders have to show annual percentage rates of interest that take into account all the costs involved in paying off the loan they may not be strictly comparable. But look at both. Remember that it is the interest rate over the full term of the loan that matters, so do not be taken in by short-term catch-all promotions. If the rate is variable, it may change within months and what was cheapest when you borrowed may prove dearest in the long run. Some lenders offer a special low rate for the first year or so and that may look attractive. But the gains in the first year can very quickly be offset if the interest rate in subsequent years is higher than the competition.

At least in the long term it usually makes good financial sense to borrow to buy a house

It is, of course, always possible to switch lenders later but that can be costly enough – anything from €750 to €1,500 although some lenders will absorb some or all of the cost as an incentive to switch to them. But even if there is a cost involved, switching shouldn't necessarily be ruled out because of it. Remember if you can save half a percentage point on a €200,000 mortgage, the annual saving is €1,000 gross or €800 after allowing for tax relief. So the cost of switching can be recouped over a few years. And most mortgages run for 25 or more years.

It's worth asking if interest is calculated on a daily, weekly, monthly or annual basis. Traditionally with building societies, interest was calculated on the basis of the amount outstanding at the end of each year. But now most lenders calculate interest on a daily basis. The differences are built into the APR but it's worth knowing the mechanism used. It's important if you are considering paying off a mortgage early or even making additional lump sum repayments. If interest is calculated daily then you should get an immediate benefit from such repayments.

Fixed or Variable: It is impossible to know which is best in advance. As a rule of thumb, a fixed rate mortgage will tend to be more expensive in the long run. The lender will fix a rate on the basis of how interest rates are expected to move and then add a margin on to cover his risk.

So the borrower pays a little extra for the assurance that whatever happens to rates, his interest rate remains unchanged. But just as a bookie sometimes loses, so can a bank. It is impossible to accurately foretell the future and if rates go higher than expected, a fixed rate mortgage will prove to be the cheapest.

The only certainty is that one type of mortgage will definitely prove cheaper in the long run than the other but it's impossible to know in advance. So a choice has to be made on the basis of limited information and many borrowers will find that their repayments would have been lower had they chosen otherwise. But that doesn't necessarily mean that they made the wrong choice.

The borrower should not be trying to second-guess developments on the money market. At the time the mortgage is taken out, the money market believes that the fixed rate mortgage will prove more expensive than the variable rate one.

The fixed rate provides the borrower with a guarantee that repayments will not go up. He or she has to pay a premium for that insurance. The lender has to raise the money from depositors who expect to do better by fixing their rates. In other words, the market expects variable interest rates to be lower over that period than the fixed rates. The market may be wrong, of course, but the borrower does well to heed its view unless (s)he believes (s)he knows better than the money market moguls or else simply wants to gamble against the market.

The choice between a fixed rate and variable rate mortgage should not be made in the hope of picking the cheapest option. If that is the sole objective then the variable rate will most often prove the cheapest. That has to be true even if the market is only right half of the time since there is an insurance premium built into the fixed rate. That said, fixed rates are still the best option for many borrowers — those for whom a hike in interest rates would prove traumatic because of the impact higher repayments would have on their lives. The security of having fixed repayments can be well worthwhile if variable rates do rise. Buying that insurance is the only good reason for picking a fixed rate loan and it's as relevant now as it was in the past.

The choice between a fixed and variable rate mortgage has to be made without adequate information

In general, for those on a tight budget, a fixed rate mortgage is a good option for borrowers who could suffer severe difficulties if interest rates rise. Even if it doesn't prove cheapest in the long run they will have benefited from fewer sleepless nights. A variable rate mortgage is likely to be best for borrowers who can well handle a rise in interest rates and who are not of a worrying nature.

Lender: Different lenders may be prepared to lend different amounts. The traditional norm favoured by the Central Bank was to limit mortgage loans to $2^1/_2$ times the sum of a principal income and half of a secondary income. But that was at a time of very high interest rates. Most lenders will lend more than that although a renewed realisation that house values can fall as well as rise, has made them more

Mortgage types — the options

■ The range of mortgage options now available is very wide. The following is an outline of the various mortgage types.

Annuity: This is the most popular type of mortgage where each repayment covers the interest and also pays something off the loan. The amount owing goes down each year, slowly at first and then progressively quicker. But you are 15 years into a 20 year mortgage before you have paid off half the loan.

Endowment: With the basic endowment mortgage the loan is not repaid until the end of the term. The borrower pays interest each year on the full amount and also pays money into an investment fund which should, at the end of the term, mature yielding at least enough to pay off the loan. Their attractiveness depends on how the investment fund performs.

Current account: Combines a normal current account with the mortgage account. Any money in the current account is automatically offset against the mortgage debt thereby reducing interest charges. Personal loans when agreed are at the mortgage rate of interest. Also sometimes known as an offset mortgage they may be linked to both savings and current accounts.

Tracker: The interest rate rises or falls in line with a standard rate usually the European Central Bank rate. Other variable rate mortgages allow the lending institution to vary rates at its discretion.

Fixed Interest: The interest rate is fixed for a set number of years irrespective of movements in the market so that the borrower knows exactly what the repayments will be during those years. At the end of the set period, interest rates may be fixed for another period or the borrower may switch to normal variable rates. The borrower gambles that the fixed rate will prove lower than the market rate.

Pension linked: This is an endowment type mortgage linked to a pension scheme rather than an insurance policy. For a self-employed person it provides better tax relief since all of the contributions to a pension fund can be allowable for tax relief. The loan is repaid from the accumulated pension fund on retirement. This option is unlikely to be available to those in standard company schemes.

cautious. Lenders may also have a different propensity to raise interest rates in the future. In Britain, mutual building societies have tended to have lower mortgage rates over the longer term than more profit-orientated lenders. But there can be no guarantees in this regard.

Endowment versus annuity: Endowment mortgages enjoyed a brief spell of popularity a number of years ago but now account for only a small proportion of new mortgages. Most mortgages are of the traditional annuity type. The difference between the two relates to the way that the loan is repaid. With an annuity mortgage, each repayment goes partly to pay the interest on the loan and partly to reduce the principal amount borrowed. Over the years the amount owed declines. The decline is relatively small in the early years and even 10 years into a 20 year loan three-quarters of each monthly repayment is still interest. After that it goes down at a relatively faster pace so that by year 15 only a little more than half the repayment is interest.

With an endowment mortgage the borrower only pays the interest on the loan. The money that could have been used to reduce the loan is invested instead in a savings type life assurance policy designed to mature at the end of the loan — say 20 years hence. The hope is that it will yield enough to pay off the loan. There may even be something left over. But there is always the risk that the proceeds from the policy won't be enough to pay off the loan. So endowment mortgages involve a mixture of borrowing and investment.

Speeding up your mortgage repayments doesn't always make good financial sense, see page 44

The risks involved may be worth taking but it is important to realise what they are. Instead of paying money off the loan it is being put into an investment fund. If that fund yields a return higher than the interest on the loan then you are winning but there is no guarantee that it will. The choice of investment fund is obviously of prime importance. Some are more risky than others. Unit-linked policies have, in general, performed reasonably well over the longer term although they can move sharply down at times. And the variation between best and worst is great. There is no sure way of picking the winners although you can reduce the risk by picking a with-profits policy.

The availability of tax relief on pension contributions adds to the attractiveness of pension mortgages which operate in the same way as endowment mortgages except that the investment is into a personal pension fund rather than a life insurance policy. They are of particular interest to the self-employed, and high earning individuals who are not in company pension schemes. That extra benefit reduces the rate of return needed on the investment fund in order to make the whole package worthwhile.

Local authority loans

Local authorities — county councils and corporations — have for many years provided house purchase loans for those on relatively low incomes and can also pay mortgage subsidies to tenants and tenant-purchasers of local authority houses who give up their houses to buy a private home. In 2008, a new scheme known as 'Home Choice Loan' was introduced to provide loans for first-time buyers of new homes who are unable to borrow sufficient finance from a bank or building society. 'Home Choice Loans' are administered by four local authorities, Cork and Dublin City Councils and Galway and Kilkenny County Councils. The finance is provided by the Housing Finance Agency and applications are made through a network of mortgage brokers throughout the country. Loans up to 92% of the market value of the property, subject to a maximum of €285,000 are available to first-time buyers of new houses and are repayable over a maximum of 30 years. To qualify, buyers must earn at least €40,000 a year and have been in permanent employment for at least two years. Where the loan is being taken out by a couple at least one of them must have an income of over €40,000.

Those on lower incomes may qualify for a local authority loan under the older scheme. To be eligible, the applicant's income has to be below a set level which is €36,800 in the case of a single purchaser. The joint income of a couple can be such that two-and-a-half times the larger income plus the lower income is no more than €92,000. So, for instance, one could have an income of €26,500 and his or her partner could have an income of €24,000 and qualify. That maximum income limit does not apply to approved applicants for, or tenants of, local authority dwellings. Neither does it apply to tenants of rent subsidised housing owned by a voluntary housing group provided the accommodation is returned to the group.

Standard Loan: There is no minimum income requirement but the local authority must be satisfied that it is sufficient to meet the repayments. The maximum loan is normally €165,000. Within that limit, loans may be up to 97% of the purchase price or the market value of the house (whichever is less).

The interest rate is variable and will not exceed the standard building society rate. Loans for new houses can be repaid over 30 years while the upper limit for second-hand houses is 25 years. Normally neither the borrower, nor his or her spouse, should ever have bought or built a house before. An exception is made for people living in substandard conditions.

Shared Ownership: Tenants, or tenant purchasers, of local authority houses wishing to give them up to buy a private house, or people on a housing list, or those who meet the income criteria mentioned above may qualify for a local authority loan to buy at least a 40% share in a private house of their own choosing. The rent is set at 4.3% of the value of the portion of the house owned by the local authority but that is reduced where the purchaser's income is below €25,500. So the outgoings between rent and mortgage repayments can be significantly less than if the purchaser had to be fully financed by way of a loan. The maximum reduction is €1,523 a year for those with incomes below €10,792 while the minimum is €317 for those earning between €13,968 and €15,237.

There are moves to coordinate access to the existing affordable housing schemes operated by local authorities throughout the country.

Costs of buying

Obviously, first of all, you need the cash for the deposit. In the new economic climate, post credit-crunch, you may find it hard to get more than 80% on an old house and even on a new house if you are not in a very secure job. If it is an old house which you are going to renovate, it may be possible to increase the mortgage later as alterations and additions are made. Check this with your lender. But there are also other costs. Auctioneers fees are paid by the seller, so there is no need to worry about those, but there will be fees to the building society or other lender, legal fees and maybe stamp duty. There will also be costs involved in satisfying yourself that the house has no structural flaws.

Let us look at these in turn.

- **Fees to the lending agency:** These are not likely to break you, but it is as well to bear them in mind since they can stretch a slim budget. They include mortgage fees, survey fees, and search fees. The rates vary but the following provides a rough guide:

  - Mortgage Law Costs: 0.5 to 0.65% of the loan – some lenders charge a fixed fee of up to €300, others allow you to use your own solicitor.

  - Application Fee: From nothing to 0.2c per €1,000 of the mortgage to a fixed €60 fee depending on the lender.

  - Survey Fees: About €1.50 per €1,000 although some times a fixed fee is charged. There may also be travelling expenses for the surveyor.

  - Search Fees: These should not amount to much more than about €150.

Cost of buying a home

- The following example assumes the purchase of a €400,000 house by a first time buyer with a mortgage of €250,000. This is only an illustration of the possible costs. It's a new home and no stamp duty is payable – see table on page 121.

Legal fees*	€3,000
Survey fees	€400
Land registry fees	€625
Search fees	€120
Total	**€5,145**

* There is no set scale of fees. They are negotiable. Check in advance and don't be afraid to shop around.

Stamp duty on home purchase

■ First time buyers are exempt from stamp duty whether the house being bought is new or old. Also exempt are new houses or apartments under 125 square metres in area purchased by an owner-occupier. New homes, with a floor area greater than 125 square metres, are charged to duty either on the site value, excluding VAT, or on one quarter of the total cost of the house and site, whichever is the greater. There is a claw back of these exemptions if the house is rented within two years.

Total price	Tax rate
Less than €125,000	Nil
Next €875,000	7%
Excess over €1,000,000	9%

These rates are charged on slices of the property value and apply to investors and owner-occupiers who are not first time buyers. No duty is payable where the total consideration is less than €127,000

■ **Stamp duties:** First time buyers of residential properties are exempt from stamp duty. To be considered a first-time buyer, the purchaser must never have bought or built, either jointly or individually a home for his or her own use either in Ireland or abroad. An exception is that he or she may own another house that has been acquired either by way of gift or inheritance. No rent should be derived from the property for two years after completion of the purchase with the exception of up to €10,000 a year which can be earned tax-free from renting a room in the principal private residence of the taxpayer.

Stamp duty on transfers of residential property is applied to slices of the property value. For instance, on a house sold for €1.2 million, there is no duty on the first €125,000. Duty at the rate of 7% is charged on €875,000 and at 9% on the remaining €200,000. Before November 5, 2007, the higher rates of stamp duty were applied to the total price paid and that is still the case with stamp duty on other property and land transactions. The new regime only applies to residential property. There is also a stamp duty of 0.1% on mortgages over €254,000.

- **Legal Fees:** There are too many possible pitfalls in buying a house for you to dispense with the services of a solicitor. Ask him in advance what his fees will be – most solicitors will tell you as a matter of course. There is no fixed rate of charges, but about 1% of the house price plus VAT at 21.5% is not uncommon. The VAT only applies to the fees — not to the stamp duty which the solicitor may also collect. It pays to shop around and negotiate.

- **Indemnity bond:** If you borrow more than 80% of the house value the lender may require you to take out an indemnity bond. It can cost about 3% of the additional amount borrowed over and above 80% of the property value. That can be costly but some lenders don't require them.

Checking the house

There are, of course, other — mainly non-financial — matters to be borne in mind. These are the fairly obvious considerations of the location, house size, age, etc. In other words, is the house good value for money? Is it suitable for your particular requirements and are there any flaws which might make it bad value for money? Your solicitor is only concerned that the contract of sale does not put you at a disadvantage. Make sure that a check is also made for planning applications or approvals that might affect the value of the house.

The importance of location and size are matters for your own judgement, but you should never buy a house without having someone give it a professional once-over, unless it is a new house and the purchase contract provides for the making good of any structural defect appearing in the first two years. The lending agency will always send out its own surveyor to examine a house before agreeing to grant a mortgage. This provides some protection, since a mortgage will not be forthcoming unless the house is reasonably sound. But remember the lending agency is only concerned that the value of the house covers 80% of the price which it is lending to you. So with a second-hand house it is a good idea to engage your own surveyor to carry out a more detailed examination. With a new house, ask your solicitor to ensure that the purchase contract contains a guarantee that any structural defects becoming evident in the first two years will be put right at the builder's expense. For preference deal with a builder who is in the National House Building Guarantee Scheme. If not, have a survey done.

Having satisfied yourself that the house is sound — or at least that you know of any major defects — the next thing to check is the possibility of any new building which might affect its value in the future. That is as important with second-hand as it is with new houses. It could be that the person selling knows that a large block of apartments is planned on a site overlooking the, seemingly private, back garden; or that a new motorway is to be built along your side wall or a new airport runway will put you under a flight path. So you need to check the planning applications and approvals for the area. This can be done at the offices of your local planning authority. There you can examine maps of your area showing the zonings — whether agricultural, commercial or residential — and see details of any planning approvals granted or applications pending. Such a visit is well worth making.

Rent-to-buy schemes

Rent-to-buy schemes which provide potential home buyers the chance to rent a property with an option to buy at a later stage are being promoted by builders and developers faced with a depressed market. Such schemes have some obvious attractions but there are potential pitfalls. At their simplest, such schemes give potential buyers the right to buy a house or apartment at a fixed price at any time over a set time frame. It may be two, three or more years. Sometimes the rent payable is higher than the current market rate but usually some, or all, of the rent is put towards a deposit on the property is and when a decision to buy is made.

Within that general concept, there is plenty of room for variation. There's the price at which the option to buy is set. There's the rent to be paid, whether it's below or above the market rate. And there's the amount of the rent, if any, that will be put towards the purchase price. You need to ask yourself a number of question.

- **Just how valuable is the right to buy at a fixed price in the future?**

It could be worth a lot if prices go up significantly but, if they don't, you'll be left with either leaving a house that you may have settled into or buying at a price higher than you might pay for an alternative.

- **Is the rent reasonable?**

Would you be paying more or less if this wasn't a rent-to-buy scheme? Even if you think you are going to get all or part of the rent back when you eventually buy the property, it's important to be aware of the real costs and benefits involved. You might be better paying a lower rent and saving in a regular saver account some of which are paying more than 4% on up to €1,000 saved each month.

- **Do I have to pay a deposit up front?**

If you do, be very careful. Some schemes let you into the house under a caretaker's rather than a rental agreement.

That means that you are effectively living in the house rent-free. In this case, the Revenue consider that you are getting a benefit-in-kind which is taxable. You will be liable for tax on the market rent you would have paid. In the absence of evidence to the contrary, the Revenue will take that to be 8% of the market value of the home. So on a €200,000 apartment you could be paying tax on €16,000 a year.

- **What happens if I can't get a mortgage, or can't afford one, when the time comes to buy?**

The right to buy is likely to lapse and although you may be allowed to continue renting, you'll have gained nothing and may have lost out through paying over-the-odds in rent.

State housing grants

While first-time home buyers are no longer entitled to a State grant there are still some grants and subsidies available to home buyers and owners. There is the Affordable Housing Scheme under which houses or sites can be made available by local authorities to eligible applicants at a price that at one stage was well below market value. But market values have fallen sharply. There are also mortgage subsidies for tenants and tenant purchasers of local authority houses who wish to purchase private houses, and grants for improving or extending the houses of people on local authority housing lists. Full details of all of these schemes can be obtained from the Department of the Environment, Housing Grants Section, Ballina, Co Mayo. Some home improvement schemes are operated through local health authorities. The following is an outline of some of the schemes available. Mortgage interest relief is detailed in the next section on page 130.

Affordable housing

You don't have to be particularly poor to qualify for affordable housing. Single people with incomes of up to €58,000 a year can qualify for homes under the scheme while couples can have considerably higher joint incomes. Someone who gets a house under the scheme could end up living next door to neighbours on far lower incomes who had to buy their houses at higher prices. But because of the decline in house prices, the home bought on the open market may actually be cheaper than one bought under the affordable housing scheme.

There are two different schemes. Under one scheme the houses are provided directly by local authorities. Each authority uses its own criteria when deciding who gets the available houses but to be eligible at all you must be in need of housing and your income must be below a set level. You normally need to be a first time buyer and to have been in permanent employment for at least a year. In the case of a single income household, the gross income in the preceding tax year must have been no more than €58,000 but a lower limit may be imposed. It depends on the type of affordable house involved.

Different local authorities seem to apply different rules as regards income. That basic rule is that a single applicant should have earned no more than €58,000 in the previous tax year while a couple could have had an income of up to €75,000 but there seems to be some flexibily in applying these rules. Applications have to be made through local authorities and not necessarily where you are currently living. If you are currently living in Cork but would be willing to move if you did happen to be offered a cheap home, then you should apply to every local authority in the country.

Local authorities use different criteria for allocating houses under the affordable housing scheme

You'll find the contact addresses and phone numbers in a booklet issued by the Affordable Housing Partnership. You can get that by phone (01) 656 4100 or on its website at www.affordablehome.ie

Local authorities allocate homes under the scheme in different ways. But if you are not in, you can't win. You have to apply or at least express an interest in being considered. You need to make those expressions of interest to each local authority in whose area you are willing to live if allocated a house under the scheme or, more correctly, schemes. To add to the confusion there are actually three different schemes but the one application covers them all.

So who is eligible to apply?

The first category are those in need of housing and whose income falls below certain levels. You normally need to be a first time buyer and to have been in permanent employment for at least a year. Irrespective of income you may also qualify if you are on a local authority's housing waiting list or if you are a local authority or housing association tenant or tenant purchaser willing to give up your existing home if you are allocated an affordable home under the scheme.

Those eligible will usually qualify for a local authority loan and may also be entitled to help with their repayments if the gross household income is less than €28,000 a year. There's an annual subsidy of €2,550 for those with incomes up to €13,000 diminishing on a sliding scale to €1,050 a year for those with incomes between €25,501 and €28,000. People who are surrendering local authority or housing association homes, who are taking out a mortgage to buy an affordable home and who are claiming no other subsidies, can qualify for a mortgage allowance which amounts to a total of €11,500 payable over five years.

The local authority is entitled to claw back all or some of the discount given on an affordable home if it is sold within 20 years. During the first 10 years, the percentage claw-back equals the percentage discount originally given. For instance if a home sold under the scheme for €225,000 is deemed to have a market value of €300,000 the discount is 25%. If, within the first 10 years, the home were sold for say €280,000 the local authority would claw back €7,000 i.e. 25% of the sale price. After the 10th year the percentage claw-back is reduced by a 10th each year so in the 11th year the claw-back would be 22.5% (25% minus 2.5%). In the 12th year it would be 20% (25 minus 5%) and so on.

It is proposed to replace this claw-back arrangement with a new scheme whereby the State will take a permanent charge on the house creating an obligation on the purchaser to repay an equity stake should the house be sold. The name will change but the amount repayable will be unchanged.

While developers no longer have to include affordable housing in new developments it is possible that some will. If they do, different income rules apply. In general, you can qualify if 35% of your income is not sufficient to enable you to buy a home and that allows the €58,000 single limit and the €75,000 limit for couples being exceeded. If in doubt get your application in. If you are interested in such housing it would be as well to let your local authority know with a request to be informed if and when any become available. If you can't raise the necessary finance from a bank or building society and meet the income criteria you may be eligible for a local authority loan. Subject to your income you may also qualify for mortgage subsidies. The same claw-back provisions also apply. Demand for affordable housing well exceeds the supply and will for the foreseeable future. But some houses are available and if you don't express an interest, or don't apply, you certainly won't get one.

Grants schemes previously provided by the HSE were combined with local authority schemes towards the end of 2007 and are now administered by the local authorities. There are two grant schemes that can cover all or part of the cost of adapting a home to ease mobility problems suffered by the elderly or disabled. There is also a grant scheme aimed at assisting older people to have essential repairs or home improvements carried out. But entitlement to a grant doesn't mean that you actually get it. Applicants are prioritised and available funds are in many cases rationed.

The Mobility Aids Housing Grant provides 100% of the cost, to a maximum of €6,000, of mobility aids such as grab-rails, ramps, level access showers and stair-lifts. To qualify, household means must not exceed €30,000 but there are some disregards for dependants living in the home.

Grants of up to €10,500 are available under the Housing Adaptation Grant scheme, the maximum grant depending on the household income. Where the household income is less than €30,000 a year, the grant covers 100% of the cost of the work subject to that maximum. The maximum grant decreases on a sliding scale for each extra €5,000 a year in household income. Those with incomes between €54,001 and €65,000 can qualify for a grant of 30% of the cost subject to a maximum of €3,150.

Home Energy Saving Scheme

A range of grants is available towards the cost of insulating homes built prior to 2006, upgrading boilers and purchasing green energy devices under this scheme which is administered by Sustainable Energy Ireland. The insulation grants range from €250 for roof insulation to €4,000 for external wall insulation. Up to €700 is paid in respect of a boiler upgrade. To be eligible for a grant, a minimum of €500 has to be spent on the work. Full details can be obtained from Sustainable Energy Ireland, PO Box 119, Cahirciveen, Co. Kerry. Phone 1850 922000, or on its web site www.sei.ie.

Mortgage tax relief

Tax relief is allowed in respect of the interest on loans taken out to buy, maintain, or improve the taxpayer's principal residence, the residence of a former or separated spouse, or the residence of a dependant relative (other than a child) who is living in the house rent free. There is an upper limit on eligible interest for first-time buyers during the first seven years of €10,000 for single taxpayers; and €20,000 for married couples, widows and widowers. Since January 2009 first-time buyers get tax relief at 25% of eligible interest paid during the first and second years and at the rate of 22.5% during the third, fourth and fifth years. Tax relief in the sixth and seventh year is given at the standard rate of 20%. From the eighth year onwards home buyers, who are at that stage defined as non-first-time buyers, are allowed tax relief at the reduced rate of 15% and only on a maximum of €6,000 a year (married and widowed) and €3,000 (single).

The tax relief is given at source but only if the Revenue know of your entitlement. It's up to you to ensure that you are getting it

As a result of changes announced in the 2010 budget the relief is being extended to 2017 for those taking out qualifying loans between 2004 and July 2011 and at lower rates for those taking out loans between July 1, 2011 and the end of 2013. The relief is to be abolished entirely from the end of 2017. The tax relief is normally granted at source i.e. by way of a reduction in the repayments to the mortgage lender so it is important to ensure that the lender has been authorised by the Revenue to provide the relief. It is also important to ensure that your tax office has the full details of your mortgage account. If it hasn't been allowed at source, of course, you can claim it.

Where a taxpayer moves house and there is a delay in selling the original house, both houses can be considered to be the sole or main residence for up to one year. And during that year the interest on any loan taken out to buy the new house is allowed for tax relief in addition to the tax relief on the old loan — the limit is doubled.

Investors who buy property to rent out can claim tax relief on all of the interest payments at their top rate of tax. There are also capital allowances available to investors who

■ Mortgage interest relief is given on certain mortgages. To qualify, the borrowed money must have been used to buy, maintain, or improve the taxpayer's principal residence, the residence of a former or separated spouse, or the residence of a dependant relative (other than a child) who is living in the house rent free. First time buyers get extra relief during the first seven years of their mortgage. Relief on other qualifying mortgages is allowed at lower rates for seven years from the date it was taken out or until the end of 2017 for loans taken out during or after 2004.

Maximum relief

	Allowable interest
First time buyers	
Single	€10,000
Married, widowed	€20,000
Others	
Single	€3,000
Married, widowed	€6,000

Rates of relief [1]

First time buyers	
Years 1 and 2	25%
Years 3, 4 and 5	22.5%
Years 6 and 7	20%
Others	15%

A first time buyer is defined as someone who has bought their first home in the past seven years. Non-first time buyers can qualify for relief for seven years from the time a qualifying loan was taken out. But it is only considered a qualifying loan if it has been used to improve the taxpayer's principal residence, the residence of a former or separated spouse, or the residence of a dependant relative (other than a child) who is living in the house rent free.

How much is the maximum relief worth in saved tax

	First time buyers			Other owner occupiers
	Years 1 and 2	Years 3 and 4	Years 6 and 7	
Married or widowed	€5,000	€4,500	€4,000	€900
Single	€2,500	€2,250	€2,000	€600

■ Note: 1. Lower rates are to apply to loans taken out between July 1, 2011 and end 2013

provide residential property in certain designated areas and for owner-occupiers there is additional tax relief available on homes built or refurbished in certain designated areas. This includes the Upper Shannon Region Rural Renewal Scheme which covers all of Co Leitrim and Co Longford and parts of Co Cavan, Co Roscommon and Co Sligo. Also covered are 100 designated small towns. To qualify the property must be the sole or main residence of the individual claiming the relief. If it is a converted premises, there must be a certificate of reasonable cost obtainable from the Department of the Environment. Properties must be of a minimum size. Tax relief is allowed each year for 10 years on 5% of the construction cost in the case of a new premises and 10% in the case of a refurbished premises. For example the construction costs of a new apartment selling for €280,000 might be about €180,000. The buyer is entitled to claim tax relief on 5% of that for 10 years. So relief is allowed on €9,000 a year. That relief is in addition to any mortgage tax relief calculated on the basis outlined above.

Rent relief

Since April 1995, it has been possible to claim tax relief on the rent paid for private sector accommodation. It is not available for rent paid on local authority houses or flats. The maximum amount that can be claimed since 2008 by someone over 55 is €4,000 single, €8,000 widowed or married. The relief is restricted to the standard rate. The maximum allowance for those under 55 is €2,000 if single and €4,000 if married or widowed. It's a tax relief that is often missed because it has to be claimed. It is, of course, possible to backdate a claim — see chapter 13.

Rent a room

Rental income up to €10,000 (€7,618 for 2007) may be received tax-free by owner-occupiers who rent out a room or rooms in their own principal residence. That relates to the total payment received. The person who is paying the rent may also be entitled to claim tax relief on it. Since 2007 the relief is not allowed if the person paying the rent is a 'connected' person, for instance a child.

7 Inheritance, probate and and making a will

Live as if you were to die tomorrow. Learn as if you were to live forever —
Mahatma Gandhi

The failure to draw up a will can cause many problems for dependants. It has also resulted in many bitter family feuds. Unless there is a properly drawn up will in existence, your property will be divided up, after your death, according to the dictates of the 1965 Succession Act. Such a division may not be in keeping with your wishes and could cause major problems for your spouse. Advance planning can prevent such difficulties arising and can also reduce the amount your dependants may have to pay in inheritance tax. That is particularly so if some of the beneficiaries are distant relatives or friends.

The first concern is to ensure that your wishes are known. If there is no will, the law lays down how the estate is divided up. By making a will you ensure that your property passes to the people you choose — not to the people dictated in court according to the strict rule of law. There is the added advantage that you can appoint your own executor and the administration of the estate will be much easier.

What may happen when there is no will

Surviving Relatives	Distribution of estate where there is no will
Spouse and children	Two-thirds to spouse, one third to children in equal shares with children of a deceased child getting their parent's share.
Spouse, no children	Whole estate to spouse.
Children, no spouse	Whole estate to children in equal shares with children of a deceased child getting their parent's share.
Father, mother, brothers and/or sisters	One-half to each parent.
Parent, brothers and/or sisters	Whole estate to parent.
Brothers and sisters	All get equal shares with children of deceased brothers and sisters getting their parent's share.
Nephews and nieces	All get equal shares.
Other relatives	Nearest equal relatives get equal shares.
No relatives	The State.

A valid will can be made by anyone over 18 years of age — or younger if he or she is married. It must be in writing. While a simple will can be drawn up at home, it is well worthwhile getting a solicitor to oversee the task. The few euro it costs can save a lot of trouble in the long run.

There is usually no need to name a solicitor as executor

If you do decide to draw up your own will, remember to word it simply and clearly. Date it, sign it, and get your signature witnessed by two people. This means that you should sign it in their presence. They do not have to read the will.

Neither of the witnesses should be a beneficiary under the will. It is normal to appoint an executor, or executors, to carry out the instructions outlined in the will although it is not essential. The executor can be a beneficiary under the will although he, or she, need not be.

For a simple will, where the main beneficiaries are members of the immediate family, it is common to name the principal beneficiary as executor. In most cases, this is the husband or wife. If either is reaching old age and might find the task difficult, it is useful to name a co-executor — perhaps an elder child or trusted family friend. It is not necessary to name a solicitor, accountant, or bank as executor. Usually a member of the family — or a friend whom you trust — is the best choice. He or she can hire a solicitor if needed at the time.

All married people should have a will drawn up. It costs little to have the job done correctly by a solicitor. Once made, the will should be reviewed from time to time

The will should, of course, be lodged in a safe place, and be sure that the executor, and some other people know where it is lodged. This is particularly important for people whose families are widely spread. There are many wills lying in solicitors' offices throughout the country forgotten and, for all practical purposes, lost. Once made, the will remains in force until a new will is made or the person who made it gets married. On marriage, an existing will becomes void and a new one should be drawn up. Remember also to review your will from time to time particularly if your life situation changes. Even if you do not want to change the provisions you may want to change the executor and it can be useful to reconsider the inheritance tax implications.

Power of attorney

A power of attorney is simply a legal authorisation to act on behalf of someone else. So a person who is physically incapacitated — perhaps not mobile enough to fully look after his or her business — may grant a power of attorney to a relative, friend, or adviser to carry out a range of transactions. This is known as a general power of attorney although it can be limited to certain transactions. A person may be given a power of attorney, for instance to handle a specific transaction like arranging the sale of a house. The person granting the power of attorney must have the mental capacity to withdraw the power of attorney should he or she wish and, indeed, should he or she lose that capacity the power of attorney lapses. In such a situation it may be necessary to apply to have the person made a ward of court with someone appointed to look after his or her affairs.

So besides drawing up a will, it may also be worthwhile considering the possibility of losing the ability to take care of one's affairs as a result of an accident, disability or illness. These eventualities can be planned for by arranging to grant an *enduring* power of attorney to someone you can trust to act in your best interests and with your views in mind. Such an enduring power of attorney comes into force if and when the person who has signed it becomes mentally incapable of acting on his or her own behalf. It involves planning, of course, although many people in the early stages of Alzheimer's disease will be able to legitimately draw up a power of attorney. Before it comes into force, an enduring power of attorney has to be registered following an application to the High Court. Such application is made when the person who drew up the power of attorney has become or is becoming mentally incapable. Legal advice is always advisable.

Both spouses should make wills

It is now usual for both spouses to share ownership in the family home. But there are still families where the bulk of the assets — perhaps home and/or farm — are held in the husband's name. It may be thought unnecessary, in such cases for the wife to make a will but nothing is further from the truth. In not making a will the assumption is that she will always have time to do so, if necessary, after her husband's death. Yet this can lead to problems in an unfortunate situation where both die together — in a car accident, for instance.

It could happen in such a case that the husband dies first leaving his entire estate to his wife but that she then dies without having time to make a will. The estate would then be equally divided among the children — if there are any.

That may be in accordance with their parent's wishes. But it might not, if one child, for instance, was still living at home and hoped to be left the house.

There is only one important restriction on the maker of a will. A spouse cannot be cut out of the estate unless he or she agrees to be, for instance as part of a separation agreement. Irrespective of what the will says, the spouse is legally entitled to one-third of the estate where there are surviving children, and one-half of the estate where there are no children. Apart from that restriction, however, a person may dispose of his or her property as he or she thinks fit, although the courts can overturn the provisions of a will if, for instance, a child claims that he or she has not been adequately provided for.

Living wills

While a will outlines how property is to be divided up following death the objective of what has become known as a "living will" is to influence events before your death. The idea is to let people know what you would like to happen should you become incapable of making or communicating decisions as a result of an accident or illness. Very often, a living will deals solely with views regarding health care but it can, of course, be more wide ranging. A living will has no legal standing so the wishes outlined in it do not have to be complied with but at least they ensure that relatives and doctors know your views and those views will undoubtedly be considered.

Rights to the family home

In many cases family homes are jointly owned by both spouses but even where one spouse has formal ownership the other spouse, very often a non-wage earning wife, has certain rights in the family home under existing legislation. They are not rights of ownership although in the case of a judicial separation or divorce, a court may order a transfer of property from one spouse to another. Rights in this area are provided under the Family Home Protection Act; the Married Women's Status Act; and judicial separation and divorce legislation. The Family Home Protection Act provides that both spouses must agree to the sale or mortgaging of the family home. But where the house is in just one name, the other spouse has no right to any proceeds from a sale unless he or she made some financial contribution to the purchase of the house.

There are also provisions protecting the rights of a spouse against whom a barring order is being sought. The first step in getting a barring order is to get a protection order. Where that has been obtained, neither spouse can remove or dispose of any household contents until a decision has been made on the barring order. A spouse must also be given the opportunity to take over the mortgage repayments on the family home where his or her partner has defaulted on the payments. And the courts can make orders for the protection of a home where a spouse is indulging in some actions which could lead to its loss. Under the Married Women's Status Act, the Courts can be asked to rule on the ownership of property, including a family home. But the Courts will only grant ownership rights to a spouse who can show that he or she made financial contributions to the purchase of the house or to other household costs. Work done in the home or time spent rearing children is not taken into account.

The courts have much wider powers of discretion under the judicial separation and divorce legislation. Where a couple has been granted either a judicial separation or a divorce the court can make orders requiring the transfer of property from one spouse to another. In this case it does not matter whether or not a spouse has made a financial contribution. The courts may also make maintenance orders. Such orders can be reviewed from time to time, but orders made about property are permanent and a court will only review them if it can be shown that it was deliberately misled when the original order was made.

Wills and tax planning

Tax is another thing to consider when making a will. While the burden of inheritance tax has been greatly eased in recent years and probate tax abolished, the tax liability on inheritances can be onerous for the growing number of people inheriting from more distant relatives. There is a section on tax planning for inheritances in chapter 13 on page 273.

The duties of executors

The person making a will — the testator — should always seek the consent of a person named in the will to act as executor. It is, of course, quite in order to name more than one person, but there is no obligation on the persons so named to act. A person who does not wish to accept an executorship may renounce it by signing a form of renunciation before a witness. This can obviously create problems so it is essential to ensure that the executor named in the will is willing to act. An executor may benefit under a will but he is not entitled to any payment for his services unless it is specifically stated in the will that such a payment should be made. The executor can, however, claim for expenses actually incurred in administering the will.

You don't need to hire a solicitor to take out probate on a will. You can do it yourself

If it is decided to accept the executorship, the first move is normally to obtain a Grant of Probate from the courts. This will formally authorise the executor to collect the deceased's assets and carry out the provisions of the will. But the will itself is sufficient authorisation and even without a grant of probate, the executor can immediately take charge of the deceased's assets and start to carry out the provisions of the will. A listing of all the deceased's assets should be made and valuations obtained where necessary. It is also necessary to obtain details of any outstanding debts. Usually these are easily ascertained but, if they are not, the executor can protect himself against further claims by putting a notice in the daily newspaper asking all creditors to supply details of their claims by a certain date.

If a creditor has not made a claim by that date, he loses the right to pursue his claim against the executor although he can still proceed against the beneficiaries under the will. If the executor does not put the statutory notice in the newspaper, he may protect himself by getting the beneficiaries to give an agreement in writing to indemnify him against any claims which emerge after the distribution has taken place.

Taking out probate

The Probate Office in the Four Courts, Dublin 7 (phone 01 8725555 ex 179) has a special application section for those who wish to take out probate themselves. Application for probate can be made there or to one of 14 District Probate Registries. There is no need to get a solicitor to do the job, particularly if it is a simple will. On request the probate office will send out an application form which should be completed as fully as possible and returned. The probate office will immediately acknowledge receipt of the form and will ask the applicant to call in for a preliminary meeting. At that stage the applicant should present full details of the estate, a death certificate and the original will, if there is one. Statements of deposit accounts held by the deceased should be produced as well as details of assurance policies and all assets owned by the deceased. A second meeting will be arranged to finalise any outstanding matters and the applicant will then be required to sign the completed documents, swear to the truth and accuracy of their contents, and pay a fee.

The fees are charged on a sliding scale, €135 for first €125,000 and €12 per €31,250 thereafter.

Tax clearance is not always needed to withdraw money from a deceased person's account

In some cases, it may take more than two meetings to finalise the matter but once probate has been granted, the executor will find it easier to transfer funds from bank accounts into his or her own name. It is best for the executor to open a separate bank account for this purpose. The executor has further duties in making returns to the taxman and settling any tax claims outstanding or arising as a result of the will. This includes making income and inheritance tax returns. Because of the tax implications it may be necessary to get tax clearance before withdrawing money from bank or other saving accounts.

Tax clearance

In the case of a joint husband/wife account, a surviving spouse is not required to present a tax clearance no matter

how large the estate but the financial institution may require sight of the death certificate and/or will depending on
the type of account i.e. whether or not two signatures were
needed for withdrawals.

Tax clearance is needed to access an account in the deceased's sole name or in the joint names of the deceased and
someone other than a spouse where the account has more
than €31,750 in it, but such a clearance is granted quickly by
the Capital Taxes Branch, Revenue Commissioners, Stamp-
ing Building, Dublin Castle, phone (01)6475000 or Locall
1890 201105. The financial institution may also have its
own rules about having sight of the will, death certificate or
grant of probate. For more details on joint accounts see
chapter 2, page 16.

8 Enforcing your rights as a worker and citizen

I am involved in a freedom ride protesting the loss of the minority rights belonging to the few remaining earthbound stars. All we demanded was our right to twinkle
— *Marilyn Monroe*

The rights of employees have been greatly enhanced in recent years, mostly in line with EU directives, with the introduction of legislation providing minimum rights and protection in matters like hours of work, minimum notice of dismissal or redundancy, redundancy payments, holidays, discrimination, unfair dismissal, etc. The laws apply to both full time and part-time workers. The definition of part-time includes those working under a contract of employment or apprenticeship and those employed through an employment agency. That even includes the right to overtime pay if they work extra hours provided equivalent full-time workers get extra pay for working overtime.

Some employers have been known to try to reduce their exposure to the employment protection laws by either contracting out work to self-employed workers, or by hiring employees under contracts which effectively prevent them acquiring their full range of rights.

To qualify for some employment rights, employees have to have a minimum amount of service. But under the Protection of Employees (Fixed-term work) Act that came into force in July 2003, workers on fixed term contracts may not be treated less favourably than other employees unless justified on objective grounds other than the fact that the worker is on contract. Under the Act, an employer proposing to renew a fixed term contract of employment must explain to the employee in writing the reason for retaining the job as a contract rather than a staff job.

The Act also places a limit on the amount of time an employee may be required to work on fixed term contracts. Any renewal contract offered to workers on fixed term contracts should not extend their total period on contract to more than four years. Any contract, thereafter, is considered by law to be a permanent contract unless the employer can show reasons why it should be otherwise. The employer would have to show that a non-permanent contract was necessary in pursuit of a legitimate objective and that there was no other way of achieving it.

You can't totally rely on others, inspectors, employers or even trade unions to defend your rights. You must be aware of your entitlements and ensure you get them

What constitutes a legitimate objective has yet to be fully determined. Disputes can be referred to a Rights Commission of the Labour Relations Commission. The Rights Commission's decision can be appealed to the Labour Court for a legally binding determination. See page 159 for details of addresses and phone numbers.

Even before the 2003 Act, there were limits to what employers could do with contracts. In general the contract must be seen to have a purpose other than simply to allow the employer avoid unfair dismissal legislation. A 1993 Act specifically provided that employers cannot avoid the Act by using fixed term contracts and that a break of less than three months between two consecutive contracts does not constitute a break in service. This may be true even for work of a seasonal nature. It may not be possible for employers to prevent workers building up entitlements under the Unfair Dismissals and Redundancy Acts.

The Employment Appeals Tribunal has upheld claims for continuity of service by seasonal workers who showed a pattern of such work over a number of years. A contract worker is not normally covered under the unfair dismissals legislation unless he or she did work other than that specified in the contract of employment.

Explanatory leaflets may be obtained from the Department of Enterprise, Trade and Employment, Conditions of Employment Section, Dublin 4

While workers in large firms with union representation can be fairly certain that their entitlements are not allowed to go by default, non-union workers, particularly in smaller firms, may find that their employers, either by accident or design, fail to give them their full entitlements.

The following gives a brief guide to the more important legislative provisions. Explanatory leaflets may be obtained from the Department of Enterprise, Trade and Employment, Conditions of Employment Section, Dublin 4 which also gives further assistance and advice. In the case of disputes, you can seek redress through a Rights Commissioner who can be contacted through the Department. The rights of part-time workers under these labour laws should not be confused with social welfare entitlements. Part-time workers earning more than €38 a week have some cover under the PRSI system. See chapter 11.

Redundancy entitlements

The economic downturn has brought with it an increase in the numbers losing jobs through redundancy. It can be a traumatic experience even for those who can convince themselves, as they should, that it is the job that's redundant, not they themselves. The law provides some protection but that doesn't make the experience any easier. Under the redundancy payment scheme and the Protection of Employment Act, an employer is required to give at least 30 days notice to the relevant minister of any intention to make collective redundancies. Workers are entitled to minimum notice and to minimum lump sum payments based on the number of years service with the firm.

Who is covered? The scheme covers employees who are in employment which is insurable for all benefits under the Social Welfare Acts or who were in such employment in the four years prior to redundancy; are between the ages of 16 and 66; and who are normally expected to work for at least eight hours a week for the same employer. Domestic servants and agricultural workers — who are not relatives and who do not reside with their employers — are also covered.

An employee becomes eligible for redundancy pay if he has been employed by the same employer for at least two years after attaining 16 years of age and is dismissed as redundant, laid off, or kept on short-time at less than 50% of normal time for four consecutive weeks or a total of six weeks in a period of 13 weeks.

The lump sum: The statutory lump sum is based on two week's pay for every year of service over the age of 16 but no more than €600 a week is taken into account. In addition to the payment, based on service, there is an additional top-up of one week's pay. The number of years service is calculated backwards from the date of dismissal with any period of service less than a full year taken into account on a pro-rata daily basis.

Where a company is not going into liquidation but is simply rationalising its operations or just cutting back on staff it has become usual for the affected workers to demand and for the employer to pay, redundancy lump sums well in excess of the statutory requirements — in some cases up to seven weeks pay for every year of service. The employer can claim 60% of the statutory lump sum from the Department of Enterprise, Trade and Employment provided two weeks notice has been given.

Tax and the lump sum: The taxation on redundancy lump sums can be quite high. As mentioned above, the statutory redundancy payment is not liable for tax. In addition at least €10,160 of any other extra redundancy payment is also tax free. That €10,160 is increased by €765 for each full year of service. That's the minimum entitlement. Another €10,000 may also be taken tax free but that figure is reduced by the amount of any tax-free lump sum taken from a pension scheme. That's the lump sum received or that will eventually be received when the redundant worker retires. Any refund of pension contributions is taxed at a flat 20%.

The calculation of the actual exemption starts off at €20,160, plus €765 for each full year of service. The

Lump sums well in excess of the statutory minimum are often paid

€20,160 figure is reduced by the amount of any other tax-free payments received or credited. That does not include refunds of pension contributions but it does include tax-free lump sums from pension schemes. And it also includes a valuation put on any deferred payment from a pension scheme such as an entitlement to a future lump sum. In no case is the €20,160 reduced below €10,160.

To see how these calculations might work, let us first take the case of a man who is made redundant and leaves his pension contributions in the scheme as he is required to do. He has a right to a tax-free lump sum and a pension when he reaches retirement age.

You can have your average tax rate over the past three years applied to any taxable lump sum

A valuation is put on that lump sum taking account of the amount that will be paid out and the number of years to go before it is paid. Let's suppose that such a lump sum is valued at €4,500. The basic tax exemption on the redundancy lump sum of €20,160 would be reduced by that €4,500 to €15,660. If the value of the pension lump sum was €15,000, the exemption would only be reduced to €10,160 since in no case is it reduced below that level.

There is an alternative method of calculation which can give a higher tax-free figure for workers with long service. It is up to the worker. He or she has the option of calculating the tax-free lump sum on the following basis known as the Standard Capital Superannuation Benefit. The average annual salary over the last three years is multiplied by the number of years service divided by 15 and from that is deducted any tax-free lump sum from a pension scheme.

Whichever method produces the smallest taxable lump sum can be used.

Initially, any remaining taxable lump sum, after deducting the tax-free element, is treated as income in the year in which it is received and taxed as such but the taxpayer can opt to have tax levied instead at the average rate paid over the three tax years prior to the year in which the lump sum is paid.

The tax paid over the three years preceding the year in which the lump sum is paid is divided by taxable income over that period to give an average tax rate. Taxable income is defined as before tax credits and other reliefs that are given as a reductions of tax.

Someone who has opted for joint assessment with a spouse may, in making this calculation, use either the joint incomes and tax payable by both spouses or, alternatively, only the total income and tax payable by the spouse in receipt of the redundancy payment.

A claim to have this average tax rate applied must be made to your tax office and if a refund is payable you normally have to wait until the end of the tax year. No part of a redundancy lump sum is normally liable for PRSI but the taxable portion is liable to the health levy.

It may be possible to shelter part, or all, of a redundancy lump sum by using it to make an additional voluntary contribution to a pension scheme. Employees can claim tax relief on at least 15% of income each year invested in an approved pension fund. The limit goes up to 30% for those over 50, 35% for those over 55 and 40% for anyone over 60. If the contribution is above those limits it may be possible to claim relief against income in the previous year or to carry it forward and claim the relief against future income.

It may be possible to save tax by putting part of a redundancy lump sum into a pension fund

The drawback of making extra contributions into a pension fund is that the money cannot be accessed before retirement. There is more about additional voluntary contributions to pension funds on page 174.

In some cases, a person leaving a job after less than two years service may be entitled to a refund of pension contributions. But usually only his own, not any made by the employer. It depends on the rules of the scheme. Such repayments, if taken, are taxed at 20%. As an alternative to a refund, a person may actually take a pension on leaving the job and as part of that pension get a tax-free lump sum of up to $1\frac{1}{2}$ times final salary.

To qualify for a pension on retirement, a person must normally be of retirement age — at least 60 in most cases. In some occupations, retirement is allowed at an earlier age and the age limit is lifted in the case of retirement due to disability. To qualify for a tax free lump sum of $1\frac{1}{2}$ times salary from a pension scheme requires 20 years service.

Holiday entitlement

All workers, except of course the self-employed, are entitled to paid holidays. Minimum rights are laid down in law and many are entitled to more than the minimum thanks to locally negotiated agreements. Legal entitlement to paid holidays was improved in 1997 under the Organisation of Working Time Act which replaced an earlier 1973 Act. It covers all those working under a contract of employment or apprenticeship, employed through an employment agency, and most state employees other than the gardaí and defence forces. There is no qualifying period of service.

A 'leave year' normally means a year beginning on January 1 but any 12 month period may be used provided it is used consistently. Minimum paid holiday entitlements can be calculated in one of the following ways:

- Four working weeks where the employee has worked at least 1,365 hours in the year – this method is not used where a worker changes jobs during the leave year.

- One-third of a working week for each calendar month in which the employee has worked at least 117 hours.

- Alternatively the calculation can be based on eight per cent of the hours an employee works in a leave year subject to a maximum of four working weeks. In other words eight hours leave for every 100 hours or pro rata.

For the purposes of these calculations, hours worked includes overtime, time spent on maternity or parental leave as well as holidays and public holidays taken during the calculation period. Holiday pay should be paid in advance at the normal weekly rate.

The final decision on when holidays are taken rests with the employer but under the Act he or she is required to take account of a worker's need to reconcile work and family responsibilities and his or her opportunities for rest and recreation. That sounds good but it may mean very little in reality. A more specific provision is that the employer is required to give at least one month's notice to the employee or his trade union and the leave must be given either during the leave year or within six months after it ends.

If an employee on leave sends in a medical certificate stating that he or she is ill, the time covered by the certificate is not considered as leave. If board and/or lodgings is part of a worker's remuneration, his holiday pay must include compensation for the loss of these during his annual leave.

After eight months work an employee is entitled to an unbroken period of two weeks holidays which may include public holidays. This entitlement may be ceded by mutual agreement. But it is illegal for an employer to make a payment instead of the minimum statutory holiday entitlement unless the worker is actually leaving employment. So a worker who is continuing in employment must at the very least be given his or her minimum entitlements. There is nothing illegal, however, in asking a worker to accept a payment for giving up additional holiday entitlements over and above the statutory minimum.

In addition to the annual holiday entitlement, all full time employees are entitled to extra pay or leave in respect of public holidays. Part-time and casual workers must have worked at least 40 hours in the five weeks ending on the day before the public holiday. The entitlement is to one of the following: a paid day off on the day, a paid day off within a month of the day, an additional day of annual leave, an additional day's pay.

> **After eight months work an employee is entitled to an unbroken period of two weeks holidays**

By law the decision on which compensation to give is up to the employer although that may be changed by mutual agreement. The level of compensation may also be increased, of course, by negotiation.

If an employee asks an employer within 21 days of a public holiday to nominate which of the above options he or she wants to apply and gets no response the worker is automatically entitled to take a paid day off on the public holiday. There are nine public holidays: New Year's Day, St. Patrick's Day, Easter Monday, First Monday in May, First Monday in June, First Monday in August, Last Monday in October, Christmas Day, and St. Stephen's Day.

Working hours

The maximum working week has been progressively reduced since 1998 under the provisions of the Organisation of Working Time Act. Subject to a wide range of exceptions it is now set at 48 hours. That has applied since March 1, 2000. The Act doesn't apply to members of the defence forces, the Garda Síochána, junior hospital doctors, transport employees, those working at sea, workers who control their own working hours, or family members working on a farm or in a private house. The maximum working week may be averaged over 12 months if workers enter into a Labour Court approved collective agreement. In the case of seasonal workers it can be averaged over six months. Otherwise it can be averaged over four months.

Rest periods

Every worker is entitled to:

- An 11 hour rest period in every 24 hours.

- One period of 24 hours rest per week preceded by a daily rest period i.e. A total of 35 hours.

- Rest breaks of 15 minutes where up to four and a half hours have been worked or 30 minutes where up to six hours have been worked.

Night workers are defined as those who normally work at least three hours between midnight and 7am and who, during the year, work at least half of their hours during the night period. For night workers whose jobs involve special hazards or heavy physical or mental strain an absolute limit of eight hours in a 24 hour period applies. Working time is nett. of breaks, on call or standby time.

Minimum wage

Most workers, over the age of 18, are entitled to be paid at least the national minimum wage which has been €8.65 since July 2007. Those taking up new employment are only entitled to 80% of the minimum wage during their first year and 90% during their second year of employment.

Reduced rates also apply to those under 18 who are entitled to 70% of the basic minimum wage until they reach 18 rising to 80% on their 18th birthday and 90% a year later.

Reduced entitlements also apply to workers who are still in training and attending prescribed courses. They are entitled to be paid for their work hours at a rate of at least 75% of the minimum wage during the first year of training rising to 80% in the second year and 90% in the third year. The progression up the scale is faster where the training course takes less than three years, for instance if a course only takes one year there is an entitlement to 80% after four months — a third of the total duration — rising to 90% after eight months. Tips, gratuities, and extra payments for overtime, Sunday, holiday working or unsociable hours can not be considered as part of the minimum wage entitlement.

Workers in some sectors of the economy are entitled to minimum rates of pay in excess of the minimum wage as a result of what are known as Employment Regulation Orders or registered collective agreements.

The areas covered by Regulation Orders include the aerated waters and wholesale bottling sector, agricultural workers, catering, contract cleaning, hairdressing in Dublin and Cork, hotels outside of Dublin and Cork, law clerks, provender milling, retail, grocery and allied trades, the security industry, shirt making, tailoring, women's clothing and millinery.

There are registered collective agreements covering the drapery, footwear and allied trades in Dublin and Dun Laoghaire, the construction industry, electrical contracting and the printing sector in Dublin.

Details of all of these orders and agreements can be viewed on the Labour Court web site at www.labourcourt.ie. The responsibility for enforcing compliance rests with a State agency, the National Employment Rights Authority, O'Brien Road, Carlow, telephone Lo-call 1890 80 80 90. Its website www.employmentrights.ie provides information in a range of different languages.

Sunday work

Workers who don't already get special compensation for Sunday work are entitled to a Sunday premium equivalent to that applying to similar workers elsewhere. The premium payable should be based on the closest applicable collective agreement that applies in similar employment.

Zero hours on-call

Where a worker is requested to be available for work he or she is entitled to be paid for at least a quarter of the on-call hours, even if not called upon to work, subject to a payment for a maximum of 15 hours. So if a worker is required to be available for 48 hours a week, he or she is entitled to a minimum payment for 12 hours (a quarter of 48) even if not required to work at all.

Unfair dismissal

The Unfair Dismissals Acts are aimed at protecting workers from being unfairly sacked by laying down criteria of what is unfair dismissal and providing an adjudication system for redressing such action. The Act applies to most workers who have at least a year's continuous service with the same employer. It does not cover those who have passed retiring age or those excluded from the redundancy payments scheme because they are under 16 or over 66.

Neither does it cover people working for a close relative and living in the same house or on the same farm, members of the defence forces, gardaí, FÁS trainees, apprentices, or most State and local authority employees. Normally it is up to the employer to prove that a dismissal is fair and justified on the basis of the capability, competence, or qualifications of the worker, conduct, redundancy, or that a continuation of employment would breach another statutory requirement.

Dismissals are deemed to be definitely unfair if it is shown that they result from the worker's trade union membership or activities outside working hours or within working hours if normally permitted by the employer; race; religion; politics; pregnancy or related matters such as breastfeeding; membership of the Traveller community; the exercise or proposed exercise of rights to maternity, adoptive or parental leave; age or unfair selection for redundancy.

The normal requirement of having a year's service does not apply in cases involving trade union membership or activities, pregnancy, and maternity or adoptive leave.

An action against unfair dismissal should be taken within six months. This may be done by contacting a Rights Commissioner, through the Department of Labour, phone (01) 6765861, or by writing to the Employment Appeals Tribunal, Davitt House, Dublin 4. The time limit can be extended to 12 months in exceptional circumstances.

Where the dismissal is unfair, the Commissioner or Tribunal can order any of the following: reinstatement in the old job, re-engagement in the old job, or in a suitable alternative, or financial compensation up to a maximum of two years pay. Cases taken on the grounds of gender discrimination can be taken directly to the Circuit Court with no limit on the compensation that can be awarded.

Minimum notice

Any worker who has completed at least 13 weeks continuous employment with the one employer is entitled to receive minimum notice of dismissal. The notice depends on the length of service as outlined in the table below. An employee who has worked for over 13 weeks is required to give at least one week's notice of leaving the job to his employer.

13 weeks to 2 years	1 week
2 to 5 years	2 weeks
5 to 10 years	4 weeks
10 to 15 years	6 weeks
Over 15 years	8 weeks

Equality rights

Under the Employment Equality Act it is illegal for employers to discriminate against workers or potential workers in matters of pay, conditions of employment, recruitment, training and/or promotion on the grounds of sex, marital status, family status, sexual orientation, religious belief, age, disability, race, or membership of the Traveller community.

Discrimination in the provision of services, etc. is prohibited under the Equal Status Act.

Discrimination by individual employers is outlawed, as is discrimination in collective agreements, in advertisements, by employment agencies, in vocational training or by bodies such as trade unions and professional or trade organisations.

Harassment in the workplace is outlawed by the Act. That includes sexual harassment and harassment related to any of the other grounds for discrimination. Harassment is defined as any act or conduct that is unwelcomed and offensive, humiliating or intimidating including spoken words, gestures, or the production, display or circulation of written material or pictures. The obligation is on employers to take all "reasonable" steps to ensure that harassment doesn't take place.

There are some exceptions allowed for in the Act. Sexual discrimination is allowed where the sex of the employee is an essential part of the job in areas such as acting or modelling for an artist. It is also allowed in the case of some foreign postings to areas where women, for instance, might not be accepted locally in certain jobs.

> **The obligation is on employers to take all "reasonable" steps to ensure that harassment doesn't take place**

Discrimination in the provision of childbirth facilities or in the employment of care workers is also allowed, as is positive discrimination to maintain a desirable gender balance in the garda and prison services. Discrimination on the grounds of age is outlawed for all those between 18 and 65 years of age. Age-related pay scales are no longer allowed. An employer may discriminate against an elderly worker in relation to training if it can be shown that the cost of the training would not be recouped before the worker retires.

There is a critical exception in the case of disability. An employer may discriminate against a disabled person if the cost of ensuring equal treatment is anything other than nominal. The original Bill enacted in 1997 was found to be unconstitutional because it required employers to bear greater than nominal cost in providing facilities for the disabled. Another exception allows for discrimination on religious grounds in education and medical institutions where the discrimination is required to maintain a religious ethos. For public service jobs it is also permissible to require proficiency in the Irish language, residency in Ireland and/or Irish citizenship.

The Act also allows employers to discrimination in a positive fashion. It allows for actions specifically geared towards employing people over 50 years of age, people with disabilities, and members of the Traveller community. Employers may discriminate against men in measures or actions aimed at promoting equal opportunities for women in terms of recruitment and promotion including the provision of special training for women.

Having laws that outlaw discrimination doesn't, of course, ensure that discrimination will be abolished. Equal pay for women wasn't achieved overnight following the enactment of the equal pay laws in 1974. Indeed some would claim that it hasn't yet been achieved.

To qualify for equal pay under the 1974 Act, it was necessary to show that someone doing equal work was being paid more by the same or associate employer "in the same locality" but that is no longer required.

The Equality Authority, which oversees the law, doesn't itself rule on equality issues but its job is to work towards the elimination of discrimination and the promotion of equality of opportunity in employment on all of the nine discriminatory grounds covered by the Act.

So the first port of call for people with a grievance should be the Equality Authority. It can be contacted at 1890 245545. It can help individuals and groups to make their case and get redress. A person who believes that he or she has been discriminated against has the right to seek and get information necessary in drawing up a case from the supposed discriminator.

The Equality Authority provides advice on pursuing equality rights. It can be contacted at 1890 245545

Most cases go to the Employment Tribunal which can award pay arrears for up to three years in equal pay cases and compensation of up to two years pay. The maximum compensation is €12,700 in other cases. To comply with a judgement of the European Court of Justice, cases involving discrimination on the grounds of gender can go straight to the Circuit Court with no limit on the compensation that can be awarded.

Emergency time off

Employees are entitled under the 1998 Parental Leave Act, to limited time off for family emergencies resulting from an accident or illness. The entitlement is to paid leave. Emergency leave can consist of one or more working days subject to a maximum of three days in each 12 months or five days in 36 months. The employee must show that because of an injury to or illness of a family member his or her presence is indispensably required.

Also entitled are non-parents, including same-sex couples, who are in a relationship of domestic dependency.

Maternity and parental leave

There is a basic entitlement to 26 weeks maternity leave during which time Maternity Benefit is payable if PRSI contribution requirements are met. There is no obligation on the employer to continue to pay the worker although many do top up the social welfare benefit to the equivalent of full pay. At least two of the 26 weeks must be taken before the birth although that can be increased at the discretion of the worker provided at least four weeks are taken after the birth.

There is a further entitlement to a maximum of 16 weeks leave during which no Maternity Benefit is paid.

Full maternity leave entitlement is also available to women who suffer a still birth or miscarriage any time after the 24th week of pregnancy. Employers are entitled to adequate notice. Four weeks notice must be given of the intention to take maternity leave and four weeks notice must be given of the intention to return to work. The worker continues to earn holiday entitlements including bank holiday entitlements, during the full period of maternity leave.

Leave entitlements can only be transferred to a father in the tragic situation where a mother dies within 24 weeks of giving birth but a father is entitled to some unpaid parental leave. That's in addition to maternity leave and applies to all parents or those acting in *locus parentis*. The entitlement is to a maximum of 14 weeks parental leave, unpaid and without any social welfare entitlement. It is normally taken in blocks of at least six continuous weeks before each child is eight years old. That is extended to 16 if the child is disabled.

In the case of an adopted child, who is aged between three and eight at the time of adoption, the leave must normally be taken within two years of the adoption order. As with maternity leave the worker retains employment rights and is entitled to return to the same job under the same contract of employment unless the employer can show that it is not "reasonably practical". In such a case the worker is entitled to suitable alternative employment.

Four weeks notice must be given of the intention to take maternity leave

Existing social welfare rights are also protected by the granting of credited PRSI contributions during the period of leave. The employee, who must normally have at least one year's service must give six weeks notice of taking paternal leave and the employer has the right to postpone it where it would have an adverse impact on the business. In some cases those with only three months service may be entitled to pro-rata paternal leave.

An expectant mother is entitled to take time off without loss of pay for ante and post natal medical examination and tests and both she and the expectant father are entitled to limited time off, again without any loss of pay, to attend ante-natal classes. She may attend one set of ante-natal classes under this provision with the exception of the last three classes in the set when she would normally be on leave.

Fathers have a once-off right to attend the two prenatal classes immediately prior to the birth. Employers are entitled to be given two weeks notice in writing of appointment dates.

Adoptive leave is granted on much the same basis as maternity leave. The entitlement is to 24 weeks on social welfare and a further 16 weeks without social welfare payments. The adopting parent is usually a woman but a man can qualify in certain circumstances where his partner has died or where the child is being placed solely in his care.

The conditions as to notice etc. are similar to those that apply to maternity leave. Adoptive parents are also entitled to time off without loss of pay to attend pre-adoption classes or meetings. Attendance must be a requirement of the adoption and notice must be given.

Adoptive leave is granted on much the same terms as maternity leave

Breastfeeding mothers who have given birth within the previous six months are entitled, without loss of pay, to either a single one hour break or two half-hour breaks during each standard working day. Alternatively an employer who can't provide breastfeeding facilities must facilitate an adjustment of the mother's working hours. There is provision for both maternity and adoptive leave to be postponed in the event of the child being hospitalised or the mother falling ill.

Where a child is hospitalised an employer can be asked to postpone some of the maternity leave but the request can be refused. If it is granted, the mother returns to work and takes the remainder of the leave starting not later than seven days after the child is discharged from hospital.

If the mother falls ill during the extended period of maternity leave i.e. the period during which no Maternity Benefit is payable, she may request the employer to end the maternity leave period. If granted that allows her to claim Illness Benefit but there is no entitlement to reclaim the maternity leave foregone.

Apart from maternity and adoptive leave all employees are entitled under the 1998 Parental Leave Act to limited time off for family emergencies resulting from an accident or illness. The entitlement is to paid leave. The two are completely separate although provided for under the same Act. See page 156.

Terms of employment

All employees are entitled to get a written statement of the terms and conditions of employment within two months of starting a job. Those who were in jobs before the Act came into effect, on May 16, 1994, are entitled to a statement within two weeks of requesting it. The statement should include a job description, expected duration if temporary, starting date, hours of work, details of pay, overtime, bonus and holiday entitlements, and details of sick pay and pension arrangements.

Trade union members can refer disputes over any of their employment rights to their union representation but those who are not in trade unions have to seek redress themselves. Further information on entitlements can be got from

- **The Department of Enterprise,**
  Trade and Employment,
  Employment Rights section
  Davitt House,
  65 Adelaide Road,
  Dublin, 2.
  Telephone (01) 6313131 or 1890 201615

Other disputes can be referred to the Rights Commissioner Service of the Labour Relations Commission at

- **Rights Commissioner Service**
  Labour Relations Commission,
  Tom Johnson House,
  Haddington Road,
  Dublin, 4.
  Telephone (01) 6609662

For assistance on matters of discrimination contact

- **Equality Authority**
  Clonmel Street
  Dublin, 2.
  Telephone (1890) 245545

Most equality claims are decided by

- **The Equality Tribunal**
  Clonmel Street
  Dublin, 2.
  Telephone (1890) 344424

9 Insuring against the loss of home or possessions

To get the best insurance quote you have to shop around.
Now, there's a very quotable quote — Anon

The single largest asset owned by most people is a house or apartment. Fire, burglary, accident, or even storm damage can, and does, result in substantial losses every day of the week. It is up to the individual to decide whether he wants to bear the full risk of such losses himself or spread it around by taking out insurance. For this is what insurance does — spreads the risk. A large number of people pay a small premium so that the few who actually suffer loss can be reimbursed. And you could be one of the few.

Now that a bit of competition is coming back into the house and car insurance markets, it's more important than ever to shop around. There are significant savings to be made. Don't rely solely on a broker to do the shopping around for you. There are very good deals to be got by phoning around or by seeking online quotes. Don't assume that the first quote you get is the best available. Discounts can make a big difference where they apply and not all companies are the same. Most, but not all, give discounts for smoke detectors and burglar alarms. Senior citizens can also claim discounts from some insurers. 'Senior' can mean over 50 in some cases and over 55 in others. A couple of insurers also give discounts to people who also insure their cars with them.

The cheapest policy is not always the best, of course. Cover can vary significantly and it is often difficult to compare policies before you buy since you don't get the full documentation until you have paid the premium. But there are a few questions you can ask.

- Does the policy cover accidental damage to household items? Are you covered, for instance, for damage to the TV if you simply let it fall moving it from one room to another? Not all policies cover accidental damage.

- If one item of a suite of furniture is damaged does the policy cover replacing the whole suite or just that item even if a good match cannot be obtained?

- What limitations are placed on the cover for high value items including cash?

- What portion of any claim will you have to meet yourself? This is known as the excess. You may be able to choose a figure yourself. The higher it is, the lower the premium should be.

- Are there any discounts for having an alarm or because of my age? – over 50s sometimes qualify.

These are just some of the questions to consider when choosing a policy. Once you get the policy document make sure to read it carefully. Make sure you know what is and isn't covered. The cover may be more extensive than you realise. For instance it may cover the replacement of locks if you lose your keys or cover for items lost from your car.

You may have more cover than you realise in some areas. But every policy also imposes a range of restrictions on your cover in other areas. It's as well to be aware of them too. Take the case of John who brought a complaint to the Insurance Ombudsman. His house was burgled while he was attending a street party and he made a claim for about €2,000 to cover the items stolen.

You may even get a lower quote from your existing insurance company if it thinks that you are a new customer or if you approach it in a different way, on the internet, for instance

■ The Society of Chartered Surveyors, 5 Wilton Place, Dublin 2 issues annual guidelines for valuing houses for insurance purposes. Copies are free on request but please enclose a stamped addressed envelope. The following is a summary of their 2009 figures in euro per square foot. Based on March 2009 costs they are designed to cover rebuilding costs including site clearance.

House type		Dublin	Cork	Galway	Waterford	Limerick
Terraced —	2 bedroom 750 sq. ft.	€197	€148	€148	€145	€152
	3 bedroom 1,023 sq. ft.	€187	€139	€139	€138	€141
Semi —	3 bedroom 1,023 sq. ft.	€195	€148	€142	€147	€151
	4 bedroom 1,270 sq. ft.	€178	€133	€132	€132	€130
Detached —	4 bedroom 1,270 sq. ft.	€184	€135	€133	€136	€140
Bungalow —	4 bedrooms 1,572 sq. ft.	€174	€132	€127	€127	€142

The insurance company refused to pay on three grounds. An inspector had difficulties gaining access to the house after the burglary. Some of the goods taken belonged to a woman with whom the claimant had been living. The policy only covered goods belonging to members of the claimant's family. And the alarm was not turned on. That was a breach of a policy condition. The Ombudsman found in favour of the company on all but the first ground. It transpired that the claimant's wife had moved back into the house after the burglary and she had refused the inspector entry. That wasn't enough to refuse the claim, the Ombudsman decided. But not turning on the alarm was a sufficient reason for not paying up since the claimant had got a 10% discount on his premium on the understanding that the alarm would always be turned on when the house was not occupied, even for a short period. And the policy clearly stated that only property belonging to the claimant and his family was covered.

So paying the insurance premium isn't enough. You need to read the fine print to see what is and isn't covered and you also must abide by any conditions such as turning on alarms. You also need to answer the questions on the proposal form truthfully and fully. In another case the Ombudsman found in favour of an insurance company that had refused to pay out on a claim for damage resulting from a chimney fire. The claimant had not disclosed that she had previously claimed for similar damage from another company.

Greater losses can result from a failure to fully value the contents of your house or to underestimate the costs of reinstating the house after a fire. Overestimating will push up your premiums but underestimating can result in any claim being scaled down as a result of the 'average clause' included in most policies.

The average clause causes many misunderstandings and problems, so it is as well to understand what it is about. It can best be explained by a simple example. Suppose your house is worth €400,000, but you only have it insured for €200,000. If your house is completely destroyed, you would only expect to get €200,000 from the insurance company since you are only half insured. But suppose your house is only damaged. If the damage is estimated at, say, €40,000 then the insurance company will still consider that you are only half insured and pay out €20,000 – half of the €40,000 damage.

A house owner who complained to the Financial Ombudsman when his insurance company applied the average clause lost his case. His claim for €145,000 was reduced to €132,000 because, according to the company, his property was underinsured. He had relied on indexing the amount of cover but the Ombudsman found that this was not sufficient. In coming to his decision he took account of the guidelines issued by the Society of Chartered Surveyors.

Because of the average clause, it is important to reassess your insurance needs each year as you renew your policies. You don't have to be absolutely precise but you do need to

> **Don't assume that your building society insurance provides adequate cover**

> **It is important to reassess your insurance needs every year taking account of replacement costs**

be fairly close to the correct valuations. In the case of building insurance, of course, you need to insure for the reinstatement cost of the house. That may bear no relationship to the market value.

Similar houses in different areas may have very different market values but exactly the same reinstatement costs apply to both. The Society of Chartered Surveyors, 5 Wilton Place, Dublin, 2 issues annual guidelines for valuing houses for insurance purposes. Copies are free on request but please enclose a stamped addressed envelope.

In the case of older houses or those with unusual once-off designs it's as well to get some professional advice on reinstatement costs. Don't rely on the market value. It is seldom, if ever, a good guide to valuation for insurance purposes.

It pays to shop around or get a broker to do it for you. Don't forget, of course, that there are some companies that don't deal through brokers. You need to check them out yourself. Make sure your home is adequately insured, but don't be scared into over-insuring it.

There are four general areas of risk which the average householder should consider covering by insurance. These are: damage or loss of the house itself; damage or loss of contents — furniture, etc; liability for damage to third parties arising out of defects in the building; and all risks insurance for specific items, i.e. jewellery, etc. Very often all four types of risk can be covered by the one general policy, although individual policies covering any one type can be taken out.

The house itself

Read the proposal form and the policy carefully to discover just what's covered and what's not

For the sake of the relatively small premium involved it is not worth taking the risk of not insuring your house. If the house is rented, check if you are liable for insuring it. With a short lease you possibly are not. With a long lease you may be. If you are buying a house with a mortgage, the bank or building society will require you to insure it and in some cases will have done it for you.

Most policies cover damage to the basic structure of the house itself, the garage and certain outbuildings, together with walls, gates and fences. Also covered is damage to fixtures and fittings such as washbasins, toilets, pipes etc.

Public liability cover, up to a fixed sum, is usually included as standard to cover your liability for injury or loss suffered by another person as a result of an accident which occurred on your property. It is also usual to have some cover for the cost of alternative accommodation if the house is left uninhabitable. It may be necessary to specifically request and pay extra to get cover for damage to underground water pipes running between your house and the boundary of your land, damage to radio and television aerials and breakage of glass, etc. The basic policy usually covers:

Fire, explosion, lightning, thunderbolt, falling aircraft or other aerial devices: Damage resulting from terrorist attack may be excluded.

Flood damage: Flood damage may not be covered in some areas. Storm damage to fences and gates or damage to television aerials may be excluded.

Burglary, housebreaking or any attempt there at: The buildings policy simply covers damage to the house itself — not the contents. The cover does not apply if the house is left unfurnished, or even if it is furnished, is left uninhabited for more than a set period. If you are leaving your house vacant it is best to check with the insurance company to ensure that you are covered. If you are leaving it unfurnished you will have to take out a special policy.

Bursting or overflowing of water tanks or pipes: Again it is usual to exclude some small part of any claim under this heading — the first €50 say — and the conditions on leaving the house vacant are the same as above.

Impact: Damage caused by impact with the buildings, walls, gates, fences of any road vehicle, horses or cattle not belonging to or under the control of yourself or your family.

Loss of rent: If the house is left uninhabitable you are usually covered in this regard up to a set percentage of the sum insured on the building — often 10%.

Liability to Public: If you are proved liable for damages caused to another person by an accident which occurred on

■ There's a temptation to believe that taking out insurance somehow safeguards your property. That if you have insurance on your mobile phone, for instance, there is a reduced chance of it being stolen or lost. Of course there isn't. That's obvious when you think about it. And if you really think about it taking out insurance on your mobile phone doesn't really make sense at all.

The real trauma involved in losing your mobile phone has a lot more to do with the inconvenience of losing the information in the phone's memory than it has to do with the cost of replacing the phone itself.

If you comply with all the conditions, an insurance policy may reimburse you for most of the cost of replacing the phone. But it won't compensate you for the trouble and strife involved in getting a replacement and programming it to your particular needs.

And having insurance doesn't, in any way, reduce the odds against your phone being damaged, lost or stolen – unless, of course, there is really something in that old belief that a slice of bread always falls buttered side down.

Is it really worth paying €5 a month to cover a potential loss of maybe only €100. You wouldn't dream of taking out insurance to cover the possibility of losing the €100 or so you may occasionally carry around in your pocket. So why take out cover on your mobile phone? You should be able to cover that sort of financial loss yourself without too much difficulty.

But many people do take out insurance on their mobile phones simply because they are not paying too much attention when filling out the application form and it's very often easier to say yes rather than no. The person selling the phone will usually have an incentive to sell the insurance. It's a lucrative business for the insurance companies and they pay generous commission.

While many people take out this form of insurance, few people bother to read the fine print. Very often the first €30 or so of any claim is disallowed. That's called the excess. Usually the owner of the phone is required to take good care of his or her phone.➜

your property, the normal building policy will provide cover up to about €65,000.

When you are taking out insurance you should read the proposal form carefully to see what risks are excluded and decide whether or not you want extra cover. It is a good idea to look at your insurance policies at least once a year,

Companies will, for instance, refuse to pay out if the phone was left unattended, say in a car or in a jacket left on the back of a chair.

This type of condition also applies to credit card insurance which is even less useful than insurance on a mobile phone.

Under the terms and conditions of most credit card agreements there is an upper limit on the cardholder's liability if the loss of a card is reported promptly. It's usually no more than about €60 and often only half that. In many cases the card companies don't even bother collecting that money.

Of course there is no limit on a cardholder's liability if he or she has been negligent or has acted in a fraudulent manner. Negligence might include simply leaving a card unattended but it certainly includes carrying a PIN number around with the card. The cardholder's potential liability can be very high if both card and PIN number fall into the wrong hands, particularly in some countries abroad where the upper limit on cash withdrawals is very high.

That's the type of liability against which it would be nice to have insurance. But it's not covered by the standard policy or indeed any policy that I know off. The standard policy costs about €16 a year. It isn't much. But it can't be good value when the most you are likely to ever claim is about €60.

Credit card companies also offer payment protection policies. They are similarly bad value. Yet it is all too easy to tick off the "yes" box when filling out the application form for the credit card or when buying a mobile phone.

The typical charge is 60 cent a month for every €100 outstanding. At first glance that seems to be a small amount but it adds up to 7.2% a year on your debt. That's a lot, particularly for what you get. The typical policy provides a benefit if the cardholder is disabled or loses his or her job. But it only provides for the phased repayment of the debt, perhaps over 12 months. The debt isn't automatically cleared. In all these cases, save yourself some money by thinking twice before saying yes to taking out insurance.

preferably long before the renewal date so as to give yourself ample time to shop around for a better deal.

House contents

Premiums for house contents insurance vary greatly depending on where the house is, the company providing the cover and the type of cover given. Many companies give discounts where the occupants are over a certain age, for being in a neighbourhood watch scheme, or for having an approved alarm system. A discount may also be available if you agree to pay the first part of any claim yourself. One of the main reasons for the increased cost of house insurance is the increased risk of loss.

So can you afford not to be insured or to underestimate the value of your house contents?

If the contents of your house are not insured, you may be running a serious risk of loss — tot up the value of the contents of your kitchen for instance. Could you afford to replace them yourself? If it would impose an undue burden, then you would do well to be insured. Do not assume that you are insured just because the bank or building society that holds your mortgage looks after your insurance. It is normally only interested in having the buildings insured. Insuring the contents is generally left up to yourself. The normal contents policy covers loss arising from the same causes as the building policy. Extras which may be included as standard in some policies include:

Tenant's liability to landlord: Useful if you are in a rented house, this clause provides cover for damage caused to fittings, etc., for which the tenant may have to reimburse the landlord.

Employer's liability: This covers claims by people employed to work in the house – anything from full-time domestic staff to tradesmen, who may be doing repairs about the house.

Liability to third parties: This provides cover for claims arising from accidents occurring in or about the house to visitors or their property.

Most policies also include provision for replacing items on a new for old basis provided it is not more than (usually) five years old. Suppose, for instance, your cooker gets burnt it will be replaced with a new cooker of the same type. Some companies, however, only provide this as an extra, so check.

There can be some important exclusions which need to be borne in mind. There may only be limited cover for loss or damage to articles temporarily removed from the house. Usually if the value of any one article — a piece of jewellery for instance — is more than 5% of the total sum insured, a special policy will be required. Cash and bank notes are often only covered to a maximum of 5% of the total value insured. But there may be an even more onerous money limit, as low as €30. Usually the following items are not covered at all: deeds, bonds, bills of exchange, promissory notes, cheques, securities for money, stamps, documents of any kind, manuscripts, medals, coins, motor vehicles, accessories, and livestock.

Some insurers offer discounts for homes with alarms but be careful before applying for such a discount. There may be a condition attached that the alarm is always switched on when there is no-one is the house. If the policy does contain such a condition then you may not be insured at all if you forget to turn on the alarm. Most companies now have what is known as a "best endeavour" clause rather than a complete exclusion clause so that you are covered as long as you did not blatantly refuse to turn on the alarm. But before looking for a discount or accepting one make sure that onerous conditions do not apply.

> **Accepting a discount for having a burglar alarm may require you to meet fairly onerous conditions. It's not always the case but do take care**

Personal liability

You, as a house owner or occupier may be held liable for damages caused by your negligence. A passer-by may be hit by a tile falling off your roof. A guest might trip over a carpet. Most household policies provide some cover for such claims. With some policies the cover extends to incidences unrelated to the house.

You can cause damage in many different ways. You could hit someone with a golf ball, close a door on someone's fingers, or cause an accident by walking out on the road in front of a cyclist. If you are found to be negligent in such cases, you could be liable to pay damages. Apart from the cover given by some household policies it is also possible to take out stand-alone personal liability insurance to provide you with cover against such claims up to a maximum sum. It's possible to get cover of up to €100,000 for an annual premium as low as €1.

All risks

As mentioned above, the normal policy on house contents does not provide cover for articles whose value represents more than 5% of the total sum insured. So if you have a valuable piece of jewellery, a camera or a painting, you may find that you are not covered for its loss. If you have such valuable items, an all-risks policy is worth having. Usually a valuation certificate is required for each article worth more than about €120. Rates vary considerably and range upwards of €1 a year for every €100 insured — a lot more for bicycles. Some insurance companies have a minimum all-risks premium so it may cost no more to put a few items on the policy than it does to simply cover one item.

10 Planning for your retirement

Many of the things you can count, don't count.
Many of the things you can't count, really count — Albert Einstein

On average a person can expect to spend over one year in retirement for every three in the paid workforce. For many it can be longer. The average is based on someone working from 18 to 65 and then living another 16 years. That's about the average life expectancy at age 65. But people are living longer and more active lives, entering the labour force later and retiring earlier. It's no wonder we're told that it is never too early to plan for retirement.

Many people spend a lot of time planning their careers but there is frequently a reluctance to even think about the post retirement years. Quality of life depends on a range of factors from health to wealth. The latter is the easiest to plan for. Planning is about anticipating change and preparing for it. Planning for retirement involves preparing for the changes that will take place in your income and expenditure patterns when you give up work. Your income is reduced but your spending needs are unlikely to decline to the same extent. A new income source will be needed. So where is

> **The quality of life in retirement can be much improved by a bit of advance planning**

that income to come from? The majority of workers retiring in the future will be entitled to a contributory old age pension when they retire. But even at the full rate that's far from enough to provide a comfortable living. The more you can put aside to supplement it the better. If you're self-employed, it's entirely up to yourself. If you're a PAYE worker you may be in a company pension scheme and be inclined to leave it at that. But you can always top up your benefits if they are inadequate. All the options involve saving. Some people save by investing in their own businesses or directly in shares or property. But the most common way is through a pension scheme.

With a change in the tax relief regime planned, there is an incentive for those on the standard rate of tax to postpone making pension contributions

Within generous limits you can get tax relief on every cent you put into a pension scheme. If you are paying tax at the top rate of 41c in the euro that effectively means a top up of at least €50 for every €50 you save. That's taking account of the income tax, PRSI and health levy that you would pay on the money if you didn't pay it into the pension fund. There are some set-up and management costs to take into account but you'd have to pay those anyway on most alternative investments.

The tax saving is less for those paying tax at the standard rate of 20c in the euro. But it still represents a top up of €30 for every €70 saved. If you take €100 in pay, you end up with €70 after tax, PRSI and the health levy is deducted. Invest that money in a pension fund and you paid none of those. The full €100, less perhaps some small administrative charge, goes into your fund.

At the end of 2009 there is a major disincentive for those paying tax at the standard rate to contribute to a pension fund because of the expectation that the tax relief will be improved as part of a major review of pension policy that has been ongoing for year but is coming to fruition. For those paying tax at the standard rate it clearly makes sense to wait while for those paying tax at the top rate, there's an incentive to act now before any reduction in the generous tax relief that they can currently enjoy.

There is, of course, one major drawback to investing in a pension fund. The money has to remain untouched until retirement. But that's not a drawback if your objective is really to save for your latter years. Restrictions on what can be done with the accumulated funds on retirement have in recent years been greatly eased in respect of personal pension funds and additional voluntary contributions to occupational schemes. Saving is about accepting present pain for future gain and that future gain is almost certain to outweigh the current pain in foregone spending, particularly when saving for retirement. So should YOU be saving for retirement?

Should you be saving?

Only you can decide the level of income you would like to have in retirement. Obviously the more the better but securing an adequate pension requires a lot of saving. The standard civil service pension can be used as a benchmark against which to judge your current entitlements or to set as an ideal to strive for. It provides:

- A pension of one-eightieth of final pay for each year of service up to a maximum of 40/80ths i.e. half final pay,

- A tax-free lump sum up to one and a half-year's salary is also payable on retirement.

- Post retirement increases in line with pay increases, and

- A continuing pension for a surviving spouse equal to half the original pension.

Good private sector schemes provide similar benefits. The pension may be calculated on the basis of one-sixtieth of final pay up to a maximum of 40/60ths or two-thirds. That pension is reduced, however, to take account of any tax-free lump sum taken on retirement. So the end result may be close to the standard civil service scheme. But only a minority of private sector schemes provide that type of benefit and the proportion is declining rather than increasing as new entrants in many firms are often offered less attractive pension entitlements than the existing workforce.

You may need to save 15% of income over your working life to secure a good pension on retirement

A recent study concluded that a man aged 20 would need to invest about 15% of his income each year to fund a civil service type pension at age 65. That's assuming he achieves a reasonable rate of return on the invested money. If he wanted to retire at 60 he'd need to invest 19% of his income

■ There is no time limit on the making of additional voluntary contributions to a pension scheme. They can be made any time during your working life. The earlier you start, of course, the better the return will be in terms of an enhanced pension. The sooner the money goes in the longer it has to grow. But so long as you qualify for tax relief, particularly at the top rate, it's never too late to make contributions. It's possible to make very good returns on contributions made even in the last few weeks before retirement and can be well worthwhile if you qualify for tax relief.

Even if you are going to qualify for the maximum pension under your particular scheme, that may be less than the maximum allowed by the Revenue Commissioners. Your scheme, for instance, may only take account of basic pay while the Revenue allows you to fund for a pension based on a wider definition of pay including overtime, shift allowances and the value of benefits-in-kind. Your scheme may only provide for a pension of two-thirds final pay **including** your social welfare pension. Most defined benefit schemes do. But the Revenue allow you to fund for a pension of two-thirds final pay **plus** social welfare and still qualify for tax relief. There may even be scope for claiming tax relief on additional contributions even if you are going to qualify for the maximum public sector pension of half final pay plus a tax free lump sum of one-and-a-half times final salary. The Revenue recently conceded that with interest rates so low, this level of pension entitlement falls short of the maximum allowed for tax relief.

Those who make last-minute AVCs can backdate a claim for tax relief over two years on a maximum of 40% of pay in both the current and previous tax years. That 40% applies only if you are over 60 and includes any basic pension contributions that are being made. So if you are already putting 5% into the scheme, you can claim tax relief on a further 35% for each year. On retirement the money accumulated in the AVC may, in some cases, enhance the tax-free lump sum that can be taken immediately. If the maximum tax-free lump sum is already being taken the AVC money can be transferred into an approved retirement fund (ARF or AMRF).

Provided the pensioner has other income of at least €12,700 a year, the money in that fund can be drawn down at will. Otherwise it has to be left until he or she is 75. Money drawn out is subject to tax in the normal way but many pensioners are exempt from tax and few are subject to tax at the top rate. So in many cases the AVC money that qualified for tax relief when it was put into the fund can be drawn out tax free.

or 23% if he wanted to start drawing his pension at 55. A woman would need to invest more since women tend to live longer than men. However slightly less than one in two workers is in a company or other occupational pension scheme in Ireland. While over 80% of public sector workers are covered, the figure is a much lower 38% in the private sector. It's as low as 19% in the distribution sector. The majority of self-employed workers don't make any pension provision for themselves either.

Reviewing your pension options

There is a wide range of options from which to choose. The factors that you need to consider depend initially on whether you work for yourself or for someone else.

■ You work for someone else

If you are already in a company or occupational scheme you need to ask:

- How good is the scheme?

- What pension can I expect?

- Am I entitled to other benefits?

- Can I improve my entitlements by making additional contributions?

If you are not in a scheme you need to think about:

- Joining one if there is one to join,

- getting your employer to set up a scheme, or

- contributing to your own personal pension plan or PRSA.

■ You work for yourself

If you are self-employed, then your only option is to contribute to your own pension fund. There are a number of questions that you need to consider. For instance, if you work for your own company you may be better off setting up a company scheme and have it make the contributions. But either way ask yourself:

- How much should you be investing?

- Should you make regular contributions or invest occasional lump sums?

- Where do you invest your money? There are many companies and a range of funds to consider. There's even the option of administering your own fund. The following sections will help to provide answers to those questions.

Occupational pension schemes

Less than four out of every 10 private sector workers are in company pension schemes. That includes those who are in industry-wide occupational schemes. Even if you are one of the lucky ones, it doesn't mean that you can look forward to an adequate pension. Much depends on the type of scheme and its rules. They can vary greatly from one to the other. If you are not in a scheme and there isn't one for you to join, you can either get your employer to set one up or else contribute to a personal pension plan of your own in the same way as a self-employed person might.

Employers have to at least collect contributions from pay for those workers who want to save for retirement through a PRSA although they do not have to make contributions themselves. (See the next section). If you are in a company or other occupational pension scheme how good is it? If it doesn't rate too highly there are actions you can take to get a better pension.

How good is your scheme?

There are two basic types of pension scheme, defined benefit and defined contribution. In a defined benefit scheme, the pension payable is usually based on final salary and years of service. Worker contributions, if required, are usually fixed as a percentage of pay. The employer accepts an open-ended commitment to make whatever additional contributions are necessary to fund the guaranteed level of pension. Most older schemes are of this type.

In a defined contribution scheme, as the name implies, it is the level of contribution that's fixed. Usually both employer

■ Pension scheme members enjoy a wide range of rights and protections including:

INFORMATION ENTITLEMENTS: Members of pension schemes are entitled to the following information: basic information about the scheme's benefits, contributions etc; copies of the trust deed and rules of the scheme; an annual statement showing the individual's current entitlements; annual reports giving audited accounts; actuarial reports; and an investment report. Some of that information must be given automatically to members, prospective members and their trade unions. All of it must be available at least on request. Schemes with more than 100 members must produce a statement of investment policy, principles and objectives

TRUSTEES: Members in schemes covering more than 50 people are entitled to elect at least two trustees if requested by 15% of members or a trade union.

PRESERVED PENSIONS: A pension fund member with over two years qualifying service is entitled to a preserved pension if he leaves the job. Its value will go up by the rate of inflation or 4% a year whichever is the lower figure. Alternatively pension entitlements may be transferred into a new pension scheme, a PRSA or into an approved pension bond. Refunds are not allowed.

CONTRIBUTION PAYMENTS: Contributions stopped by an employer from pay have to be lodged to the pension fund within 15 days of the end of the month in which the deductions were made.

INDEX LINKING: Pensions don't have to be index-linked to inflation on wage increases but the actuarial reports on pension schemes have to comment on the effects that indexing would have on the fund.

FUND SURPLUSES: In the event of a wind-up or transfer, employers and trustees have to consult with members on the treatment of any surplus that may be in the fund. But having consulted they can take any action allowed under the scheme rules.

WORKERS ON LOW PAY: The minimum pension payment must be at least equal to 120% of the member's personal contributions plus interest.

PENSIONS BOARD: The Pensions Board can be contacted at Verschoyle House, Mount Street, Dublin, 2. Phone (01) 6393622.

PENSIONS OMBUDSMAN: Complaints with regard to the mal-administration of schemes can be made to Paul Kenny at The Office of the Pensions Ombudsman, PO Box 9324, 36 Upper Mount Street, Dublin, 2. Phone (01) 6131900

and employee contribute a set percentage of pay. The eventual pension depends both on the amount contributed over the years and the performance of the funds into which the money is put. The pension level is not guaranteed and the employer is not faced with an open-ended commitment as in the case of a defined benefit scheme.

The best defined benefit schemes provide:

- An initial pension of 2/3rds final pay after 40 years service,

- A built-in widow/er's pension which can be as much as the full pension,

- Annual increases after retirement in line with pay rises, and

- No reduction in the pension to take account of State pension entitlements.

A company pension scheme can provide a pension of two-thirds final salary plus social welfare

That's the standard to aim for. It is broadly in line with the maximum benefits allowed by the Revenue Commissioners. Contributions aimed at funding benefits over and above that level aren't eligible for tax relief. The Revenue rules are fairly liberal with regard to fine print conditions attaching to pension schemes. Some schemes are much more restrictive in the definition of final pay, for instance, than the Revenue rules require.

If your **defined benefit** scheme provides less than the maximum allowed by the Revenue rules, or if you won't have sufficient service to qualify for the maximum pension, then you should qualify for tax relief on additional voluntary contributions made to enhance your benefits. If you are in a **defined contribution** scheme you need to be constantly checking the build-up of your fund and the benefits you can expect. Your annual statement is required to show a reasonable forecast of what you can expect on the basis of expected contributions and investment returns.

Improving your entitlements

If you decide that your pension entitlements are inadequate and you don't have much hope of having your pension scheme improved, then your only option is to start saving to secure improved benefits for yourself by making additional voluntary contributions (AVCs). Most private sector schemes allow members to either contribute more money to the existing pension fund or, alternatively, to contribute to their own personal fund such as a Personal Retirement Savings Account (see page 182). There are pros and cons for both options. Setting up a scheme of your own involves costs that may be avoided by contributing extra money into the company scheme. But a personal scheme is more flexible particularly in the choice of investments.

But whatever option you choose, there is no doubt that if your aim is to boost income in retirement there's a clear advantage in saving through a pension fund. That way you can get tax relief on every cent you save up to generous limits laid down by the Revenue Commissioners. Contributions up to the following percentages of pay are allowed in full for tax relief on condition that they won't provide you with benefits in excess of the very generous maximum levels set by the Revenue Commissioners.

The maximum earnings taken into account in applying these percentages is €275,239 in 2008 and €150,000 since 2009. For a high earning 60 year old, the maximum contribution allowed for tax relief is €60,000 – 40% of €150,000.

Age	Limit	Age	Limit
up to 30	15%	30 but less than 40	20%
40 but less than 50	25%	50 but less than 55	30%
55 but less than 60	35%	60 or over	40%

There is an added advantage in that the fund built up through AVCs doesn't have to be used to buy a pension on retirement as was once the case. Up to a quarter of the fund can be withdrawn immediately on retirement tax free, subject to a maximum of one-and-a-half years salary. Salary is defined by Revenue to include overtime and other additional earnings that may not be taken into account in the benefits provided by the occupational scheme. Up to a few years ago, the rest of the money accumulated through additional voluntary contributions had to be used to buy an additional pension for life. Now there are other options. For details see page 184.

Setting up your own pension fund

Whether you are self-employed or working for someone else you can set up your own personal pension plan. If you work for yourself, it may be your only option but if you are an employee, you may see it as an alternative or addition to an occupational scheme. If you are self-employed and work for your own company, you can have it set up a company pension scheme even if you are going to be the only member. The alternative, which is also open to employees, is to contribute to your own pension scheme or open a PRSA. The following are points to consider in making the choice.

■ Company schemes

Where the self-employed person works for his or her own company, there are advantages in having the company set up the scheme. The net cost is likely to be lower and the restriction on the size of contributions that qualify for tax relief is less onerous. There can also be tax advantages in having your company pay all the contributions rather than paying them yourself into a personal plan. Also, where an employer is willing to make some contribution to an employee's pension, it can be more tax efficient to set up a formal scheme rather than paying the worker the extra money and letting him or her take out a personal pension plan.

Apart from the possible tax advantages within a company scheme there can be more flexibility in opting for early retirement. The balance of advantages depends on individual circumstances. Where a company scheme is deemed best it may even be worthwhile setting up a company simply to avail of that option but that has other implications. Professional advice is advisable.

■ Personal pension plans and PRSAs

If you are self-employed, or in a job with an inadequate pension scheme or no pension scheme, then you can contribute to your own personal pension plan or Personal Retirement Savings Account (PRSA). You pay all the contributions and you decide where the money is to be invested. If you want to save for your retirement then it's about the best option available.

- You get tax relief on the contributions.

- The tax relief also applies to contributions made to a life insurance policy that is part of the plan.

- You can withdraw 25% of the fund tax free on retirement.

- Subject to some conditions the remainder of the fund does not have to be used to fund a pension.

It's not difficult to set up a personal pension plan. The options have been widened greatly with the introduction of Personal Retirement Savings Accounts (PRSAs) which, although aimed mainly at employees without pension cover, are also an option for the self-employed. Tax relief is allowed at the top marginal rate so someone paying tax at the top rate gets tax relief of €41 for every €100 invested in the fund. The relief is less for someone liable for tax at the standard rate. There may also be a saving in PRSI contributions.

■ Self-administered pension schemes

If you are putting sizeable sums into a pension fund it is possible to control your own investment strategy and even have the fund borrow to finance property or other investments. The costs of establishing and managing such a fund are significant and only worthwhile if the fund is fairly large so they are really only an option for relatively high earners. Self-administered pension schemes usually have fewer than 12 members, but Revenue approval for borrowing is only given to single member schemes. There are restrictions on the assets that can be held by such schemes. It is not permissible to buy, sell, lease or rent property to or from any beneficiary of the scheme. In other words you can't get the pension fund to invest in your house or in property used by your business. Neither can it invest in "pride of possession" assets such as works of art, a holiday home, antiques, etc.

Picking the right plan

There is no single pension plan that is best for all people. There's even an element of luck involved in making the choice since there is no way of knowing in advance how various investments are going to perform in the future. But

■ Personal Retirement Savings Accounts (PRSAs) offer a low cost, flexible way of saving for retirement. They can be used by the self-employed, employees who are not in occupational pension schemes and even by employees who are in pension schemes but who want to improve their pension entitlements by making additional voluntary contributions (AVCs). They may or may not be more attractive than existing AVC arrangements. It's important to look at the costs and how the money is being invested.

A PRSA is simply a personal investment account subject to the restriction that the funds cannot be accessed until retirement. They are issued by insurance companies, banks and other financial institutions and are open to everyone even those who are not employed subject to a minimum contribution of €300 a year. They are flexible in that there must be a facility to vary contributions from year to year. Tax relief at the contributor's top tax rate can be claimed on contributions put into a PRSA. The proportion of income on which the relief can be claimed varies with age.

Age	Proportion of pay	Age	Proportion of pay
Under 30	15%	50 to 54	30%
30 to 39	20%	55 to 59	35%
40 to 49	25%	Over 60	40%

Irrespective of income, an individual contributing to a non-AVC PRSA can claim tax relief on up to €1,525 a year. An individual not liable for tax can carry that relief forward to set against a future tax liability. The maximum income taken into account is €275,239 in 2008 and €150,000 in 2009. The charges on standard PRSAs may not exceed 5% of each contribution plus an ongoing management charge of 1% of the accumulating fund. Those are maximum levels. Some companies charge less.

There is no cap on the charges in respect of non-standard PRSAs and no reason to believe that they will on average perform any better than their standard counterparts.

Employers who do not operate company pension schemes for all their employees or who do not offer an AVC arrangement are required to set up at least one standard PRSA for their workers. They must arrange to stop contributions from pay but they do not have to contribute themselves. They do, however, save employer's PRSI on the contributions made by their workers since they are not considered to be income for tax or PRSI purposes. On retirement, usually after age 60, a quarter of the value of the PRSA can be taken as a tax-free lump sum. The remainder can be used to buy a pension or be put into an Approved Retirement Fund (ARF) – see page 186.

you are more likely to make a good choice by asking the right questions and getting good advice. The following are some of the basic choices that have to be made.

■ Personal pension plan or PRSA

There are technical differences between the two but these are of less importance in making a choice than the actual specifics of the individual options. So the decision is best made on the basis of other criteria such as cost, flexibility, the investment options available.

■ Cost

The costs involved in building up a pension fund usually include a set-up cost applied to each contribution and an annual management charge applied to the ongoing value of the fund. The rates vary from company to company and may also vary from fund to fund. On standard PRSAs, the charge on contributions can be no more than 5% while the annual management fee can be no more than 1%. No other charges are allowed on standard PRSAs.

■ Regular premium or lump sum?

Most of the newer personal pension plans and all PRSAs allow you to alter contribution levels from year to year. That flexibility can be very important to someone whose income may fluctuate. An alternative is to make annual lump sum contributions into a pension fund. Each investment is a separate transaction. The lump sums may go into different funds or even different companies. If you work for a company and made regular contributions through the payroll, you will automatically get the tax relief. If you make lump sum contributions on your own you have to pay the gross amount up front and claim the tax relief.

The advantage of contributing occasional lump sums is flexibility. The main disadvantage, apart from the delay in getting your tax relief, is that it is all too easy to forget the initial good intentions and fail to make the investment each year. With a regular contribution plan there is an element of compulsion.

■ Type of fund?

The final decision is where to invest your money. There are many companies and a wide range of funds to consider. Professional advice is well worthwhile. The investment performance of the fund can make a very significant difference to the size of pension you eventually enjoy. So too can the set-up and ongoing management charges. They differ from company to company and sometimes even from fund to fund. Equities are an ideal choice for investments made well before retirement.

Over the longer term, equities have yielded a far better return than bonds or bank deposits although over the shorter-term, and sometimes even over the medium terms, share values can be volatile as has been very evident in recent years. As a good rule of thumb it makes some sense to invest in equity funds for the best long term returns before moving into safer investment options closer to retirement. The risk varies with the type of fund and you can always mix and match to build up your own portfolio. It is up to you to work out your own attitude to risk. Then take advice, and make your choice remembering that it is prudent to reduce your exposure to risk as you approach retirement age.

Collecting your pension

Members of occupational pension funds often face difficult choices when they reach retirement age. There's possibly little that can be done about the overall value of pension entitlements at this stage but there are usually decisions to be made about how the entitlements should be taken. Is it best to take the maximum possible lump sum? Is it best to accept a reduced initial pension to secure entitlement to a survivor's pension for your partner? If you have been making additional voluntary contributions, is it best to use the accumulated fund to buy an enhanced pension or to transfer it into an approved retirement fund?

Choices have to be made and there is no way of knowing in advance what decision is going to prove the most financially advantageous. But you stand a better chance of getting it right by carefully considering all of the options in the light of your best assumptions about those factors over which you have no control. Let's have a look at each of those questions in turn.

■ Tax free lump sum

The generous tax relief allowed on pension contributions is justified as an incentive to encourage people to save for retirement. The Revenue requires that the bulk of the money be used to provide a pension for life but the rules do allow a portion of it to be taken as a tax-free lump sum. Different rules apply to the self-employed and those with personal pension plans but here we are only considering workers in company pension schemes.

The size of the tax-free lump sum depends on the length of service up to a maximum of one-and-a-half times final pay after 20 years service. The choice is between taking the lump sum and getting a lower pension or not taking the lump sum and qualifying for a higher pension. The actual sums will vary from individual to individual. So which is best?

As a rule of thumb it is better to take the tax-free lump sum. With most pension schemes the actual pension is only guaranteed for five years. If you die within that period it continues to be paid until the end of the five years and then stops. If you die after five years it stops right away. Usually if you were to invest the lump sum in a deposit account it wouldn't yield enough to make up for the pension foregone. But you'll have the lump sum and have got it tax free while the pension would be taxable although that is only relevant if you are liable for tax. If you live a very long life it might work out that you would have been financially better off by not taking the lump sum. But you will have enjoyed extra flexibility by having the money under your control.

■ Widow/er's pension

Some pension schemes have a widow or widower's pension built in. There's no choice to be made. Very often the surviving spouse gets half of the original pension for life. But if there isn't an automatic survivor's pension built in, you may be given a choice between taking a smaller pension and the knowledge that the surviving spouse will continue to get half of it on your death or a larger pension that will die with you. For someone with inadequate pension entitlements to start with, it can be a very hard choice.

If your spouse dies before you the choice will have been immaterial and you may have given up some of your pension for nothing. It's a very personal decision and can't be made solely on financial grounds although the extent of any other resources that would be available to a surviving spouse is obviously relevant. It's a decision that no-one should be asked to make particularly at a time when they are facing a traumatic change in their lives.

■ AVCs, PRSAs and personal pension fund

If you have built up your fund through a personal pension, a PRSA or with AVCs, you face a range of options on retirement. Those options also apply to someone in a company scheme who owns more than 5% of the company. In these cases a quarter of the fund can be withdrawn as a tax-free lump sum. The remainder can be used to buy a pension for life — an annuity, or invest in an approved retirement fund (ARF) or an Approved Minimum Retirement Fund (AMRF). The choice is up to you although the Revenue Commissioners do set some limitations. Any money that hasn't been taken as a tax-free lump sum or used to buy an annuity has to be invested in either an ARF or an AMRF. Either way it remains the property of the pensioner and apart from a requirement of keeping a minimum of €63,500 in an AMRF until you are 75, pensioners can draw down the money as they like.

The requirement to keep €63,500 in an AMRF until age 75 doesn't apply if the pensioner has another income of at least €12,700 a year. Any money not required to be kept in a fund as a result of this rule can be drawn down. The only disincentive against drawing down too much, too quickly, is that money taken out of the fund is subject to income tax in the normal way. In 2007, a notional 1% of the value of an ARF fund was deemed for tax purposes to have been withdrawn, whether it is taken out or not. That notional 1% was added to the taxable income of the ARF's owner. If he or she is exempt from tax then no tax is payable. The notional withdrawal was increased to 2% in 2008 and 3% from 2009 onwards.

Suppose, for instance, you have €100,000 in an ARF fund. The Revenue will assume that you have withdrawn €1,000 in 2007 whether you have or not. If you are exempt from income tax (a couple, either of whom is over 65, is exempt from tax in 2009 or 2010 if their joint income is less than €40,000) then no tax is payable. At the other end of the scale a high earner would be liable for tax at 41% on the notional €1,000. In most cases it will make sense to actually withdraw the notional amount of the ARF fund that was deemed taxable each year i.e. 2% in 2008 and 3% thereafter.

An ARF or AMRF must be managed by an approved fund manager such as an insurance company, bank or an investment intermediary who are licensed to hold money on behalf of clients and there are some restrictions on how the money can be invested. It used to be possible to invest some of the money in personal use assets such as yachts or holiday homes. But that is no longer allowed. Any money left in the pension fund on death becomes part of the deceased person's estate. There is no tax on its transfer into a ARF in the name of a surviving spouse. In other cases, liability for income tax, inheritance tax or both can arise. It depends on the individual's circumstances. The rules are complicated. If there is a lot of money involved get professional advice.

> **Anything left in the fund on death becomes part of the deceased person's estate**

Marital breakdown

The rights of spouses to benefits from a pension scheme are not defined in any law. But the laws covering judicial separation and divorce allow the courts to make orders allocating such benefits between spouses in the event of separation or divorce. So part or all the pension rights of one spouse may be allocated to the other even though he or she had not made any financial contribution to it. The actual application of these powers depends on the courts and individual circumstances. All pension rights are covered from both defined contribution and defined benefit company schemes, personal pension plans and State schemes.

11 Using your rights as a consumer

Nothing is cheap that is superfluous, for what one does not need,
is dear at a cent — Plutarch

Consumers enjoy a far greater degree of protection from mis-selling, fraud and incompetence than they did even a short few years ago and rights were further enhanced by the enactment of the Consumer Protection Act 2007. Its enforcement was passed into the hands of the National Consumer Agency which took over the powers and functions of the Director of Consumer Affairs. It is planned to extend its remit to cover the financial services area and merge it with the Competition Authority. Those changes may aid administration but are unlikely to change consumers' basic legal rights.

While many of the provisions of the 2007 Act were simply a consolidation of previous legislation, it also transposed into Irish law the EU Directive on Unfair Commercial Practices, the provisions of which greatly extend consumer rights. It makes it unlawful for businesses to exploit consumers by the use of unfair commercial practices. A practice is considered unfair if the trader is not acting in good faith or without the standard of care and skill that would be reasonably expected by an "average consumer". The European Court of Justice defined an "average consumer" as one reasonably well informed and reasonably observant and circumspect. That's a general provision and the Act includes some examples:

- The provision of false and misleading information with regard to anything from the prior usage of a second-hand item to the country of origin.

- Trying to pass off products as something they are not by use of misleading or counterfeited trade names.

- Withholding or concealing material information of a product or service or of its full price.

- Measures aimed at pressurising, intimidating or taking advantage of vulnerable consumers.

- Persistent sales techniques.

There are bound to be grey areas with regard to all of those and it may require test court cases to determine where the boundaries lie between unfair and acceptable. Some of those cases may be taken by consumers but the Agency may take some cases itself to test the waters and create precedences.

There are some practices, however, that are deemed unfair in all circumstances and therefore prohibited. They include making false claims such as:

Some commercial practices are deemed unfair in all circumstances

- Having the endorsement of a regulatory body.

- Being about to cease trading.

- Providing a cure for illnesses.

- Promising free prices when it costs money to claim them.

- Claiming that a product is in short supply to promote sales.

- Sending out false invoices.

- Demanding payment for unsolicited goods.

- Directing advertising at children.

FINANCIAL SERVICES	Financial Regulator Dame Street, Dublin 2. Tel. 1890 777 777
	Financial Services Ombudsman 3rd Floor, Lincoln House, Lincoln St, Dublin 2. Tel: 1890 88 20 90
Insurance companies	Irish Insurance Federation, Russell Court, St. Stephen's Green, Dublin 2.
GOODS AND SERVICES	National Consumer Agency 4 Harcourt Road, Dublin 2 Tel. 1890 432 432 www.Irishconsumer.ie
DATA PROTECTION	Data Protection Commissioner, Station Road, Portarlington, Co. Laois Tel. 1890 252 231
SOLICITORS	The Law Society, Blackhall Place, Dublin 7. Independent Adjudicator of the Law Society, 26/27 Upper Pembroke Street, Dublin 2.
PENSIONS	The Office of the Pensions Ombudsman, PO Box 9324, 36 Upper Mount Street, Dublin 2. Tel. (01) 6471650.
EUROPEAN UNION	The European Ombudsman, 1, avenue du President Robert Schuman, B.P. 403, F - 67001 Strasbourg Cedex.
ESB	ESB Customer Complaints Commissioner, 39 Merrion Square, Dublin 2.

Also prohibited under the Act is pyramid selling and "gifting" schemes. While most of the Act only covers transaction that are of a business to consumer nature, these activities are banned even when they involve consumer to consumer transactions and they can attract severe penalties. Pyramid selling offences carry a fine of up to €150,000 and/or imprisonment for a term of up to five years. Those convicted of other breaches of the Act also face hefty penalties of up to €600,000 and 18 months in prison.

The Agency has other options besides taking errant traders to Court. It can impose compliance notices or seek an undertaking that doubtful practices will be discontinued. Such undertakings may include an agreement to compensate affected consumers. So the Agency can directly help consumers and should be the first port of call for those with complaints.

Aggrieved consumers can alternatively seek redress through the courts and, under the Act, they can be awarded both damages for any lost suffered and also exemplary damages. The Agency can take cases on behalf of consumers but it is more likely to take test cases on practices that affect large numbers of consumers rather than just one individual. It has considered taking such an action against airlines over their pricing and information practices particularly on their web sites but it seems to prefer getting agreement on change without the need for Court actions.

Pyramid selling and gifting scheme are specifically banned by law

For instance, it managed to get compensation for Barbra Streisand fans who were less than impressed by the organisation of her Irish concert and it also lodged a formal and very detailed submission on proposed changes to Dublin's toll bridge charges.

But the Agency can and does tackle individual complaints and because of its powers to seek undertakings from traders including agreement on compensation payments, it is, in all cases, a good place to start if you have a complaint to make. Its website is a mine of information on consumer rights and it has also published a range of booklets and leaflets. It can be contacted through the website www.Irishconsumer.ie or on its phone helpline at 1890 432 432.

Financial services

It is proposed to transfer the Financial Regulator's consumer protection role to the National Consumer Agency. But until that happens the Regulator, which operates under the aegis of the Central Bank, continues to oversee the activities of all financial intermediaries, financial advisers, insurance intermediaries, brokers, etc. It doesn't deal with complaints but does provide information for consumers. There is an ombudsman who adjudicates on disputes involving financial institutions and another dealing with the maladministration of pension schemes.

Consumers have plenty of legal safeguards but they are useless unless they are enforced

The Financial Services Ombudsman can make awards of up to €250,000 to individuals which are binding on both parties subject to an appeal to the High Court. The scheme covers banks, building societies, insurance companies, credit unions, mortgage, insurance, credit intermediaries, stockbrokers, pawnbrokers, moneylenders, bureaux de change, hire purchase providers and health insurance companies. He can consider complaints relating to events that occurred within the previous six years. Before going to the Ombudsman, you must first make a complaint to the company itself. All the banks and building societies have designated managers to deal with complaints. Obviously you should try to sort out any problem at local level first, then take it to the head office of the bank or building society. If you are still not satisfied, you can then take the matter to the Ombudsman.

He is unlikely to look at a complaint unless it has been through the complaints procedures of the institutions involved. He is open to complaints from individuals, organisations and sole trader and will also consider complaints from companies whose annual turnover is under €3 million. He can't consider matters of company policy. For instance, he will not adjudicate on a complaint about the general level of bank charges. But he can, of course, deal with a complaint about the application of those charges in an individual case.

If your claim is for less than €2,000, another option is to take a case to the Small Claims Court. It need cost no more than €9 and is no more complicated that making a complaint to the Ombudsman. While the Ombudsman normally operates in private, cases heard in the Small Claims Court are open to the public and the prospect of adverse publicity may help to speed up a settlement. See page 196 for details about how to go about it.

The Consumer Credit Act provides protection against unscrupulous lenders while a range of regulations make it compulsory for life insurance companies and intermediaries to give consumers more information on, among other things, the costs involved in buying their products. Through the Small Claims Courts consumers have a low cost means of processing claims of up to €2,000. Some of these protective measures have the backing of law while in other cases professional bodies operate their own regulatory codes.

> **Where a claim involves less than €2,000 the Small Claims Court offers an alternative to the Financial Services Ombudsman**

Financial advisers

The operations of all financial advisers are regulated by the Financial Regulator. Only those authorised advisers who are also authorised cash holders can handle a client's money. With all other advisers, the money transaction takes place directly between the consumer and the investment company itself.

The Regulator has drawn up very detailed codes of how intermediaries must operate including a requirement that they draw up a statement indicating why they believe that a suggested product is suitable for the particular client. For more details see page 42.

The law also requires companies to produce a wide range of information to customers on the true cost of a product, the amount of commission and other remuneration that will go to the intermediary, the exact purpose of the product and the penalties that may be incurred on early encashment. For further details see page 88.

Solicitors

Solicitors are members of the Law Society of Ireland and it is to that body that complaints should first be directed after, of course, they have first been made to the individual concerned. The Law Society has its own complaints procedures. Complaints may be referred to the Disciplinary Tribunal of the High Court or, in the case of excessive fees, to the Taxing Master, at the Four Courts, Dublin 7.

In all cases the first complaint is made to the Law Society

Where a complainant is dissatisfied with the manner in which the Law Society has dealt with a complaint, he or she may refer it to the Independent Adjudicator of the Law Society whose role is to ensure that complaints are dealt with fairly and impartially by the Law Society.

The Adjudicator only considers the Society's handling of a complaint against the solicitor, not the actual complaint itself. The Adjudicator cannot award compensation and cannot consider any matters which have been dealt with by the Society's Compensation Fund Committee, the Disciplinary Tribunal of the High Court or the Taxing Master. Complaints have to be made in writing and should include a copy of the Society's decision and confirmation that the subject matter of the complaint has not already been considered by the Disciplinary Tribunal of the High Court.

Access to personal files

Many companies, organisations and public bodies gather personal information on individuals and can hold it on file in any form of structured filing system. Subject to certain limitations they have a right to do so but the individual has a right to access that data, in so far as it relates to themselves, and to have it changed if it is factually incorrect. Those rights are given under the Data Protection Act and, in the case of public bodies, the Freedom of Information Act which also gives rights of access to a much wider range of information.

Under the Data Protection Act, individuals have a right of access to most personal files relating to themselves held on computer by companies and other organisations. Public sector organisations, financial institutions, providers of credit ratings, holders of direct mail lists, and those who keep sensitive information about such things as racial origin, political or other beliefs etc. are required to register with the Data Protection Commissioner. That register is open to the public and contains details of the type of information held.

The right of access covers not only the files of those companies and organisations required to register but anybody with personal information on file. In response to a written enquiry you have the right to be told what sort of information is kept on file and to see files relating to yourself. You are also entitled to be informed of the source of any data kept about you although the holder of the data can refuse to tell you if getting the information would involve "disproportionate effort" or affect trade secrets or copyright.

Some data including police and prison files is exempt. Your first approach should be to the person or organisation you think is holding files on you. You should write to them along the following lines -

"Please send me a copy of any information you keep on file about me. I am making this request under the Data Protection Act."

You should give any information which might help the individual or organisation to identify you. You should get the information within 40 days and you may be asked to pay up to €6.35. If you experience any difficulty or if you want to see the register of data holders you can contact the Data Protection Commissioner at Canal House, Station Road, Portarlington, Co. Laois phone (057) 868 4800 or 1890 252 231.

> **You have a right to see any information being held about you by individuals or businesses**

If the information on file is wrong you have, of course, the right to have it corrected and you may have the right to have information completely erased. Corrections must be made to factually wrong data but you have no right to have opinions changed. If, for instance, a school is keeping assessments of its pupils the individual has a right of access to the data and could have actual markings changed if they were wrong. But there is no right to have teachers' opinions with regard to ability, etc. changed.

Where information is being unnecessarily kept, there is a right to have it erased. As mentioned above, the holder of data must have a stated reason for holding it. If the information held is not necessary for that purpose, then you can have it erased. For instance, information on a person's religious beliefs may be appropriate to files held by a hospital, but would be unnecessary to the files of a finance company.

Pursuing your rights in court need only cost €9

■ Have you ever bought faulty goods or paid for less than adequate service? Who hasn't? Complaints often go unheeded. So what else can you do? Well you can take your case to the Small Claims Courts and it need only cost you €9. The maximum amount that can be claimed under this procedure is €2,000 and the dispute must normally relate to the purchase of goods or services for private use from someone selling them in the course of business. Also covered are claims for minor damage to privately owned property. Precluded are claims for accidents, damages or for the recovery of payments under a loan or hire purchase agreement. Complaints related to the non-return of rent deposits or similar landlord/tenant issues are dealt with by the Private Residential Tenancies Board.

The scheme is administered by the Small Claims Registrar at local District Court Offices throughout the country. You can look up the address and telephone number in the telephone directory or on the internet at www.courts.ie. The first approach is to the Registrar who will provide help in drawing up a statement of claim. A special form makes the job relatively easy. A non-refundable fee of €9 is payable at this stage. A copy of the claim is sent to the person against whom it is made — the respondent — and he or she has 15 days to reply. If no answer is received, the claim is automatically treated as undisputed and the District Court will make an order for the amount claimed to be paid within a stipulated time.

If the claim is disputed, the Registrar will try to reach an agreed settlement between the parties at an informal meeting. This is held in private. Both parties may be asked to outline the facts of the case and they may be asked questions by the Registrar. His aim is not to make a judgement but rather to reach an agreed settlement. Either side can bring forward witnesses or present expert reports. But the parties have to pay for these themselves. If the Registrar fails to get a settlement agreed, the matter is referred to the District Court and is heard before a judge. The hearing may not be in private and will, of course, be more formal. The parties may be asked to answer questions on oath. The Registrar attends the Court hearing to outline the facts.

There is provision for witnesses to be summoned to appear before either the Registrar or the Court. The Registrar will help in issuing the summons but it is up to the individual requesting the witness to pay any expenses involved. There is nothing to stop either party hiring a solicitor to represent them but the whole idea is to keep the cost down and there is no need for a solicitor. People who don't get their awards can go back to the Small Claims Registrar and have the matter passed to a sheriff or county registrar for collection. But even that is not a surefire way of getting the money. Not all the decrees passed to sheriffs for collection are enforced. Still most claimants win something. For €9 it's worth a try.

There are many files out there that may be worth looking at and checking. Your employer may have some files, so too might your trade union. Most schools keep files on pupils. Then there are the banks and other financial institutions that maintain credit ratings. They are certainly worth checking if you have had any difficulty getting approval for a loan.

Holders of data have to exercise great care in how they gather and keep it. The data must be obtained fairly, it must be accurate, and it must be kept up to date. It must also only be used for a stated purpose. The purpose for holding the data has to be stated in advance and data said to be kept for one purpose cannot be used for another. The information kept must be adequate for the purpose; it must be relevant and not excessive. It must be erased when it is no longer needed for its stated purpose.

Employers are not allowed to use the Act to force employees or job applicants to reveal personal data about themselves. They cannot, for instance force job applicants to produce their detailed personnel files from previous employers.

You can't generally prevent people from keeping information about you on file but you can ensure that it is accurate

Freedom of Information Act

The Freedom of Information Act came into force in 1998 and provides wide ranging rights to access information held by public bodies. It doesn't apply to private companies or organisations. Rights under the Act play a role in consumer protection in so far as all citizens are consumers of many State services. In this regard an individual has a right to access his or her own personal files and to have them amended if they are incorrect or misleading.

There is also a right to access official files dating back to April 21, 1998 when the Act came into force subject to some limitations. To get access to the information you are looking for you should write to the head of the relevant government department or organisation saying that you are making the request under the Freedom of Information Act.

A fee of €15, or €10 for anyone with a medical card, must accompany the request unless the information sought relates to personal data relating to yourself. You may also be charged for the cost of gathering and photocopying the information. Decisions to refuse access to information can be appealed first to the body concerned and then, if necessary to Emily O'Reilly, Information Commissioner, 18 Lower Leeson Street, Dublin 2, phone (01) 6785222.

Credit ratings

Most financial institutions use credit reporting bureaux to maintain credit ratings on customers and potential customers

The Irish Credit Bureau, of which most of the leading finance houses are members, provides members of the public with details of their personal credit rating as shown on the Bureau's books. It has been doing this since before the enactment of the Data Protection legislation. The information provided includes the name of the company which registered the information, the relevant account number and what is called the "conduct grading" of the account — likely to be only one word "satisfactory" or "unsatisfactory".

Most banks, finance companies, building societies and many credit unions are members of the Bureau. It can be contacted at Newstead House, Newstead, Clonskeagh, Dublin 14. Another agency is Experian Ireland, Park House, North Circular Road, Dublin 7. If you are finding difficulty in getting loan finance and you have no idea why, then you should contact the Bureau, Experian Ireland and your bank and ask for details of the information they have on you. Mistakes have been made. The Ombudsman for the Financial Institutions granted an award for damages to a man who had been refused business loans as a result of a mistake in the information held on a bank's files. The fact that he had paid off a loan early was mistakenly entered as something else on his file and he was effectively blacklisted. So it can happen.

Office of the Ombudsman

The Ombudsman, Emily O'Reilly, who is also the Information Commissioner, investigates complaints from individuals about government departments, local authorities, the HSE and the postal services. The office is independent of government and has powers to inspect files, require officials to give information, and make recommendations for redress including compensation. While she has no power to force acceptance of her recommendations, if they are not accepted and acted upon, she can report the fact to the Dáil and Seanad. Complaints, in writing, can be sent to her office at 18 Lower Leeson Street, Dublin 2, phone (01) 6785222, within a year of the action, or lack of action, that is the subject of the complaint.

ESB complaints

The ESB has its own ombudsman type operation to deal with complaints that cannot be resolved by their own internal procedures. The ESB Customers Complaints Commissioner has the power to issue binding recommendations to ESB Customer Services and may recommend that the company follow a particular course of action or make an ex-gratia payment. Before going to the Commissioner it is necessary to have exhausted all of the ESB's internal procedures. There is no cost involved to the complaining consumer and he or she can reject any recommendation and pursue other remedies such as taking the matter to court. See page 190 for contact details.

Consumer Credit

There is a common misconception that banks don't like lending money and are somehow doing customers a favour when they advance them a loan. Nothing is further from the truth, of course. Banks, building societies, finance houses, moneylenders, and pawnbrokers all make their profits by lending money. It's important, of course, that the money is repaid. So lenders do need to be convinced that the borrower won't renege on the repayments. But the borrower is the customer and the lender wants the custom and there is enough competition in the market now for borrowers to use their power as consumers. That means shopping around for the best possible deal. That's not too difficult to do. The Consumer Credit Act gives consumers a right to the full range of information needed to compare products. Let's have a look at some of the provisions:

- **Information:** All loan agreements have to be written in plain language and contain a minimum amount of information on interest rates, charges, repayments, what happens if there is a default, etc. If there are two possible meanings to any clause, the Courts have to favour the one most beneficial to the borrower. That provision applies to all consumer agreements under a different Act which ensures that the Courts will not uphold "unfair conditions".

A condition is considered to be "unfair" if, contrary to the requirement of good faith, it causes a significant imbalance in the parties' rights and obligations under the contract to the detriment of the consumer. The borrower must also be given time to read and understand the agreement.

- **Refused a loan:** A person who is refused a loan has the right to request and get information including the name and address of "any single person" from whom the lender sought information on the financial standing of the would-be borrower. The request has to be made within 28 days of the refusal and the lender has 14 days to comply.

- **Interest Rates:** The only interest rates that can be quoted in advertisements and agreements are annual percentage rates (APRs) worked out under a fixed formula so that the consumer can compare rates on a like-with-like basis. A legal provision, which doesn't apply to bank or building society loans, allows the borrower to apply to the Circuit Court claiming that the terms of an agreement are "excessive". The Court will take all the circumstances into account including "the age, business competence and level of literacy and numeracy of the consumer". The Court can effectively rewrite the agreement reducing or eliminating further repayments.

- **Cooling-off Period:** All loan agreements except for housing loans, credit cards and overdrafts must allow for a 10 day cooling-off period during which the consumer can withdraw from it. But the borrower can waive that right.

- **Early Repayment:** The borrower must be compensated for making an early repayment of the loan. The formula on which such compensation is based has to be agreed by the Central Bank or the Director of Consumer Affairs. The same compensation has to apply where the borrower is forced to pay off the loan early because of some condition of the loan.

- **Enforcement:** The lender is barred from contacting a consumer at his or her place of work except in some cases where the borrower has a live-in job. Any contact at home, by phone or personally, has to be between 9 am and 9 pm. The lender has to give 10 days notice in writing of any action he wants to take under the agreement. He also has to detail the action and the date on or after which it is intended to take that action. Where the action has been prompted by a breach of the agreement on the part of the borrower no action can be taken for 21 days. If the borrower gets back on track within that time the lender must not include any reference to it in the customer's credit record.

- **Lender's Liability:** A lender may be liable to make good any defect in the goods or services bought with a loan. In certain circumstances where the loan is arranged through the supplier and the money is paid directly to the supplier of the goods or services the lender can become liable. The customer has first to pursue his or her rights against the supplier of the goods or services but where that fails the claim can then be pursued against the lender.

Buying house insurance

Mortgage lenders often suggest that borrowers take out house insurance with a particular company or even from one of a group of companies but they cannot force a borrower to do so. However they can require that insurance be taken out and they may impose a charge if the insurance is taken out with a company other than one of those recommended. Taking out house insurance through a building society or bank need not, of course, be a bad thing. Some lenders offer very attractive house insurance packages which are cheaper in many cases than the alternatives.

European Union

There is a European Ombudsman who investigates complaints about mal-administration by institutions and bodies of the European Community. These include the Commission, the European Parliament, the Committee of Regions, the European Investment Bank, and the European Investment Fund. You don't have to be personally affected by the mal-administration, but you must first contact the institution or body concerned to inform it of your complaint. A letter of complaint is sufficient. Complaints should be made in writing. There is a standard form which may be used if you like. You can get a copy from the Ombudsman's office — see page 190 for the address. The Ombudsman tries to find a mutually acceptable solution to the complaint. He can recommend how it might be solved. If the recommendation is not accepted, the Ombudsman can make a special report about the case to the European Parliament.

Goods and services

If the retailer, shopkeeper, or what have you, refuses to rectify a claim, the final judgement on who is right has to be made in court. The Small Claims Court offers a low cost route where the amount involved is less than €2,000. If you have a complaint, your claim is against the retailer or service provider. If you fail to get redress you could try the Small Claims Courts.

The National Consumer Agency can investigate various practices and take direct action against traders who do not comply with the general provisions of the Act and it can help a consumer to get redress but in the absence of an agreed settlement the final recourse has to be to the Courts.

In matters concerning the supply of good and services consumer protection legislation relates mainly to dealings between a trader and an end-consumer. Most of the protections do not apply to deals between two traders — a retailer and wholesaler, for instance so a consumer may not be covered by the full Act if he does a deal at a "trade price".

When something goes wrong it is almost always the retailer who is, in law, responsible for putting things right. It is he who sold the goods and it is between him and the consumer that the contract was made — a contract for sale, remember, need not be in writing. Even if the manufacturer provides a guarantee against defect in the product it is still the retailer who is responsible to see that things are put right. The law gives the consumer five areas of protection.

- **The goods sold must be made of "merchantable quality".** The goods must be capable of being used for the purpose for which they are normally sold. It does not matter if the retailer did not know about the fault. He has a responsibility to the consumer but if there are defects he may cover himself by pointing them out. Goods marked "seconds" or "slightly defective", for instance, would not be expected to be of top quality. The buyer also has responsibilities — he or she is expected to have examined the goods and have no complaint if the defects could reasonably have been noticed before purchase.

- **The goods must be fit for their intended purpose.** In some cases the purpose is obvious but in other cases the consumer may be relying on the retailer for advice and he is expected to have some skill in this matter. If he says the product or service will do the job, or serve the purpose, then you have a claim against him if it turns out otherwise.

- **The goods must be as described.** Goods can be described in advertisements, pictures, or orally by the salesman and if these descriptions are not in keeping with the truth, the purchaser has a claim for redress. The trader may also be liable for criminal prosecution under the 1978 Consumer Information Act.

- **The goods must conform with the sample.** This provision applies when the consumer buys on the basis of seeing a sample of the goods.

- **The trader can be assumed to be able to pass ownership.** This is a difficult area of law but, in general, the trader is assumed to be able to pass ownership of the goods to the purchaser. If, for instance, there is an unpaid hire purchase debt on the goods and the hire purchase company comes looking for them, the buyer may have a claim against the seller.

These rights are enshrined in law and in general, the trader cannot limit them. If a consumer has a valid complaint, then in general, he has a right to get his money back. He may, in some cases, be entitled to compensation and may have a claim against the manufacturer if the goods are so defective that they cause damage. But that is another area of law. Re-

■ Everyone is equal before the law, they say, but getting access to the courts can be a problem for those on limited means. And many relatively wealthy individuals may consider their means to be limited when contemplating the likely costs of a court action. Awards in the Small Claims Court outlined on page 196 cannot exceed €2,000 so it's not an option in many cases. Some solicitors will take on compensation cases on a "no foal, no fee" basis. But the claimant may have to pay the defendant's legal costs if the claim is lost. That can amount to a big risk. The Legal Aid Board is an alternative for those on low incomes. The vast bulk of cases handled by the Board involve: judicial separation and divorce, maintenance, domestic violence, custody and access to children, landlord and tenant disputes and disputes over hire purchase agreements. The Board also provides a legal service for asylum seekers. Some types of cases are specifically excluded from the scheme although there are exceptions to the rules. Exclusions includes land disputes, cases before employment, social welfare or income tax tribunals, defamation cases unless linked to something else, debt collection, conveyancing except in family law cases, licensing disputes and election petitions.

The Legal Aid Board can refuse aid if it believes that there is no reasonable chance of success. There is a right to appeal a refusal to give aid but only to a committee of the Board itself. Its decision is final. Applications for aid can be made to any one of the legal aid centres throughout the country. You'll find the addresses in your local telephone directory. The Legal Aid Board can be contacted at Quay Street, Cahirciveen, Co. Kerry, Telephone (066) 947 1000.

tailers cannot rely on such notices as "no exchange", "no money refunded", "returned goods only exchanged for credit notes", or "no liability accepted for faulty goods". Indeed such notices are illegal.

Unfair consumer contracts

If a contract is unfair, it is unenforceable even if read, freely entered into and graced with the consumer's signature. The law no longer assumes that the consumer is a completely free agent. That was made very evident in regulations introduced by the government at the beginning of 1995 to comply with an EU Directive. The regulations apply to contracts entered into by personal consumers with suppliers of goods or services and they greatly enhance the rights of consumers.

A consumer cannot be assumed to have signed his or her rights away just because of a signature on a practically unintelligible contract written in legalese and produced in small fine print. That doesn't mean that contracts can be signed with impunity and repudiated afterwards. The old adage of *caveat emptor* (let the buyer beware) still applies.

The regulations don't apply to core provisions of a contract such as the price or other terms that were individually negotiated with the consumer. They are aimed more at the type of standard clause often written into contracts to protect the seller or supplier without providing any benefit to the consumer — the type of clause included in the fine print and imposed on the consumer in a take-it or leave-it fashion. Such clauses are not automatically unfair and unenforceable. Only a court can decide that but the regulations lay down guidelines.

The Courts can decide that a clause voluntarily accepted by a consumer is, in fact, unfair and not enforceable

They require all consumer contracts to be written in plain and intelligible language. Consumers must be given a reasonable opportunity to read the contract and fully understand what's involved. Any term that allows the supplier to hold onto a deposit if the consumer pulls out of the deal must be matched by a similar clause providing equal compensation for the consumer if the supplier fails to deliver.

An individual consumer may go to court to have a clause in a contract declared unfair. This may arise where a consumer is looking for compensation and the supplier is relying on the fine print of a contract to avoid payment. Alternatively it may be used by a consumer as a defence against a seller or supplier who is looking for extra payment.

So how does a Court decide if a clause in a consumer contract is unfair? It has to take a range of factors into account including the balance between supplier and consumer in terms of rights and obligations and the strength of the consumer's bargaining position. A contract that imposes severe sanctions on a consumer for late payment, for instance, without imposing similar penalties on the supplier for late delivery might well be considered unfair, for instance.

In each case the final decision is up to the courts so it can be expensive finding out. But as outlined on page 196 the Small Claims Courts provide access to legal redress for claims up to €2,000 for a flat fee of €9. So if you are being held to a clause in a consumer contract that you believe to be unfair and you are willing to cap your claim at no more than €2,000 then the Small Claims Courts are worth a try. There's little to lose.

Using your rights

It is one thing having rights as a consumer, but it is another thing altogether using them. The consumer may have a claim against the trader but how does he get redress, and what form will this redress take. The Office of Consumer Affairs has suggested the following guidelines:

- If the goods are incapable of doing what they are supposed to do from the very beginning, it is likely that the consumer is entitled to a full refund, and may refuse all offers of repair, replacement, or adjustment.

- If goods are not as described, the consumer is not bound to accept them. This is an important provision since it can be difficult for a retailer to claim that even a minor instance of false description was not important.

- The consumer's right to reject goods could be lost if he does not act promptly on discovering the cause of complaint. It could also be affected if he altered the goods or if he does anything which implies that he has accepted them.

- If the goods have been used for some time before the fault is detected, a repair may be all that the consumer can expect but the repair should be a permanent one which restores the goods to the quality that they should have been when sold allowing, of course, for wear and tear.

- If the consumer is entitled to his money back, a credit note is never good enough.

12 Social welfare who qualifies for what?

The want of money is the root of all evil — Samuel Butler

The social welfare system is every bit as complicated as the tax system and there are few people with a full knowledge of its working. There is plenty of money to be earned from having a detailed knowledge of how the tax system works but users of the social welfare system can seldom afford to pay for advice. There are, however, many sources to draw on for information and advice. Booklets and leaflets on various aspects of the system are available from Information Service, Department of Social and Family Affairs, Áras Mhic Dhiarmada, Dublin 1. Information and advice can be obtained from local social welfare offices and Citizens Information Centres throughout the country. You'll get a list of your local information centres under Citizens Advice Centres in your phonebook.

Information on policy formulation, guidelines and the procedures for determining entitlement to the various payments can be accessed on the Department's internet website at www.welfare.ie. Everyone has a right to this information under the Freedom of Information Act. If you haven't got access to the internet, you can request the information at

■ For only the second time in the history of the Stat, social welfare payments were reduced in money terms in the 2010 Budget with effect from January 1, 2010 although in some years, even quite recently benefits were not increased in line with inflation so that claimants suffered a real reduction in the spending power of their benefits. See page 340 for details of 2009 and 2010 rates of benefit.

■ Payment rates for older people - basically over 65 - remain the same in 2010 as they were in 2009.

■ Most other benefits have been cut by €8.30 a week. The reductions range from €8.20 to €8.50.

■ Benefits for qualified adults have been cut by €5.50 a week so many claiming additional payments for a spouse suffer a total cut of €13.80 a week.

■ The additional payment for dependent children has been increased by €3.80 to €29.80 a week. That amounts to an increase of €197.60 a year which compensates for a €192 cut in Child Benefit.

■ Family Income Supplement thresholds have been increased by €6 per child. That's worth €187.20 a year per child which just falls short of compensating for the cut in Child Benefit.

■ Treatment benefits have been abolished except for entitlements to medical and surgical appliances and free dental and optical examinations.

■ The Rent Supplement scheme is to be reviewed but the minimum contribution required from claimants remained unchanged.

■ Jobseeker's Allowance and Supplementary Welfare Allowance payments for new claimants aged between 20 and 24 have been reduced to €100 a week for those aged 20 and 21 – the rate that has applied to 18 and 19 years olds since April 2009. Those aged 22, 23 and 24 will be paid €150 a week. Claimants with dependant children get the full rate, as will 20 to 24 year olds who participate in an approved training or education course.

any social welfare office. In this short chapter only a small number of topics are covered. But first a brief overview of the system.

Basically there are two types of social welfare payments — benefits and social assistance/allowances. Entitlement to benefits is based on meeting certain PRSI contribution requirements and also meeting some other conditions such as being unemployed, over 65 or widowed etc. Most workers earning €38 or more a week are covered by social insurance. Entitlement to social assistance is based solely on need, usually assessed by applying a means test.

A private sector employee doesn't pay PRSI on the first €127 of weekly earnings. Those earning less than €352 in any week are exempt from PRSI and those earning less than €500 are exempt from the health levy. Most public servants pay a lower rate of contribution and are entitled to fewer benefits but those who have joined the public service since April 1995 pay full rate PRSI and are entitled to the full range of benefits. Public servants paying PRSI at the lower rate are exempt from paying it on the first €26 a week. The self-employed have been paying PRSI since 1988.

With a few limited exceptions entitlement to any social welfare *benefit* is not affected by the claimant's means. Entitlement to social *assistance*, however, is dependent on satisfying a means test. An example of the difference between the two is that the State Pension (Contributory) is a benefit — there is no means test — while the State Pension (Non-contributory) is a form of social assistance subject to a means test.

> **Everyone has a right to information on the procedures used in determining entitlement to social welfare payments**

Part-time workers

Part-time workers who earn €38 a week or more are covered for all social welfare benefits including jobseeker's benefit, illness benefit and invalidity pensions. As with full-time workers, there is no PRSI on the first €127 earned each week and the exemption outlined above also apply.

To be eligible for benefits, part-time workers need to have worked for 39 weeks in insurable employment and also have 39 contributions paid or credited in the relevant contribution year. The same 39 contributions may satisfy both conditions. Having satisfied these contribution conditions, part-time workers are entitled to the same PRSI benefits as full time workers but unemployment and disability benefits may be paid at reduced rates. Those benefits are paid on a pro-rata basis depending on the part-timer's weekly earn-

> **Part-time workers who earn €38 a week or more are eligible for a wide range of PRSI benefits**

■ One of the criteria for eligibility to a contributory old age pension is the annual average number of contributions paid by the claimant over his or her working life. The fact that pre-1953 contributions were not taken into account in deciding eligibility was a major cause of grievance in the past. Many pensioners either had their pensions reduced as a result or lost their entitlement altogether. Now anybody who paid social welfare contributions prior to 1953 and who paid contributions for at least five years over their working lives is entitled to a non-means-tested pension of half a full contributory old age pension – €115.15 a week from January 2009. There are only those two requirements. The claimant must have paid at least one social welfare contribution prior to 1953 and must also have paid contributions for at least five years.

The Department files may not be as complete as they should be so there is no guarantee that you will automatically get your entitlement. If you think you are eligible it's essential to put in a claim outlining the details of your social welfare contributions.

This entitlement is not additional to other pension entitlements. For instance, a woman in receipt of a surviving spouse's pension (widow's pension) can not qualify for this pension in addition to her existing pension. Some people who are eligible for a pension under these new rules may already be in receipt of a contributory or non-contributory pension. If you are already getting more than €115.15 a week there is no sense in replacing your existing pension with a lower one. But there could still be a benefit to be gained if they are on a reduced contributory pension or a non-contributory pension. There is nothing to be lost in claiming. You can get more information from the Department of Social, Community and Family Affairs, College Street, Sligo, telephone (071) 9169800 or LoCall 1890 50 00 00.

ings during a specified tax year. For those claiming in 2010 the relevant tax year is 2008.

Contributory State pension

In order to qualify for the State Pension (Contributory) it is necessary to have a minimum annual average of contributions either paid or credited over a specified number of years. The number of years can, however, differ with the individual — a fact which can result in some anomalies. A man who paid contributions for only five years could get a full old age pension while someone who paid for over 10 years can find himself on a reduced pension or even ineligible for any pension. But let us look at the conditions in detail. To be eligible the claimant must:

- Have an average of at least 10 contributions either paid or credited for each year between the date he or she first entered insurable employment and the end of the contribution year prior to reaching age 66. Pre-1953 contributions are taken into account in some circumstances – see page 210. Apart from those special cases, an average of 48 contributions a year is required to qualify for a full pension while an average of 10 will be enough for a 'reduced' pension. Those with an average of 20 to 47 contributions a year qualify for a pension of 98% of the maximum rate while those with between 15 and 19 contributions qualify for a pension of 75%. Those with between 10 and 14 contributions get about 50%.

- Contributions credited during periods of unemployment or illness can be used to meet the contribution requirements but those seeking a standard pension need to have paid at least 260 contributions in respect of insurable employment at some time during their lives. This requirement can be met by contributions prior to 1953. It is intended to increase the requirement to 520 from 2012.

In assessing a claim, the Department first looks at the insurance record back to 1979 and if the claimant qualifies for a full pension on that basis they do not look back any further. If the claimant does not qualify for a full pension on the basis of his or her contributions from 1979, then the rules outlined earlier are applied.

Where entitlement can be based solely on self-employed contributions, prior employee contributions are not taken into account. This is an important concession since, if earlier contributions were taken into account, the claimant's working life might have to be spread over a larger number of years thereby reducing the average contributions per year.

Full rate PRSI became compulsory for most private sector workers from April 1974. Before that, non-manual workers

In assessing a claim for a contributory old age pension the Department initially looks at the records only as far back as 1979

■ It has been a long-standing complaint of the self-employed, particularly farmers, that the social welfare system discriminates against their spouses by restricting their access to social welfare entitlements. But there is a way around this problem. A person working for a spouse is not covered for social insurance. They are not allowed to pay PRSI contributions and as a result are not entitled to any of the benefits, most significantly a State pension on retirement. That's the pension that was once known as the Contributory Old Age Pension but is now known as the State Pension, Contributory.

It's mainly women who are affected by this discrimination, the bulk of them are farmers' wives. But it can affect any family business where both spouses contribute to the workload but only one is covered by social insurance.

It is possible, however, for both spouses to pay PRSI contributions and be each covered in their own right if the business is established as a limited company or if a formal commercial partnership is deemed to exist. The latter requirement is the easiest to comply with and the Department may accept that the partnership is of long standing.

So a farmer's wife, for example, coming up to retirement without having made PRSI contributions may be able to backdate contributions for earlier years and thereby qualify for a pension.

The process may not be easy but it can be well worthwhile. The Department of Social and Family Affairs has issued a booklet on the issue "Working with your spouse". It is a good starting point – it can be obtained from any social welfare office – but it is important, in all cases, for couples to get both legal and financial advice. There can be other implications in creating a formal partnership besides improving social welfare entitlements.

The rules are fairly clear and they haven't been changed. The restrictions on social insurance cover have never applied to spouses who are formal partners in the family business or where the business has been incorporated as a limited company. It applies to the spouses of sole traders i.e. the self-employed. They are not covered by social welfare whether they are formally employed or simply assist in the business.

As outlined on page 279, there can be a tax advantage in formally employing a spouse and actually paying a wage. A two income couple benefits from wider standard tax bands than a single-income couple. But to be covered for social insurance it takes more than simply getting a wage from the business. The business must be a partnership or a limited company. If that is the case and you are employed by the business you are liable to pay Class A PRSI which can entitle you to unemployment and disability benefits in addition to building up entitlement to a State pension. ➙

If you work as a self-employed person for the partnership or company, you are liable for Class S contributions which don't provide entitlement to unemployment or disability benefits. But you do build up entitlement to a pension. You must have an income of at least €3,174 a year but that's all you need. You simply pay contributions on whatever income you have at the "S" rate of 5% and you are credited with a year's contributions which goes towards building up your pension entitlements.

To qualify for a State Pension, Contributory at age 66 you need to have started making contributions before age 56. To draw the Transition Pension that is payable at age 65, you need to have started contributions before age 55.

Provided a person can clearly demonstrate that they had been working with their spouse in a partnership for a number of years then it is possible to backdate his or her PRSI liability. The PRSI due has to be paid before the claim is considered but it can be very worth while.

In assessing whether a commercial partnership actually existed, the Department takes a range of factors into account. Each case is taken on its merits. All the following criteria don't have to be met but some of them do.

- There is a written partnership agreement – the law doesn't require this but it's obviously a fairly conclusive indication that a partnership does exist.

- There is a joint business account on which each partner writes cheques.

- The existence of a partnership is apparent to those doing business with it.

- Each partner makes a significant contribution to running the business.

- The profits and losses of the partnership are shared by the partners.

- Business stationery reflects the existence of a partnership.

The first step in pursuing this option is to get a copy of the booklet. It's available on the internet at www.welfare.ie or alternatively from any social welfare office. You can order one by phone from the Department's LoCall leaflet request line at 1890 20 23 25.

Further information can be obtained from the Department's Scope Section, which is based in Oisín House, Pearse Street, Dublin, 2. Phone (01) 6732585. But before contacting them, it is recommended that you read the booklet and get professional advice on the non-social welfare implications of forming a business partnership with your spouse.

■ Child benefit is payable in respect of all children under the age of 16 or 18 if the child is in full time education or disabled.

The rates of payment from January 2010 are as follows:

First and second child €150

Third and subsequent child €187

• The Early Childcare Supplement ceased in 2009 and has been replaced by a pre-school Early Childhood and Education Scheme (ECCE) which applies to children aged between 3 years 3 months and 4 years 6 months. Children are eligible to enter the scheme from January 2010 if they are aged between 3 years 7 months and 4 years 10 months on 1 January 2010.

earning above fixed income levels did not have to pay social insurance. If they did not make voluntary contributions they ended up with a gap in their contribution record. Those who came back into the PRSI net from April 1, 1974 get reduced rate pensions provided they had a minimum yearly average of at least five contributions.

For those eligible, an average of five to nine contributions provides a pension of a quarter of the reduced rate; 10 to 14 provides a half pension; while 15 to 19 provides a three-quarters pension.

The people eligible, under this concession, are those who did not stamp cards prior to 1974 because they were in white-collar jobs and went above the income levels at which social welfare contributions were compulsory. A similar scheme exists for people who stopped paying full rate PRSI on joining the public service.

The Contributory State Pension is payable from age 66. Subject to the same contribution conditions the Transitional State Pension is payable at age 65 provided the claimant has ceased working. He or she can have an income of no more than €38 a week or, in the case of the self-employed, €3,174 a year and still be eligible.

Widowed parent grant

All widows and widowers with dependent children qualify for a widowed parent grant of €6,000 on the death of a spouse irrespective of means or PRSI contributions. In addition, a bereavement grant of €850 is payable on death subject to certain conditions. It is payable on the death of an insured person, the spouse of an insured person, a child under 18 (under 22, if in full time education) where either parent, or the person that the child normally lives with, satisfies the PRSI contribution conditions, a contributory pensioner, a spouse of a contributory pensioner, a qualified adult dependant of a contributory pensioner, a qualified child or an orphan in receipt of Orphan's Allowance.

Those paying PRSI at the full rate, the self-employed rate or the reduced rate applicable to some public servants can all qualify. The normal requirement is that at least 156 PRSI contributions have been paid since entry to employment. A claim form can be obtained from any Social Welfare office or by phoning LoCall 1890 500000 or 071 9135200.

Family income supplement

This scheme provides a supplementary benefit for families on low incomes. To be eligible, it is necessary for one member of the family to be working for at least 19 hours a week and for the family income to fall below set levels depending on family size. If both partners are working, their hours can be combined to make up the 19. It is also necessary for some member of the family to be entitled to the normal Child Benefit. The aim of the scheme is to help families on low wages who might otherwise be better off on social welfare. Claiming the benefit does not affect eligibility for a medical card and it is tax free.

The family income supplement payable is 60% of the difference between actual income and the prescribed income given in the table overleaf. Actual income is defined as pay after tax, PRSI, health levy and any contributions to a pension scheme. The figures in the table are those which apply from January 2010. Once the actual income level is established, the FIS payment remains unchanged for some

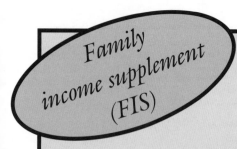

■ To be eligible your net **weekly** income from January 2010 must be less than the figure shown below. The 2009 thresholds were €6 lower per child. The payment is 60% of the difference between your net income and the income in the table.

Family size	Family income must be below	Family size	Family income must be below
One child	€506	Five children	€950
Two children	€602	Six children	€1,066
Three children	€703	Seven children	€1,202
Four children	€824	Eight children	€1,298

time. It doesn't fluctuate up and down on a weekly basis according to the earned income in the previous week. To qualify it is necessary to show that the employment will last at least three months. Job-sharers can qualify.

The rate of payment is adjusted immediately on the birth of a child. Application forms are available from social welfare offices or from: Social Welfare Services Office, Ballinalee Road, Longford, phone (01) 7043481 or (043) 40000.

Medical cards

Eligibility for a medical card is usually based on the claimant's means. There are some exceptions. Subject to some conditions, the dependants of people working in other EU countries or drawing state pensions from EU countries are entitled to medical cards irrrespective of means and until 2009 so too were all people aged 70 or over. The over-70s are now subject to a means-test on the basis of income before tax and any other State deductions and the actual return they are getting from assets. Other claimants are assessed on the basis of net income and notional system of assessing the return from assets that applies to other claimants. The over-70s who already had a card prior to January

■ To qualify for a medical card the applicant's weekly income must be below the thresholds set out below. See the main text for details of how means are assessed. The method of assessment is different for those over 70 being based on actual income from assets rather than a notional income.

PERSONAL	Up to age 66		Age 66 to 69		70 and over
	Medical card	**GP visit card**	Medical card	**GP visit card**	Medical card
Single, living alone	€184.00	**€276.00**	€201.50	**€302.00**	€700
Single, living with family	€164.00	**€246.00**	€173.50	**€260.00**	€700
Married couple	€266.50	**€400.00**	€298.00	**€447.00**	€1,400
DEPENDANTS	Under 16		Over 16		
Allowance for first two children	€38.00	**€57.00**	€39.00	**€59.50**	
Allowance for third and subsequent child	€41.00	**€61.50**	€42.50	**€64.00**	
Other dependants in full time education not receiving grants	€78.00	**€117.00**			

Additional allowances are given in respect of reasonable outgoings on rent or mortgage repayments, expenses in travelling to work (public transport costs or 50c a mile) and reasonable childcare costs.

1, 2009 were asked to submit themselves to the test if they had any doubt about their eligibility. New applicants are automatically mean-tested and subjected to means-test thresholds of €700 a week single (€36,500 a year) and €1,400 married (€73,000 a year).

The full medical card provides access to general health services free of charge. There is also a GP-only card, available only to the under-70s, which only provides free access to GP services. From January 2010, medical card holders are required to pay a prescription charge of 50c subject to a maximum of €10. To qualify for a card the applicant's means must be lower than a set threshold level.

The threshold levels, detailed in the table above, vary depending on circumstances and age. For the under-70s income is defined as net income after deductions for tax and PRSI. In assessing eligibility, the income limit is increased by 'reasonable' amounts in respect of rent or mortgage repayments, childcare and the cost of travelling to and from work. The HSE, which issues the cards, can also take factors other than means into account. These include "exceptional personal and financial burdens arising from medical or social circumstances".

The assessers are instructed to issue a card if, in the light of all relevant circumstances, they consider that the applicant would suffer "undue hardship" or if it would be "unduly burdensome" if they had to pay for medical services.

Usually the full cost of housing and childcare is taken into account. The cost of travelling to and from work is based either on the cost of public transport or a rate of 50c a mile. Savings and other assets are assessed as providing an income.

In calculating the return from assets owned by the under-70s, the first €20,000 is ignored. The next €10,000 is taken to yield a weekly income of €1 per €1,000; the next €10,000 an income of €2 per €1,000 and the remainder i.e. anything over €40,000, is taken to yield an income of €4 per €1,000. In the case of a couple, the first €40,000 is ignored.

The assessment of savings is different for the over 70s

The calculation for the over-70s is more generous. The first €36,000 is ignored (€72,000 for a couple) and the remainder assessed on the basis of the actual income produced. An asset that produces no income is ignored, even though like land, for instance, it has the potential to provide an income.

Some people are entitled to medical cards irrespective of means. For instance, the dependants of people working in other EU countries are entitled to medical cards without any means test as are those drawing state pensions from other EU countries who are neither employed nor self-employed in this country. So someone whose spouse is working in Britain or in Germany is automatically entitled to a medical card – there is no means test. The same applies to someone who has retired here and is drawing a social welfare pension from an EU country provided they do not earn more than €3,175 a year in Ireland.

Drugs payment scheme

No individual or family is required to pay more than €120 a month for prescription drugs included on a list of "essential medicines". This threshold was €100 in 2009. The scheme is based on a system of registration. The necessary forms can be obtained from GPs, pharmacies or health board offices. Immediate registration is possible when an individual or family unexpectedly incurs expenditure in excess of the monthly threshold. The aim is that all individuals will have plastic cards, similar to credit cards, to be presented at any pharmacy with the details of the transaction is automatically passed to the central computer.

Long-term illness scheme

People suffering from certain long-term illnesses, not including asthma, are entitled without charge to the drugs, medicines, medical and surgical appliances prescribed for that disease. This benefit is not means tested. The diseases covered include: mental handicap, mental illness in persons under 16, phenylketonuria, cystic fibrosis, spina bifida, hydrocephalus, diabetes mellitus, diabetes insipidus, haemophilia, cerebral palsy, epilepsy, multiple sclerosis, muscular dystrophies, parkinsonism and acute leukaemia. People suffering from any of those diseases get a long-term illness card from their local health boards.

Nursing home "fair deal"

The long promised "fair deal" scheme for providing State financial assistance to those in need of nursing home care was introduced during 2009. It provides the elderly and their families with a degree of certainty that didn't exist in the past but it is very far removed from providing nursing home care as a right for all.

Basically nursing home residents have to contribute 80% of their income and up to 5% of the value of their assets each year towards their nursing home care. But the family home will only be included in the calculation of assets for the first three years. So only a maximum of 15% of the value of the family home will have to be used to help pay for nursing home care. That three year rule will also apply to farm and family business assets but only in what seems to be limited circumstances where the person requiring long-term nursing home care has suffered a sudden illness or disability and where her or she, or a partner, was engaged in the daily management of the business up to the time of the sudden illness or disability.

There is also a requirement that a family successor continues on the management of the farm or business.

The emphasis is on "sudden" where a person did not have an opportunity to put appropriate succession arrangements in place. But it may well result in farm and business assets enjoying the same three year cap on assessment that applies to the family home. It depends on how the rule is applied.

While this three year rule provides some certainty and protection for the family home, it is not a great concession. The vast majority of residents are in nursing homes for less than three years and in many cases the 5% of assets will cover the full cost of care. This new scheme is unlikely to cost the Exchequer any more than the old one.

So how exactly does it work?

Farm and family business assets can get favourable treatment under "fair deal" scheme

To qualify, a person first has to be assessed as in need of nursing home care. The assessments is made by health care professionals employed by the HSE. Residential care is likely to be seen as a last resort. The policy is to improve community care facilities with a view to reducing the number of people needing nursing home care. Those already in nursing homes will not be reassessed even if they choose to move over to the new scheme. They also have the choice of staying on whatever subvention scheme that they are currently on.

Health minister, Mary Harney expressed the view, some time ago, that 20% of those currently in care would be better off at home. She's undoubtedly right but her comment suggests that the assessment of nursing home needs may be based on bed availability rather than on what's best for the applicant.

Those assessed as in need of long-term residential care automatically qualify for the scheme if they want to take it up. There is no age limit and, once assessed as eligible, a person can pick any available nursing home either private or public. The scheme operates exactly the same for both.

Those who opt for this scheme are required to make a contribution towards the cost of the care up to 80% of his or her disposable income and 5% of the value of any assets owned in excess of €36,000 in the case of a single person or €72,000 for a couple. The assets taken into account initially include the individual's home. But the 5% assessable on the home, and in some cases on farm and business assets, as outlined above, is only payable for a maximum of three years and will not be collected until the individual dies, or later still if a spouse or a dependant is still living in the home. In effect, the State will be providing a loan of that money and will take a mortgage charge on the home or other assets.

Let's take an example.

Mary has a pension of €212 a week. She has €86,000 in savings and owns a house worth €500,000. The first €36,000 of her savings is disregarded so Mary's total assets are deemed to be worth €550,000.

Her contribution to the nursing home cost will consist of 80% of her pension which works out at €170 and 5% of her assets which works out at €27,500 a year or €528 a week. That's a total of €698.

The €25,000 assessed on the value of her home (5% of €500,000) will not be collected until after her death and that 5% will only be assessed for three years. There is no time limit on the 5% collected on other assets such as her savings. So in the fourth year if she still has savings of €86,000, the first €36,000 would be disregarded and she would be liable to contribute 5% of the remaining €50,000 or €2,500.

If Mary's house was worth say €800,000 she'd possibly be contributing almost enough to pay the full cost of the nursing home. But she'll never have to pay more than the full cost.

Assets disposed of within five years of applying for assistance during the scheme can be taken into account in the means assessment. Unfortunately that may encourage some elderly people to dispose of assets well in advance of needing nursing home care or they may be encouraged by others to do so. But that can leave an elderly person very vulnerable. Married and other couples, either heterosexual or same-sex, who are cohabiting as life partners, for at least three years, are assessed on half their income and assets.

Free travel

Free travel is available to the following: All those aged 66 years or over residing permanently in the State; those receiving Invalidity Pensions from the State, those receiving a Disability Allowance, Blind Person's Pension, Carer's Allowance and people aged 18 or over who are registered with the National Council for the Blind. Also entitled are people who have been getting an invalidity pension or benefit continuously for at least a year from another EU country or a country with which Ireland has a bilateral social security agreement.

If you are married or cohabiting and entitled to a free travel pass your spouse or partner is entitled to travel with you free. This facility is included on the pass provided you have specifically applied for it. All wheelchair users, blind people and those on an Invalidity Pension, who are entitled to free travel, are also entitled to a free travel companion pass as are those who are being cared for by someone in receipt of a carer's allowance.

Anyone aged 75 or over, who is medically assessed as unfit to travel alone, is eligible for a free travel pass for a companion. The pass enables the holder to have any person aged 16 or over accompanying him or her free of charge on public transport. People who transfer from Invalidity Pension, Disability Allowance or Blind Person's Pension to another social welfare pension such as a widow's pension are entitled to keep their entitlement to the free schemes.

There is also an entitlement under the scheme to free travel on all bus and rail services in Northern Ireland. Spouses, partners and companions, entitled to travel with you free, are covered for cross-border journeys but not for travel on public transport within Northern Ireland. You need a special Senior SmartPass card to avail of services within Northern Ireland. You can get an application form from your local social welfare office or by ringing 1890 20 23 25.

The application form has to be returned in person to your local social welfare office. You'll need your current Free Travel Pass, evidence of your address, (an electricity or phone bill) and evidence of your identity, (a drivers licence, passport or other photo identification). It can take up to six weeks to process an application.

If you are married or cohabiting and entitled to free travel your spouse or partner is entitled to travel with you free

Household benefits package

Everyone over 70 years of age is entitled to the Household Benefits Package which includes free units of electricity or gas. With some exceptions, applicants under 70 must be living alone or with a dependent spouse or partner; an invalid; dependent children under 18, or under 22 if still at full time education; or, if the applicant is an invalid or infirm, one other person who provides care and attention for him/her. Widows and widowers, aged 60 to 65, whose late spouses had entitlement to free schemes retain that entitlement. If they meet the "living alone" condition, those over 66 may qualify if they are:

- receiving pensions from the Department of Social, Community and Family Affairs; social security pensions from other EU countries or from countries with which Ireland has a bilateral social security agreement; any other social welfare payment; or an ordinary garda widow's pension.

- pensioners who do not have social welfare pensions but whose total weekly income is not more than €38 above the contributory old age pension rates plus any appropriate allowances e.g. living alone allowance. People under 66 years of age can qualify if they are in receipt of an Invalidity Pension; Blind Person's Pension; Unemployability Supplement or Worker's Compensation

Supplement; Disability Allowance; Disability Pension/Benefit (or equivalent) for at least 12 months from another EU country, or another country with which Ireland has a bilateral social security agreement, people getting Carer's Allowance or caring for people getting Constant Attendance or Prescribed Relative Allowance.

The allowance covers 400 units per billing two-monthly billing period, winter and summer. The annual maximum is 2,400 units. As an alternative, the claimant can have a natural gas allowance of €57 per two monthly period from June to November and €123 per bill from December to May. Another alternative, but only open to those who have not got gas or electricity, is an allowance towards the cost of bottled gas.

Application forms can be obtained from any Post Office or Social Welfare Office. The package also includes an entitlement to €20.41 a month towards telephone expenses. The account doesn't have to be with Eircom. Also included is an entitlement to a free TV licence. Lifetime TV licences are issued that don't have to be renewed each year.

13 Money saving guide to the tax system

Only two things in life are certain, death and taxes — Benjamin Franklin
They don't necessarily come in that order

The 2010 Budget was billed as the harshest budget ever. In so far as the impact was felt disproportionately by social welfare recipients and State employees on low incomes, it undoubtedly reserved that billing but the April 2009 Budget took more out of the economy in tax cuts, than the 2010 budget took in pay and social welfare cuts. The extra levies and taxes imposed, in April 2009, were designed to collect €3.6 billion in a full year while the reduction in social welfare benefits and public sector pay will save the Exchequer €1.8 billion. The remainder of the €4 billion cut from Government spending plans will come by way of reduced capital spending and a range of cost-cutting exercises across Government departments.

The confusing mixture of tax, PRSI, Income Levy and Health Levy will continue to apply to income during 2010. But major changes are on the way. Finance Minister Brian Lenihan intends widening the tax net to include more low-

INCOME TAX

— **High earner restriction:** The restriction on the extent to which high earners can avail of tax breaks has been tightened to require those with income of more than €400,000 a year to pay at least 30% of their income in tax. The restrictions start to apply at income levels of €125,000 and are phased in to take full effect on incomes of €400,000 or more.

— **Domicile levy:** Annual levy of €200,000 on all individuals resident or domiciled in Ireland who have income in excess of €1m a year and Irish assets worth more than €5.

— **Mortgage interest relief** is being extended to 2017 for qualifying loans taken out between January 2004 and July 2011 and at lower rates for loans taken out between July 1, 2011 and the end of 2013. The relief is to be abolished entirely from the end of 2017.

— **Income levy:** Farmers are allowed to deduct from the gross income, that would normally be chargeable to the income levy, a provision for spending incurred in complying with the EU Nitrates Directive.

PRSI and LEVIES

— There is no change in 2010, but PRSI and the Health and Income Levies are to be combined from 2011 onwards in a new single levy that will be imposed on a wide definition of income, perhaps without any allowance for pension contributions or capital allowances, as is the case with the current income levy.

CAR SCRAPPAGE SCHEME

— During 2010, a relief of up to €1,500 in the Vehicle Registration Tax (VRT) where a car over 10 years old is scrapped and a new car in emission bands A or B (emissions of less than 140g/km) is bought. The car being scrapped must have been insured for road use for at least 12 months during the previous 18 months and have a valid NCT certificate of roadworthiness, a certificate that has expired no more than 90 days previously or have failed an NCT test in the previous 6 months.

VAT

— Standard rate of VAT reduced from 21.5% to 21% from January 1, 2010.

CARBON TAX

— Imposed at the rate of €15 per tonne on fossil fuels. It applies to petrol and auto-diesel from December 10, 2009 and from May 1, 2010 to kerosene, marked gas oil, liquid petroleum gas, fuel oil and natural gas. It will be charged on coal and commercial turf at a future date.

income earners and pensioners. He pointed out in his Budget speech that almost half of those on the Revenue Commissioners' books in 2010 would be exempt from income tax because of low incomes, while 4% of top-earners will pay almost half of the income tax collection.

That's a little bit of an exaggeration but the imbalance reflects the fact that the top 4% account for about a quarter of all the income declared to the Revenue Commissioners while the bottom 30% account for little more than 6%.

It is also intended to combine PRSI and the income and health levies into one contribution that will be applied to "a wide base". That presumably means that the definition of income used will be a wide one, perhaps similar to that currently used for the Income Levy. Its gross income before such deductions as pension contributions, capital allowances and losses.

There is a commitment, in the current Programme for Government, to introduce water charges and a tax on residential property. While water charges seem a certainty, if only because of pressure from the EU and the Green Party whose votes are needed to keep the Government in power, the property tax is unlikely to be introduced for some years. Why both are needed is not quite clear as one or the other could more simply serve the purpose of raising whatever revenue is deemed necessary to help fund local services.

The full impact of the increased income and health levies will be felt for the first time in 2010. Income tax bands and credits remain unchanged from 2009. The change in the time limits for Mortgage Interest Relief will only confer benefits in future years.

There are details of the levies and how they are imposed on page 240 while a summary of current and past tax credits and bands for earlier years are included in Appendix 1 starting on page 330. The following examines the current situation in more detail.

Reducing your tax bill

Most people believe that they are paying too much tax, on the basis that any tax is too much. There are certainly many people paying more tax than they need to – simply because they don't claim all the allowances they're entitled to, or because they are not making use of every tax avoidance measure possible. Tax avoidance is no crime. It is simply using the tax system to the best advantage. It is tax evasion which is illegal.

The following are some ideas worth considering. Further details on each option are given later, in this chapter, or in chapter 14 on page 278.

- Make sure that you are claiming all the tax credit and reliefs to which you are entitled. PAYE taxpayers are likely to lose rather than gain by not making an annual return. That is not always true but it generally is. Do you claim for any local authority charges you pay? Are you eligible for the home carer's tax credit which has wider application than many think? Have you a claim for medical expenses? You can still claim relief at your top rate on most out-of-pocket health expenses although that is being confined to standard rate relief in respect of expenses incurred after January 1, 2009. A careful reading of the following pages could be worthwhile.

- If you are self-employed, consider employing your children on a part-time basis. As a family you can save some tax that way. It may also be well worthwhile formally employing a spouse to gain the extra standard rate band enjoyed by two-income couples. Before tax bands were individualised there was no tax advantage in paying a spouse a wage even if he or she worked in the family business. But a tax saving of up to €5,754 is possible in 2010. **See page 279.**

- The cap on the tax relief, available on pension contributions introduced in 2009, only affected those on incomes of more than €150,000 a year. The limit was a higher (€275,239 in 2008). Others can still gain from full tax relief on pension contributions so, for the self-employed, a personal pension scheme offers a particularly favourable way of saving for the future. No longer has the bulk of the accumulated fund to be used to buy an annuity on retirement. It will be worth taking a fresh look at your pension entitlements during 2010. Workers can benefit by putting extra money into their own pension schemes while, for those not in pension schemes, Personal Retirement Savings Accounts (PRSAs) offer a relatively low-cost way of saving for retirement while qualifying for tax relief. But changes in the way tax relief is granted on pension contributions are in the offing, perhaps for 2011. It is likely that it will be increased for those paying tax at the standard rate and reduced for those paying at the top rate. **For details see chapter 10 page 171.**

- Despite the recession, many firms are still making profits and it is possible to get some of your income tax free through an approved profit sharing scheme negotiated with your employer. Even if the business is not profitable but is expected to be in the future, you could help the firm's cash flow by accepting shares instead of pay. You get up to €12,700 tax-free each year in the form of shares and even more through approved share option schemes. **For details see page 288.**

- You can also get certain benefits from your employer tax free. They include a subsidised canteen, child minding facilities, some leisure facilities, travel passes for a period of more than a month or a bicycle. You will find other ideas throughout this book.

Pay As You Earn

The vast majority of income tax payers come under the Pay As You Earn scheme (PAYE). They have no alternative. With very few exceptions, all employees come under the scheme which was initially sold on the basis that it spread income tax liability over the year. That saved taxpayers being faced with large bills once a year. That was the idea anyway. Of course, it also provides the Exchequer with a nice even flow of revenue throughout the year.

For centuries, long before income tax was introduced, the financial year ran from April 6 to April 5. But since 2002, the tax year coincides with the calendar year and it is your income during the tax year that dictates your tax liability. With very few limited exceptions, it is not possible to carry forward reliefs or allowances from one year to another or to average your income over a number of years. PAYE is simply an administrative method of collecting that tax in easy stages during the year, once a week or once a month.

Employers have a legal obligation to stop tax on payments to employees and they do so on the basis of instructions given to them by the Revenue Commissioners. These instructions are summarised on your "Notification of determination of tax credits and standard rate cut-off point".

The 2010 Budget was unveiled a week later than the traditional first Wednesday in December and with the tax year starting on January 1, the Revenue are unlikely to have sufficient time to get out new tax certificates before the beginning of the tax year with provision for all the Budget changes. Even though tax rates and credits have not changed, there maybe changes to your cert due to personal circumstances, a drop or rise in income for instance.

It is all too easy for PAYE taxpayers to be overtaxed. It is important to check that you are claiming all your credits and reliefs. You will not get them all automatically

It's important to check your cert. It lists the tax reliefs you have been allowed. Do not ignore it. The taxman can make mistakes and so can you. You may not have claimed all your credits and reliefs. Some of them are given to you automatically but others you will not get unless you claim them. So check your certificate.

The check list of tax credits and reliefs on page 330 contains most of the concessions applicable to the average taxpayer. A fuller list starts below. Check both.

The table on page 256 is designed to help you to work out your annual tax liability in exactly the same way the taxman would work it out. It is done on an annual basis whereas the PAYE system is geared to collecting the tax due from your pay packets over the course of the tax year. It should ensure that your tax payments over the year add up to your full liability and no more. But, in some circumstances, it may result in you paying too much or too little. If it has taken too much, then you are due a rebate. If it has taken too little and the taxman finds out, you will swiftly get a demand for the difference.

The tax on some income may not be collected under the PAYE system but total liability is calculated by charging your gross income to tax, so much at the standard rate and so much at the top rate if your income is high enough. That

■ Although tax allowances have been mostly replaced by tax credits, the few that remain create a complication in the system resulting in PAYE tax payers moving onto the top rate of tax at seemingly differing levels depending on the allowances they have to claim against the top rate. The annual tax certificate known as "Notification of determination of tax credits and standard rate cut-off point" provides you with details of your tax credits and also indicates the income level at which the higher rate of tax starts to apply. A tax credit is simply a deduction from your tax liability. The value of a tax allowance depends on whether you pay tax at the standard or at the top rate. A tax credit of €1,000 reduces your tax bill by €1,000 irrespective of what rate of tax you are on while a tax allowance of €1,000 is worth €200 (20% of €1,000) in saved tax for those on the standard rate and €410 (41% of €1,000) for those paying at the top rate.

A single taxpayer pays tax at 20% on the first €36,400 of income and 41% on anything thereafter. The basic tax credits, personal and employee, amount to €3,660. So, on an income of €40,000, the tax liability works out like this:

Gross income	**€40,000**
€36,400 taxed at 20%	€7,280
€3,600 taxed at 41%	€1,476
Gross tax	**€8,756**
Less tax credit	€3,660
Tax liability	**€5,096**

If this taxpayer claimed approved expenses of €1,000 wholly, exclusively and necessarily incurred for the job, he or she would be given an extra tax credit of €200. That provides the necessary tax relief for someone paying tax at the standard rate. But relief may also be due at the top rate. To provide for that, the tax cert will raise the income level at which he or she moves onto the top rate of tax by €1,000. As a result, an extra €1,000 will be taxed at 20% rather than 41% and provide an extra tax saving of €210. So the person on the 41% rate of tax will save €410 in tax if they have allowable expenses of €1,000 – €200 of it will come by way of a tax credit and the other €210 by way of a raising of the pay level at which they move onto the top rate. The opposite happens in the case of a benefit-in-kind, for instance, where the threshold level is reduced to take account of the extra tax that needs to be stopped. Such items will also involve a deduction from tax credits. A benefit-in-kind worth €1,000, for instance, is shown on the certificate as a €200 deduction from tax credits. That's equivalent to taxing the benefit at 20%. To collect the extra tax payable by a top rate taxpayer, the certificate will also provide for a reduction of €1,000 in the level at which tax at 41% becomes payable.

gives a gross tax figure from which is deducted your tax credits and reliefs to give your actual tax liability. Income includes all emoluments (pay) of any office or job including salaries; fees; wages; perquisites; profits; pensions; headage and other similar payments; most interest; and benefits-in-kind. Some of these may not be caught in the PAYE net but the tax liability is calculated in the same way.

People who are part-time self-employed, in addition to being in paid employment, may be liable to pay tax on their self-employed income under what is known as Schedule "D" which allows for the tax to be paid in one annual instalment — more about that later in the chapter. But the tax liability is calculated on the basis of your total income from all sources.

So what credits and reliefs can be claimed? The following apply to the 2010 tax year. They are shown as tax credits in euro.

- **PERSONAL CREDITS:**

Single person	**€1,830**
Married couple	**€3,660**

- **WIDOWED PERSON:**

Without dependant children	**€2,430**
Qualifying for one-parent credit	**€1,830**

- **ONE PARENT FAMILY:** **€1,830**

- **AGE CREDITS:**

If the taxpayer or his spouse is over, or will reach, the age of 65 during the tax year, the following extra credits apply:-

Single or widowed	**€325**
Married couple	**€650**

- **CHILD CREDITS:** **€3,660**

There is a credit of €3,660 in respect of an incapacitated child, reduced if the amount spent in maintaining the child is actually less. The child must have become incapacitated before reaching 21 years of age, or while still receiving full-time education. There is no tax relief in respect of other children. But tax exemption limits are increased depending on the number of children in a family. This can be relevant to taxpayers who are over 65 — see page 332 for details.

- **PAYE CREDIT:** **€1,830**

This credit is granted to all people liable to be taxed under the PAYE system. If a husband and wife are both wage-earning, there is a double credit. It is allowed to a child working full-time in a family firm but not to a spouse.

- **DEPENDANT RELATIVE CREDIT: €80**

This credit is granted for each relative of the taxpayer, or spouse, who is incapacitated, and, even if not incapacitated, the widowed mother or mother-in-law of the taxpayer. The allowance is also granted in respect of a son or daughter of the taxpayer who is resident with him, and on whose services he or his wife depend because of old age or illness.

It is not necessary to claim this allowance in order to claim for any contribution made to the relative's medical expenses (including the cost of maintenance in a recognised nursing home or hospital).

The Dependant Relative Credit is itself reduced by €1 for every euro by which the dependant's income exceeds the maximum contributory old age pension rate for someone aged 80 or over — €240.30 in both 2009 and 2010.

HEALTH INSURANCE:

The allowance is granted on the amount paid in premiums during the previous year. It is granted in respect of insurance against the medical expenses of the taxpayer, spouse, child or other dependants. The relief is given at source. Insurers get the tax relief directly and reduce their premium levels to take account of it. As a result even those who are not liable for tax can benefit from the relief.

- **BLIND PERSON'S CREDIT:** **€1,830**

This credit can be claimed where either the taxpayer or the taxpayer's spouse is blind. If both are blind, the allowance is €3,660. A tax allowance of €825 can be claimed in respect of a registered guide dog.

- **SPECIAL CARER'S ALLOWANCE: €50,000**
  — **allowed at the top marginal rate of tax.**

This allowance is given to a totally incapacitated taxpayer who is employing a person to care for him or herself or for an incapacitated spouse. It is also allowed where a family employs a carer to look after a totally incapacitated person. Family members contributing to the cost of the carer can share the allowance between them. The requirement is for "total" rather than "permanent" incapacity.

- **HOME CARER'S CREDIT €900**

Granted in respect of a taxpayer's spouse who works at home caring for children, the aged (defined as over 65) or the incapacitated. This allowance is not always given automatically. The Revenue does not have all the necessary information, so it may be necessary to claim it. While it is aimed at stay-at-home spouses you can have an annual income of €5,080 and still get the full credit. Over €5,080 and the credit is reduced by €1 for every extra €2 of income. If the income goes above €6,880 there is no allowance left. The social welfare carer's allowance is not included in the definition of income for this purpose.

The person being cared for need not live in the home so long as he or she lives close by — two kilometres is used as a rule of thumb for "close by". So even if the children are grown up you may qualify if you have an elderly parent living within two kilometres. Even if they still believe that they are looking after you, you can claim to be caring for them as long as either of them is over 65.

- **PERMANENT HEALTH BENEFIT SCHEMES:**

The relief is allowed against premiums paid to insure income in the event of ill health or disability. It is limited to 10% of the taxpayer's income in the year of assessment. Benefits paid under the policy are taxed as income.

- **MEDICAL EXPENSES:**

Full allowance is granted for most medical expenses paid by the taxpayer in respect of himself, his wife, or any other person for whom he claims tax allowances. Relief can either be claimed in the tax year during which the payment was

■ People with incomes below certain exemption limits are not liable for income tax, although if tax calculations were done in the normal way they would be liable. **It is important to remember that these are not allowances.** Those with income above the threshold are taxed in the normal way with, some marginal relief granted by applying the rule that they pay no more than 40% tax on any income above the exemption limit. For example, a married man aged 66 with an income of €40,100 i.e. €100 above the exemption limit, will pay €40 in tax — 40% of the €100. The exemption limits shown below are increased by €575 for each of the first two dependent children and by €830 for each subsequent child. Since the tax authorities do not automatically know how many children a taxpayer has, since the general child tax allowance was abolished, it is important that taxpayers with children make a claim if their income is below or even marginally above the relevant exemption limit. The exemption limits for those under 65 haven't changed for years and are of little relevance except perhaps to someone with a very large family.

	2009	2010
■ Single and widowed 65 or over	€20,000	€20,000
■ Married, either spouse over 65	€40,000	€40,000

made or in the year in which it was incurred. The relief is only granted at the standard rate in respect of medical expenses incurred after January 1, 2009. An exception was made in respect of nursing home charges which continued to be allowed at the claimant's top rate of tax for the 2009 tax year.

It may be possible for a family to get tax relief at the top rate in respect of an aged relative's nursing home care by making use of covenants — see page 298.

Medical expenses in respect of the following are not allowed: normal dental treatment; eye testing; or the supply of spectacles. Dental treatment which is not considered 'normal' in this context includes: crowns, veneers, tip replacing, gold posts, gold inlays, endodontics — root canal treatment, periodontal treatment, orthodontic treatment and the surgical extraction of impacted wisdom teeth. The tax relief is available on treatment performed outside the State.

Any relative can be considered part of a family for this purpose. This allowance can be shared among a number of people. This means that a number of children, for instance, contributing to the medical expenses of a parent can all consider the parent to be part of their families for the purposes of a claim for relief under this heading. In certain cases — kidney patients and child oncology patients — the Revenue Commissioners accept the cost of travelling to and from treatment centres as legitimate medical expenses for the purpose of this relief. Telephone costs and certain costs involved in home dialysis treatment are also allowed.

The claim is normally made at the end of the tax year on the form MED1 – or MED2 if in respect of dental treatment. Full details and forms can be requested from the Revenue on 1890 30 67 06. In the case of heavy or ongoing expenses, tax relief can be granted during the tax year.

- **INTEREST PAYMENTS:**

Apart from the few exceptions mentioned below, relief is only allowed in respect of the interest on loans taken out to buy, maintain, or improve the taxpayer's principal residence, the residence of a former or separated spouse, or the residence of a dependant relative (other than a child) who is living in the house rent free. The upper limit on eligible interest for first-time buyers during the first seven years of a loan is €10,000 for single taxpayers; €20,000 for married couples, widows and widowers. Since January 1, 2009, the relief is allowed at 25% during the first two years. In year three, four and five the relief is given at 22.5% and in years six and seven at 20%.

Other borrowers can claim relief on up to a maximum of €6,000 a year (married and widowed) and €3,000 (single) and the relief is only given at 15%. This relief is normally granted at source i.e. by way of a reduction in the repayments to the mortgage lender so it is important to ensure that the lender has been authorised by the Revenue to provide the relief. It is also important to ensure that your tax office has the full details of your mortgage account. Relief will continue to be granted on loans taken out during 2004 or since, up until 2017. The relief at current rates will be given on qualifying loans taken out before July 1, 2011. Lower rates are to apply to loans taken out between July 1,

■ These rates have applied since March 5, 2009 The normal overnight rate applies for the first 14 nights, the reduced rate for the next 14 and the detention rate for subsequent periods.

Rank	Night Allowances			Day allowances	
	Normal	Reduced	Deten-tion	10 hours or more	5 to 10 hours
Higher officials	€108.99	€100.48	€54.48	€33.61	€13.71
All others	€107.69	€92.11	€53.87	€33.61	€13.71

2011 and the end of 2013. A decision on the actual rates that will be applied will be made nearer the time. There will be no mortgage interest relief after the end of 2017.

Where a taxpayer moves house and there is a delay in selling the original house, both houses can be considered to be the sole or main residence for up to one year. And during that year, the interest on any loan taken out to buy the new house is allowed for tax relief in addition to the tax relief on the old loan — the limit is doubled. Interest on loans taken out to pay death duties is allowed for tax relief without any restriction. Relief is also allowed in respect of interest on money borrowed to buy newly issued shares in the company you work for but not, since December 7, 2005, in property rental income companies. More information on this latter point is given in the section on reducing your tax bill on page 278. A more detailed treatment of mortgage interest relief, with detailed examples and tables, is given in chapter 6. starting on page 130.

Where a loan is used to buy an investment residential property, tax relief at the taxpayer's marginal rate of tax is allowed on 75% of the interest.

■ RENT CREDIT:

This relief can be claimed by tenants living in private rented accommodation in respect of the rent paid. The maximum rent allowed for relief for those under 55 is:

| Married or widowed | €4,000 |
| Single person | €2,000 |

A single taxpayer, over 55 years of age, living in rented accommodation can claim an allowance of up to €4,000 in respect of the rent paid. The maximum is €8,000 for a married couple or widowed person. These tax allowances cannot be claimed in respect of rent paid to local authorities or on tenancies of 50 years or more. The relief is only granted at the standard rate.

■ PENSION CONTRIBUTIONS:

The contributions to an approved scheme are allowed in full, subject to the following maximum levels related to annual pay. Unused allowances in any one year can be carried forward. Within those limits any allowances unused on retirement can be claimed as a relief against tax in any of the previous two years.

AGE	LIMIT
up to 30	15%
30 but under 40	20%
40 but under 50	25%
50 but under 55	30%
55 but under 60	35%
60 and over	40%

There was a cap of €275,239 in 2008 on the income taken into account. That figure was reduced to €150,000 for 2009 and later. The relief is not allowed on contributions that would bring the value of a pension fund to more than the equivalent of €5 million in 2006. This cap was initially adjusted upwards in line with average earnings but not in 2009 or 2010.

■ EXPENSES:

Allowances are also made for expenses incurred by the taxpayer in performing his job. In the case of a PAYE worker, the expenses must have been wholly, exclusively, and necessarily incurred. The 'necessarily' criterion does not apply to the self-employed taxpayer. PAYE workers may claim relief against the expense of buying tools and special work clothes, for instance. Travelling expenses to and from work are not allowed. Very often, the tax inspector will agree a figure that can be claimed without any evidence of the expenses being incurred. But the taxpayer can claim more, provided he can justify the higher claim.

The table on page 237 provides an insight into the level of agreed rates which may find favour with the Revenue. They are the rates applicable to civil servants with effect from March 5, 2009.

■ YEAR OF MARRIAGE:

Married couples are taxed as single persons in the year that the marriage takes place. If they would have paid less tax as a married couple they can claim a rebate at the end of the tax year in respect of the proportion of the full tax year for which they were married. The various options facing married couples are considered in more detail in a separate section on page 283.

■ WIDOWS/WIDOWERS:

An extra credit of €4,000 is granted in the year following bereavement for widows and widowers with dependant children. It declines by €500 a year thereafter. So it is worth €3,500 in the second year, €3,000 in the third year, €2,500 in the fourth year and €2,000 in the fifth and final year.

■ TRADE UNION SUBSCRIPTIONS

A tax credit is given in respect of up to €350 paid each year in trade union subscriptions. It was €300 in 2007 but increased to the current level for 2008 and subsequent years. It is often given at source i.e. directly to the trade union who can pass it on in lower subscriptions but it is important to check as it was certainly not granted at source prior to 2008. So it needs to be claimed in respect of past years.

■ SERVICE CHARGES Maximum €400 a year

This relief is allowed on a previous year basis, so you get it this year on the service charges you paid last year. Service charges include those imposed by local authorities. for the provision of a domestic water supply, domestic refuse collection or domestic sewage disposal where, for instance, a house has its own septic tank. They also include payments made to group water schemes for domestic water supply and to independent contractors for domestic refuse collec-

You won't get the relief on service charges if you don't claim it

■ Income levies and PRSI are the only taxes paid by a large proportion of income earners. They are payable by many whose incomes are too low to be in the income tax net. Combined they can amount to a charge of 11% on income — 14% in the case of the self-employed. Details of the rates and threshold levels are shown on the opposite page. But a range of exemptions apply and the system is made more complicated by the fact that "income" as defined for the Income Levy is different from that used in calculating liability to either PRSI or the Health Levy.

■ PRSI

The rate you pay depends on your job. While there are a wide range of categories and sub-categories with differing liabilities, most people fall into one of three main categories: private sector employees; public sector employees; and the self-employed. Public servants recruited after April 6, 1995 pay PRSI at the full 4% rate.

Employees earning less than €38 a week are outside the PRSI net altogether. Those earning less than €352 in a particular week are exempt from paying PRSI that week. For those who exceed the threshold, the first €127 of weekly pay (€26 for public sector employees paying the lower rate PRSI) is exempt from PRSI. That exemption applies on a weekly basis. Self-employed workers with earnings of less than €3,174 a year are exempt from PRSI.

PRSI is levied on income after the deduction of pension contributions up to a ceiling of €75,036 in the case of an employee but with no upper threshold for the self-employed. The ceiling is applied to each individual spouse even if they are jointly assessed for tax.

■ HEALTH LEVY

There are two rates, the top rate charged on income above €75,036 a year. It is charged on the same income as PRSI but those on less than €500 a week are exempt. Also exempt are those with full medical card, widow or widower's pensions and those over 70 years of age.

■ INCOME LEVY

Those with earnings of less than €15,028 are exempt from the income levy. If that threshold is exceeded the levy is applied to all income. It is charged on a wider definition of income than either PRSI or the Health Levy i.e. income before deduction for pension contributions, capital allowances or losses. The levy is not charged on social welfare payments or redundancy lump sums that are not subject to income tax. Medical card holders and those over 65 who are exempt from income tax are not liable.

■ Income can, in addition to tax, be liable to a range of levies — income, health and PRSI. Public sector workers who took up employment since April 6, 1995 pay the same rate of PRSI as private sector workers. The self-employed pay PRSI on all of their income. The income and health levies are charged on slices of income and there is a range of exemptions for those on lower incomes. Ignoring those exemptions, which are outlined below, the rates applicable to slices of incomes are as follows:

■ **PRIVATE SECTOR**

	Income	Health	PRSI	Total
Up to €75,036	2%	4%	4%	10%
€75,037 to €174,980	4%	5%	0	9%
Over €174,981	6%	5%	0	11%

■ **PUBLIC SECTOR**

	Income	Health	PRSI	Total
Up to €75,036	2%	4%	0.9%	6.9%
€75,037 to €174,980	4%	5%	0	9%
Over €174,981	6%	5%	0	11%

■ **SELF-EMPLOYED**

	Income	Health	PRSI	Total
Up to €75,036	2%	4%	3%	9%
€75,037 to €174,980	4%	5%	3%	12%
Over €174,981	6%	5%	3%	14%

■ No PRSI is payable on the first €127 a week earned by those paying the 4% rate.

■ For those paying the lower public sector rate, the weekly exemption is €26 a week

■ Those earning less than €352 a week are exempt from PRSI and those earning less than €500 a week are exempt from the Health Levy.

■ Those on less than €15,028 a year or €289 a week are not liable for the income levy but the exemption is based on annual rather than weekly, income although the Revenue may not pursue someone whose liability for the levy arose because extra income at the end of the year caused the annual threshold to be breached after a year when weekly income remained below the weekly threshold.

tion or disposal. Usually the relief is claimed by the person liable to make the payments but it may be claimed by another person living in the home, for instance, a son or daughter living with an elderly parent who might not be liable for tax. A claim has to be presented each year. That means keeping receipts, although they don't have to be submitted unless you are asked for them.

- **COLLEGE FEES:**

The relief is given in respect of tuition fees paid in publicly funded third-level colleges in the State and approved undergraduate and postgraduate courses in both private and publicly funded colleges both in the State and in other EU countries. It also applies to tuition fees for undergraduate and postgraduate distance education courses provided by colleges within the EU and for some postgraduate courses provided outside the EU. The maximum relief is €5,000. Relief is also allowed on annual fees of up to €1,270 in respect of IT and foreign language courses that result in a certificate of competence rather than just a certificate of attendance. The fees must not be recouped by grants or scholarships and the relief may not exceed the tax liability of the taxpayer. In the case of a married couple the relief may be claimed by either spouse provided they have not opted for separate assessment. The relief is given at the standard rate.

Tax on social welfare benefits

Many social welfare benefits are liable for tax if the recipient's income is sufficiently high to put them into the tax net. The Department of Social and Family Affairs does not operate the PAYE system under which tax would be stopped at source but the Revenue often arranges for the tax to be stopped out of any other income the recipient may have. Only the first four on the following list of taxable benefits is considered to qualify the recipient for PAYE tax credit. That means that a couple is entitled to the benefit of two PAYE tax credits if one is being taxed under PAYE on earnings and the other is in receipt of a contributory old age pension. The following are the taxable benefits:

- State pension (contributory),
  State pension (transition),

Contributory survivor's pension,
Contributory orphan's pension,
Invalidity pension,
One parent family payment,
Carers allowance,
Jobseeker's benefit,
Blind person's pension,
Non contributory widow's pension,
Guardian's payment (non-contributory), and
Social assistance allowance for deserted or prisoners' wives.

A number of concessions apply:

- The first six days of illness benefit is not subject to tax.

- Child dependant additions to disability and unemployment benefits are not taxed.

- The unemployment benefit payable to systematic short-term workers is not taxed.

- The first €12.70 a week of unemployment benefit is not liable for tax.

Benefits-in-kind are not all taxed

Since the introduction of the PAYE system many decades ago, most earnings have been taxed at source but this was only extended more recently to non-cash benefits such as company cars, cheap loans and lunch vouchers. Most of these benefits are, of course, taxable. They are considered by the Revenue to be every bit as much income as basic pay and are liable to tax as such. Employers are required to value the benefits and stop tax and PRSI at source through the PAYE system.

While most non-cash benefits provided by employers for individual workers or for employees in general are liable for tax, there are important exemptions that allow employers to provide some tax-free benefits to their workers. The exemptions are all subject to conditions that are strictly applied by the Revenue but if those conditions are met the employer can confer the benefit tax free and it remains tax free in the hands of the recipient.

One such exemption applies to small benefits worth no more than €250. Only one small benefit is exempt from tax in any tax year, so it may not sound like much but so long as the conditions are met, a €250 gift voucher, given as a bonus, costs an employer just that while providing the same benefit in cash can cost up to €532.45. That €532.45 would be subject to employer's PRSI of €51.67, employee's PRSI of €28.85 and, if the top rate applies, income tax of €201.92 leaving €250 for the worker.

Workers can get some benefits tax free from their employers

The benefit doesn't have to be given in the form of a gift voucher of course so long as it isn't actual cash. However, since the vouchers can be used in a wide range of outlets they are nearly as good as cash to the recipients but in terms of euro for euro benefit, they are far less expensive for the employer. The €250 upper limit per year obviously limits the scope of this small benefit exemption for employers who genuinely want to provide workers with extra non-cash benefits at the smallest possible cost. But there are other non-cash benefits that employers can give their workers tax free. The following are some of the options:

- No benefit-in-kind tax is applied to meals, either free or subsidised, provided in a staff canteen. The facility has to be open to all employees so the exemption doesn't apply to a limited executive dining room. Neither is it extended to meal vouchers.

- Sports and recreational facilities provided on an employer's own premises can be enjoyed tax free by workers. But the facilities must be open to all employees, not just a favoured few.

- Crèche and childcare facilities can also be provided tax free, subject to certain conditions. The facilities must be up to minimum standards and the employer must either be providing the facilities, have financed the construction or refurbishing of the premises used or be actively involved in financing and managing the service. Payments made towards the cost of childcare in outside facilities are subject to tax.

- Bus, train and Luas passes can also be provided tax free and they don't have to be used necessarily for work purposes. The main condition is that they are monthly or annual passes for use on a licensed passenger transport service. The Revenue allows employees to surrender pay to an employer in return for such a pass.

- Mobile phones can be provided to workers tax free but only if it can be justified on the basis of business use. The phone may be used for private use but it must be incidental to its use for business purposes. The same rules apply to the provision of computers or broadband access if they are to be provided completely tax free.

- Employers can since January 1, 2009, supply workers with a bicycle and associated safety equipment tax free to a value of €1,000 once in any five year period. The Revenue allows employees to take a pay cut in return for such a pass. The benefit in doing it is that, if the pay was taken through the payroll it would be subject to tax and PRSI, but the value of the bicycle is not.

> **Monthly or annual bus, train and Luas tickets can be provided by employers tax free**

- Fees paid in respect of courses of study relevant to the business of the employer can also be paid tax free. The employer can either reimburse the worker or pay the fees directly. A course is relevant, according to the Revenue, where "it leads to the acquisition of knowledge or skills which are: necessary for the duties of the office or employment, or it facilitates the acquisition of knowledge which is necessary for or directly related to the performance of the employee's present duties in the office or employment or would be necessary for or directly related to the prospective duties of the employee with the employer."

- An award made to a worker in recognition of obtaining a qualification of some relevance to the job. The award must be no more than might reasonably be considered a reimbursement of the expenses incurred in studying for the qualification or sitting the exam.

- Workers can be provided with free living accommodation but only in very limited circumstances. The accommodation has to be in part of the employer's business premises and there has to be some work-related need for living there.

- The traditional Christmas party, celebrations for special occasions and events, such as sports days, are exempt

Cutting the BIK assessment on your car

■ The options available for reducing the tax liability on a company car fall into a number of fairly obvious categories.

Get green: Get a car with low CO_2 emissions.

Reduce the price: The lower the original market price of the car, the smaller will be the benefit-in-kind assessment. That comes down to a choice over the type of car you want and the status you attach to it. There is, however, one way of having your cake and eating it i.e. having a high status car and at the same time reducing your tax liability. That's by buying an old but good second hand car. Such cars are also attractive to people who want to buy their own and charge the company for the business mileage done.

Do more mileage: If you're close to one of the thousand mile cut-off points it can obviously be worthwhile to move into the higher bracket. For instance, if you do 20,000 business miles rather than 19,999 you cut the assessment to 18% rather than 24% of its initial market value.

Use the car pool: There is no benefit-in-kind assessed if the company car you use is out of a car pool. But the Revenue apply very strict rules. The car must be made available to and used by more than one employee. The car must not normally be kept overnight at or close to any of the employees' homes. Any private use must be minimal and incidental to business use.

Charge mileage: If you use your own car for business use you can, of course, claim a mileage allowance from your employer. To escape Revenue displeasure, the payment must be based on actual mileage and an acceptable mileage rate. The employer has to get Revenue approval not to deduct tax from the payments and while there is no definitive mileage rate, the Civil Service rates provide an indication of what may be appropriate.

Use a van: If you have a company van, rather than a company car, somewhat more favourable rules apply to the calculation of benefit-in-kind. Subject to certain conditions you may be able to take the van home and not be liable for BIK. But at worst, it's assessed as 5% of the original market value.

from the benefit-in-kind rules provided the expenses are "reasonable".

- Subscriptions to professional bodies provided that membership is relevant to the business of the employer.

- Medical check-ups but only where they are required by the employer.

- Long service awards but not in the form of cash and only after at least 20 years service. The award must be a "tangible article" costing no more than €50 for each year of service. No more than one award can be made every five years.

Tax and the company car

A company car is a valuable addition to any remuneration package. On the basis of AA estimates it costs over €10,000 a year to run an average sized car when depreciation, tax, insurance and all running costs are taken into account. That's a measure of what you save if the company provides you with a car and covers all the costs.

But a car is not one of those few benefits which an employer can provide tax-free to an employee. It is viewed as part of the recipient's salary — a Benefit in Kind (BIK) — and as such is subject to income tax. The benefit is also liable for PRSI and if you are a PAYE taxpayer the weekly or monthly value is included in your gross pay. It is intended to relate the BIK charge on newly provided cars to the car's CO_2 emissions, the car's original market value and the business mileage undertaken during the year. While the old system is still given with reference to miles, the new system has adopted kilometres. The rates are as follows:

Business kms	% of original market value
up to 24,000 kms	30%
24,001 to 32,000	24%
32,001 to 40,000	18%
40,001 to 48,000	12%
Over 48,000	6%

The older system, which is still in use, also takes original market value as the starting point. That is not necessarily the recommended retail price. It is based on the actual price paid for the new vehicle taking into account any discounts up to a maximum of 10%.

A maximum assessment of 30% of the market value is applied where business mileage is less than 15,000 a year. On mileage between 15,001 and 20,000 that reduces to 24%. It's 18% where the business mileage is between 20,001 and 25,000; 12% between 25,001 and 30,000 and 6% where the mileage is above 30,000.

Company vans are assessed in a different way to cars

Company vans are treated in a different way. The benefit-in-kind is simply assessed at 5% of the original market value of the van. But that is not applied if certain conditions are met. To gain this exemption, the van must be used strictly for business purposes, the worker must be required by the employer to bring the van home, private use other than simply travelling to and from work must be prohibited and the worker must spend most of his or her working time away from the employer's workplace.

But there are ways of reducing the tax liability, or avoiding it altogether, by buying your own car and charging the company a mileage rate. Or if you don't claim a mileage rate you can claim tax relief on the expense of running the car including an allowance for the capital cost of buying it.

Let's have a look at an example of those calculations: Suppose you do 19,500 business miles a year in a company car that was bought new for €20,000. The taxable benefit in kind is assessed as 24% of that €20,000 or €4,800. The tax, at 41c in the euro, amounts to €1,968. If you manage to do an extra 500 business miles to bring you above the 20,000 mile threshold the taxable benefit would be a lower 18% of €20,000 or €3,600 and the tax liability would be reduced to €1,476.

Either way it's a painful tax but it may not be a high cost to pay for the benefit of a company car. Compare it with the depreciation costs on a €20,000 car you'd buy yourself. Without putting it on the road at all, it must be costing at least €2,500 a year in depreciation. Indeed in the early years of its life, it will lose far more than that in value.

■ The Revenue Commissioners estimate that as much as €100 million of tax relief is going unclaimed each year. But they are doing something about it, starting with age and rent allowances, the relief on trade union dues and moving on to target a range of medical expenses. But the process will take time and won't be comprehensive so it remains important to check for yourself. If you have missed out it is possible to make a back claim for up to four years so the sooner you act the better. Act before the end of 2009 and you can make a claim for 2005. The following lists some of the allowances most often missed. If you have a claim all you have to do is get some tax return forms at your tax office or by phoning 1890 30 67 06. They are easy to fill out. If you can only get forms for the current year don't be afraid to simply write in the relevant dates for past years.

Rent Allowance: A taxpayer over 55 years of age, living in rented accommodation, can claim an allowance of up to €4,000 in respect of the rent paid — €8,000 for a married couple or widowed person. The allowance cannot be claimed in respect of rent paid to local authorities or on tenancies of 50 years or more. Married and widowed tenants under 55 can claim relief of up to €4,000 and single tenants €2,000.

Medical expenses: Full allowance is granted for most medical expenses at the standard rate of tax. Up to 2009 it was allowed at the taxpayer's top tax rate. Before 2007 the first €125 was disallowed (€250 for a family).

Expenses: Allowance is also made for expenses incurred by the taxpayer in performing his job. In the case of a PAYE worker, the expenses must have been wholly, exclusively, and necessarily incurred. The "necessarily" criterion does not apply to the self-employed. The allowance can be given for tools and special work clothes.

Local authority charges: Tax relief on service charges is allowed on a prior year basis but it must be claimed. An upper limit of €400 applies since 2006.

Union dues: A credit at the standard rate is allowed on up to €350 paid in trade union subscriptions. It was €350 in 2007 but increased to the current level from 2008.

Medical insurance: If your employer pays your medical insurance you may be entitled to the tax relief on it. But you do have to claim it.

DIRT: Those over 65, or permanently incapaciated, who are not liable for tax can claim back any DIRT tax stopped on deposit interest. Such people can now have their interest paid DIRT-free by simply informing the bank or other deposit taker of their status but that facility was not available prior to 2007.

eWorking from home

An increasing number of workers are operating from their homes using computers and telephone links to communicate with their employers or contractors. For tax purposes, many of them are self-employed but a large proportion are PAYE employees working for a single employer. The fact that they have control over where, and maybe even when, they work doesn't necessarily make them self-employed. They are taxable under the PAYE system and they and their employers are liable for PRSI. But the Revenue Commissioners recognise that there are some tax implications peculiar to these workers who are sometimes described as eWorkers.

It is not unusual, for instance, for employers to supply teleworkers with the computers, printers, scanners, modems, fax machines and software that they need to carry out their work. Normally when an employer gives such equipment to an employee and allows him or her to take it home it would be considered a benefit-in-kind.

Under the tax rules the employer would have to value such items and tax them under the PAYE system as if they were pay. But in the case of employees working from home, the equipment is obviously being supplied primarily for business purposes. The object is to enable the employee to do his or her work at home. In recognition of this, the Revenue is willing to bend the rules a little and ignore the fact that the computers are likely to be used occasionally for non-business purposes – anything from playing games to helping the children with their homework.

The same liberal approach is taken to the provision of a telephone line for business use or the supply of other items such as stationery and office furniture. So long as the items are supplied "primarily" for business use, the Revenue doesn't make any benefit-in-kind assessment. The employer can supply them tax-free and can claim the costs involved as a business expense.

There are other tax implications as well. While employees working from home can save a lot in travel expenses they do incur some costs in heating and lighting their home office.

They are quite entitled to claim this as an expense in their own personal tax return. Self-employed workers operating from home often claim tax relief in respect of a sixth or seventh of their household heating and lighting bills to cover that portion of the expense relating to the part of the house used for business purposes. The proportion depends on the size of the home and the proportion used for business. An employee can make a similar claim but, as with the self-employed taxpayer, they may be asked to justify it and supply receipts.

A good employer may agree to reimburse a worker for these incidental expenses that arise from working at home. And, of course, such expense payments can be made tax-free. The Revenue will allow a payment of up to €3.20 a day tax free without question. Up to that maximum, payment for expenses can be made without deduction of PAYE or PRSI and are tax free in the hands of the employee. Payments above that level require justification and receipts.

It is also possible to claim tax relief in respect of a notional rent paid for the home office but it's generally not worthwhile. Making such a claim effectively means designating part of the home as a business premises and that has all sorts of potentially nasty implications. It could create a liability for Capital Gains Tax if the home was sold. No Capital Gains Tax liability arises from the sale of a principal private residence but there is no such exemption for business premises so a pro-rata tax liability could arise.

There might also be a liability for local authority rates. The rules with regard to company cars and motoring expenses apply equally to all employees whether they work from home or at the employer's place of business. A company car is treated as a benefit-in-kind but mileage expenses can be paid tax free so long as they can be justified and don't exceed the rates paid to civil servants. Complications can arise, however, in determining the employee's normal place of work.

Tax free mileage expenses can only be paid in respect of business journeys. Travel to and from work is not included. But if someone normally works from home, can they be given tax-free mileage expenses in respect of the occasional journey to head office?

Employees working from home can claim tax relief on a portion of their lighting and heating costs

Special rules with regard to benefits-in-kind are applied to items supplied for the business use of eWorkers

The answer is possibly "yes" although the Revenue will look at each case on its own merits. They do say that where employees work part-time from home and part-time at the employer's place of business, their base is considered to be the employer's place of business. But what's the definition of part-time? Would a brief visit every week or month constitute part-time work? The Revenue's view is far from clear.

Even where a business journey starts at the worker's home, tax-free mileage expenses may only be paid in respect of the mileage from the normal place of employment if that happens to be shorter. There is nothing to prevent employees who pay their own motoring expenses from claiming tax relief on the actual cost of any business journeys. That includes fuel and also a proportion of the motor tax, insurance costs and wear and tear on the vehicle. The calculations are a bit complicated but the claim is effectively granted at the employee's top rate of tax since it is actually a deduction from taxable income. See page 265.

Calculating your tax liability

Calculating your total tax liability became easier with the introduction of tax credits although some reliefs, such as those on medical expenses and on the employment of a

Standard rate tax bands

■ The first slice of income up to these levels is charged at the standard rate of tax. Income above these levels is liable for tax at the higher rate

Category of taxpayer	2009	2010
Married, one income	€45,400	€45,400
Married, two income	€72,600	€72,600
Single parents	€40,400	€40,400
Single	€36,400	€36,400

carer for an incapacitated spouse or relative, are still available. A full explanation of tax credits is given on page 231. The basic point to remember is that an allowance of €1,000 is equivalent to a tax credit of €200 since each euro of standard rated allowance is worth so many times 20c in saved tax.

To calculate your annual tax liability, you first calculate a gross tax liability by applying the 20% tax rate to the first band of your income and the 41% rate to the remainder. From that gross tax liability you then deduct your tax credits to arrive at a figure for your actual liability. The size of your standard rate tax band differs according to your personal circumstances.

In 2010 a single person will pay tax at 20% on the first €36,400 of income and anything above that at 41%.

A very simple example would be a single taxpayer on €40,000 a year entitled to only the personal and PAYE allowances. First of all we ignore the tax credits and calculate the tax due on the full €40,000. The sums work out like this:

€36,400 at 20c	€7,280
€3,600 at 41c	€1,476
Total	**€8,756**

From that is deducted the tax credits, in this case the personal credit of €1,830 and the PAYE tax credit of €1,830. That's a total of €3,660 which when deducted from €8,756 leaves a tax liability of €5,096. Of course, there is also the 2% levy which will apply to the full €40,000 and add €800 to the total tax liability. PRSI and the Health Levy comes on top of that again.

Let's have a look at a more detailed example. Mr. Murphy is married with two children — both still at school. He is going to earn €70,000 during 2010. In addition his company supplies him with a car which is valued as a benefit-in-kind.

Mr. Murphy will pay €4,500 in interest on a house mortgage, and will be allowed that in full since it is below the upper limit of €6,000 for non-first time buyers. It comes by

■ Tax liability is based on annual income. The PAYE administrative system tries to ensure that the tax is collected in instalments during the year. But it can result in you being over or under taxed. To check you have to calculate the liability on the basis of your annual income. Here's an example of how it is done:

GROSS PAY		€70,000
Plus Benefit-in-kind (company car)		€4,500
Less Pension contributions		€2,000
TOTAL		€72,500
Allowances at marginal rate i.e. agreed expenses		€150
Income after marginal rate allowances		**€72,350**
First €45,400 at 20c in euro		€9,080
Remainder (€26,950) at 41c in euro		€11,050
Tax before deductions for tax credits		**€20,130**
TAX CREDITS		
Personal credit	€3,660	
Home carers credit	€900	
Allowable interest (€4,500 @ 15c)	€675	
Healthcare premiums (€1,000 @ 20c)	€200	
Employee credit (PAYE)	€1,830	
Service charges	€400	
Total credits		**€7,665**
TOTAL INCOME TAX		**€12,465**
Plus Levy (2% of €74,500)		€1,450
TOTAL TAX TAKE		€13,915

way of reduced repayments since it goes directly to the building society.

His employer paid €1,000 to Quinn Healthcare last year to provide cover for the Murphys and Mr Murphy is entitled to claim the tax relief on that. He has put in the claim for the relief which is allowed on the previous year's premiums. He paid €2,000 into the company pension scheme. He claims a tax credit of €400 in respect of a local service charge. The calculations are shown in the table. In doing your own calculations, you can use the form provided on page 256.

With the exception of an agreed expenses allowance of €150, all of Mr Murphy's tax allowances are standard rated. Since his wife has no income, he is only allowed a standard rate band of €45,400. But they do benefit from the €900 home carer's credit. Mr. Murphy's total income tax liability is €12,465 while the 2% levy takes a further €1,450. It applies to gross pay including the pension contributions and benefits-in-kind. The PAYE system will ensure that the tax liability is paid in either weekly or monthly instalments over the period. If there is any under- or over-payment of tax it can be sorted out in a balancing statement at the end of the year. These are not always issued so if you think you have been overtaxed it is important for you to claim.

Doing your own sums

The pro-forma table opposite and the Murphy example can help you to do your own sums. Even if you don't feel like getting the calculator out, at least have a look at the list in the panel on page 249 of some allowances and reliefs which are commonly missed. All the figures for your own calculations can be obtained earlier in this chapter and/or by reference to Appendix 1 on page 330.

Don't forget to include taxable benefits-in-kind. The private use of a car is not the only benefit-in-kind which may be valued and assessed as part of the taxpayer's income. Other such items include the provision of accommodation, entertainment, services or indeed any benefits or facilities supplied by the employer and not paid for by the employee. There are some notable exceptions, however. Childcare facilities supplied by an employer and at least partially managed by him are not treated as a taxable benefit.

Calculating your own tax liability

■ The pro-forma table below can help you work out your liability in the same way as the Murphys' liability is calculated in the table on page 252. There is a list of tax credits and bands in Appendix 1 on page 328 and there are more details of the credits earlier in this chapter starting on page 232.

GROSS PAY			
Plus Benefit-in-kind (company car etc.)			
Less Pension contributions			
TOTAL (a)			
Less	Allowances at marginal rate		
Total allowances at marginal rate (b)			
Income after marginal rate allowances (a minus b)			
First €45,400[1] (€36,400 single) at 20c in the euro			
Remainder at 41c in the euro			
Tax before deduction of tax credits (c)			
Tax credits			
Personal			
Allowable interest			
Local authority charges			
PAYE			
Total credits (d)			
TOTAL TAX (c minus d)			
Plus income levy, 2% on first €75,036, 4% on income between €75037 and €174,980 and 6% on income above that.			

Note: 1. A two income married couple has a standard rate band of at least €45,400 but where both spouses have incomes of at least €27,400 the band is widened to €72,800. The band is calculated at €45,400 plus the income of the lower earner up to a maximum of €72,800. The band is €40,400 for one parent families.

Payments towards childcare expenses are taxable, however, although legitimate expenses wholly, exclusively and necessarily incurred in the performance of one's duties are not assessed for tax. Neither is the benefit of subsidised canteen meals.

Self-employed income

A growing proportion of the workforce is self-employed. Before the rcession it was about one in six and the proportion is possibly higher now. For some it's a matter of choice. For others, who might prefer the security of a permanent and pensionable job, it's simply a matter of circumstance. There are advantages and disadvantages either way. What some people view as an advantage can seem a disadvantage to others. For instance, the ability of the self-employed to delay the payments of income tax may seem attractive to the worker whose tax is stopped each week or month under the PAYE system. But the self-employed may not see it quite the same way when the tax bill has to be met each October.

By the end of October 2010, for instance, the self-employed taxpayers will have to make the following returns and payments:

- Make a final income tax return for 2009 and pay any additional tax due for that year.

- Calculate and pay preliminary tax for 2010. To avoid penalties the amount paid must be at least equal to 90% of the total tax that is eventually found to be due or be 100% of the tax actually assessed for 2009.

- Pay any Capital Gains Tax on asset disposals made in December 2009.

The self-employed don't have to prepare accounts on a calendar year basis. The accounting period taken into account by the Revenue is that which ended during the relevant tax year. So while, for instance, the 2009 tax return mentioned above might be in respect of the calendar year 2009, it might just as easily be in respect of a 12 month period ending January 31, 2009. It's up to the self-employed person to pick their own accounting period although once picked, changing it can lead to complications.

Any delay in making the necessary returns and paying the tax due can be costly. A surcharge of 5% of any tax due can

■ Most revenue audits are targeted. Some taxpayers are picked at random but the vast bulk – perhaps over 90% – are picked because of their past record or because their tax returns trigger some alarm bells in the Revenue computers or the tax inspector's mind. It is not too difficult to imagine the type of return which might trigger an audit. All you have to do is put yourself in the tax inspector's shoes and consider what he or she might be looking for. An irregular trading pattern, for instance, might be considered a bit strange and worthy of investigation. It might reflect tax evasion but it might also be due to the nature of the business, lost contracts, illness of key workers – any number of possible explanations.

If there is an explanation like that, it is better to add a note to your tax return. It might just offset an audit. The same is true of the other possible factors which might put a tax inspector wondering – factors like the following:

Low drawings: Where the amount of money drawn out of a business by the proprietor seems unduly low by reference to previous periods or by reference to realistic spending needs the inspector may wonder what is sustaining the taxpayer's lifestyle. If there is a legitimate explanation, make it in an addendum to your tax return.

Fluctuating turnover: This may, of itself, raise questions in a tax inspector's mind unless the business is of an obvious seasonal nature. A change in the pattern is, of course, just as likely to prompt questions.

VAT: Discrepancies between VAT and income or corporation tax returns are very easily spotted now that the Revenue has encouraged a standardisation of tax periods. In small businesses, particularly, there can be a legitimate explanation. If there is, it is better to make it known before an audit is prompted than during the audit.

Careless returns: Sloppy VAT and PAYE returns will obviously raise a suspicion that accounting procedures are not all they should be.

be imposed if the return is anything up to two months late. If you are more than two months late in making your return the surcharge goes up to 10%. In addition to the surcharge interest at the rate of 0.0322% a day (about 1% a month) is charged on any outstanding tax. Apart from paying the tax the self-employed are required to estimate their own tax liability. They either have to pay an accountant to do the job or do it themselves. The DIY route has been made a lot simpler in recent years through the Revenue's Online

Service (ROS). It provides online versions of the tax forms that enable you to easily skip irrelevant portions of the lengthy tax returns.

While the ongoing computerisation of tax returns enable the Revenue to do much more sophisticated cross-checks but they have assured taxpayers that filing returns early or on the internet makes no difference to the compliance procedures applied. There is no greater chance of being chosen for an audit, for instance. Late returns on the other hand undergo a screening process that can increase the risk of being selected for audit. All returns made on paper are entered into the same computer programmes as those made on the internet.

Apart from the greater ease in making returns, other benefits include an ongoing facility of accessing your own tax data, and provision for filing early but not making payments until the final due date. Another plus-point is that any refunds due are likely to be processed more speedily. If you have access to the internet you can try it out for yourself without any commitment. You can access the Revenue website at www.revenue.ie. Just click on the Revenue Online Service (ROS) option towards the top left-hand corner of the screen. That brings you into the service and you can opt to have a demonstration including a trial filling in of forms. If you like what you see, you can immediately register to become a 'ROS customer'.

There are concessions for those who have recently become self-employed. The first deadline for those who became self-employed in 2009 is October 31, 2010. That's the date by which they have to pay preliminary tax for 2010 and any tax due for 2009. Once that tax is paid they have until October 31, 2011 to make a final tax return in respect of 2010. So in October 2010, they need to pay tax in respect of 2009 and preliminary tax in respect of 2010. In October 2011, they'll have to make their actual tax returns for 2009 and 2010 and pay any remaining tax due in respect of 2010 together with preliminary tax for 2011.

As mentioned above, the self-employed don't have to make up their accounts for the actual tax year i.e. the calendar year. That's something for those starting off to bear in mind. They can start their accounting year in whatever month they like. Someone starting up in business in July, for instance, may decide to operate an accounting year from August to July. Alternatively they may do their first accounts for the period from July to December and thereafter do accounts on a calendar year basis.

The choice depends on a number of factors. It's often simpler to have an accounting year-end during a traditionally slack period of the year. But having the accounting year coincide with the tax year and VAT accounting year can also have significant administrative advantages. Another important factor is that the choice of year-end can help delay the payment of tax. But remember some of the cash flow benefits would be offset by delays in claiming allowances. And if you change your end of year accounting date the Revenue will go back a year and calculate what your liability would have been had you used the new accounting period during the previous year.

> **The cost of capital items can be written off against profits over eight years**

You'll get an extra tax bill if the profits in that accounting period were in excess of the actual profits assessed. That doesn't mean that it can't be worthwhile changing your accounting year or picking a favourable starting date for the business. But there's likely to be many other factors involved in that decision and the cash flow benefits may not accrue for a few years in any case because the tax liability during the early years of the business are subject to special rules.

The profits assessed for the first tax year are the actual taxable income from the date of commencement to the following December 31. The profits assessed in the second year are those for the first 12 months of the business. It is only in the third year that the normal ongoing system starts to operate.

There are, of course, additional allowances which can be claimed by the self-employed. These are basically the costs of running the business. To be allowed as a tax deduction an employee must show that any expenses were incurred wholly, exclusively and necessarily for trade or professional purposes. The self-employed taxpayer has only to meet the "wholly and exclusively" requirements. He does not have to show that the expenses were necessarily incurred. That makes more expenses allowable.

The following are some of the more general possibilities.

- Wages paid to employees. See page 279 for the benefits of formally paying wages to a spouse, or children, who may be helping in the business.

- Rent paid for business premises is allowed but it may not be worthwhile claiming a notional rent allowance for a room in your private home even if it is used as an office. Instead you can claim for the cost of heating and lighting that room. Claiming for rent could result in part of your house being considered to be a commercial premises. That can have implications for local authority rates and Capital Gains Tax. There is no Capital Gains Tax on a principal residence but there could be a liability on a business premises. If it is only a matter of using one room as an office it is probably best just to claim tax relief on the "running cost" of the room — perhaps, in the case of a four bedroomed house, one seventh of your total household outgoings on heat and light.

- Repairs to premises and repairs to plant and machinery are allowable costs but not the cost of improvements or additions.

- Interest paid on business loans. Restrictions of the type applicable to mortgage interest relief on a home do not, of course, apply.

- The cost of advertising.

- Other business costs include travelling, stationery, telecommunications, postage etc. Receipts should, of course, be kept. Motoring expenses are considered in more detail on page 265.

- Bad debts are also an allowable expense. That includes doubtful debts but the expense must relate to specific debts. It cannot simply be a global provision in the expectation that a certain proportion of bills will be unpaid.

- Allowances can also be claimed in respect of capital expenditure on plant and machinery used in the business. Since December 4, 2002 the write off is extended over eight years at a rate of 12.5% a year. So if you buy a computer worth €1,000 you can write off €125 as a cost against your income for eight years. There are limits on the amount of allowances that can be claimed in respect of cars. There is more detail on this later in this section.

- In addition to these business expenses, the self-employed taxpayer who has no other income can also deduct the same personal allowances outlined above for the PAYE payer. The only exception is the PAYE allowance which the self-employed person cannot claim. The PAYE allowance is not available either in respect of a spouse working for a self-employed taxpayer. But it may be worthwhile formally employing a spouse in a family business to make use of the new wider lower-rate tax band available to two income couples. The pros and cons are examined on page 279.

Rental income

Income from the letting of flats, houses or other property is treated in the same way as the self-employed income mentioned above. It is added to the taxpayer's other income in arriving at his overall tax liability but it is not, of course, paid under the PAYE system. The one exception, is that up to €10,000 in rent can be received tax-free from the letting of a room in one's principal private residence. That was increased in 2008 from the €7,620 that applied in 2007. Since January 1, 2007 this exemption is not available where the tenant is a "connected" person, a child who is claiming tax relief on the rent paid.

In assessing the taxable income from rents, the normal personal allowances are available if they have not already been offset against other income and, in addition, the cost of the following may be deducted from the gross income before arriving at taxable income.

- Any rent payable by the taxpayer himself — i.e. ground rent on the premises.

- Any rates on the premises.

- The interest on borrowing used to acquire or improve the premises. This interest relief is unlimited — not

Cost	€32,000
Restricted to 50% of €24,000[1]	€12,000
Allowance at 12.5% (12.5% of €12,000)	€1,500
Restricted for business use (2/3rds of €1,250)	€1,000
Allowance for year one	**€1,000**
Written down value for year two (€12,000 minus €1,000)	€11,000
Allowance at 12.5% (12.5% of €11,000)	€1,375
Restricted for business use (2/3rds of €1,833)	€917
Allowance for year two	**€917**

1. *Since July 2008 assuming the car meets the middle range emission criteria. Lower emission cars would be restricted to €24,000.*

subject to the individual upper limit which applies to mortgage interest relief on a principal residence.

- The cost of any goods or services which he provides to the tenants and which are not paid for separately from the rent. An example might be providing electric light in the hallways of flats.

- The cost of maintenance, repairs, insurance etc.

- Management costs i.e. cost of collecting rents, advertising for tenants etc.

- Wear and tear allowances on the cost of furniture and fittings at the rate of 12.5% of the cost over eight years. Different rules apply to expenditure incurred before December 4, 2002. See page 262. Where the costs exceed the income from the rental property, that loss is only allowed as an offset against future rental income. It cannot be used to reduce the tax due on PAYE earnings for instance.

Any taxpayer, whether employed or self-employed, who uses his own motor car for business can claim for wear and tear on the car in addition to running expenses. It doesn't arise too often in the case of an employee since he or she is normally either supplied with a company car or has the expenses reimbursed by the employer. But self-employed taxpayers very often use their own cars.

There are restrictions on the amount which can be claimed and a new system, which applies to car bought after July 2008, precludes any claim being made in respect of cars rated for carbon emissions of more than 191 grams per kilometre. For those with emission ratings between 156 and 170 grams per kilometre the allowances and leasing expenses are based on 50% of the value of the car at the time of purchase subject to a maximumm cost of €24,000. For cars with lower emissions the allowances are calculated on the value of the car subject to a maximum of €24,000 which has applied since January 1, 2007. Lower thresholds applied in previous years

Jan 1, 2001 to 31 Dec 2001	€21,586
Jan 1, 2002 to 31 Dec 2005	€22,000
Jan 1, 2006 to 31 Dec 2006	€23,000
Since Jan 1, 2007	€24,000

For expenditure incurred after December 4, 2002 or after December 31, 2002, if the contract was entered into prior to December 4, the wear and tear allowed each year is calculated at 12.5% of the declining value of the car restricted by that initial maximum value. It is also reduced to allow for any private use of the car. A one-third private to two-thirds business is a generally accepted norm.

The table overleaf provides an example of the calculation.

No overall restriction applies to the running costs of a car used for business purposes. Where a car is used for both private and business use, the allowable business costs are apportioned generally in the ratio that business use bears to private use.

Working outside Ireland

To be liable for tax in Ireland you need to be resident in Ireland or, in some cases, to have been recently resident in Ireland. The definition of "resident" is strictly defined in this context but it is a fairly liberal definition. A person is considered to be resident in Ireland for tax purposes if he or she is in the country for 183 days or more in a tax year; or is in the country for more than 30 days in that year and 280 days or more during that and the previous tax year.

You are counted as having spent a day in Ireland if you are in the country at the end of the day so you could, in fact, spend every day in Ireland provided you left the country every night. As a non-resident you are not liable for income tax on earnings you make abroad. But for three years after becoming non-resident, you are liable for tax on income arising in Ireland and on investment income from any source. You may also be liable for Capital Gains Tax. See page 269.

Rental income is taxable irrespective of where the landlord lives

Rental income from Irish property is taxable in Ireland even if the recipient is non-resident. If the rent is paid to an Irish based agent he or she is liable for the tax. Otherwise the tenant is required to stop tax at 20c in the euro on the rent and pay it directly to the Revenue Commissioners. For example if the rent is €1,000 a month the tenant pays €800 to the non-resident landlord and the other €200 to the Revenue Commissioners.

Tax rebates for emigrants

People who leave a job in Ireland to emigrate may be entitled to a tax rebate but it has to be claimed. Such claims can be backdated for up to at least four years. The size of the rebate depends on a number of factors — most notably the date of leaving the Irish job. The potential refund is highest for those who leave jobs a few months into the tax year. It is lowest for those who leave towards the very end of a tax year. If you leave just prior to December 31 there is unlikely to be any rebate entitlement at all.

This concession separates, for tax purposes, the Irish and overseas earnings the emigrants earn during the year in which they leave the country and also in the year that they return provided they have spent at least one full tax year working abroad. Occasional visits home, of course, don't affect the entitlement. Let's first see how it works, how you can go about claiming the rebate, and also look at how to time your return to Ireland to make the maximum use of the concession.

Normally an Irish resident is liable for tax in Ireland on their worldwide income and most emigrants would be considered to be resident during the year they emigrated. So technically, they should be liable for Irish tax not only on their earnings in Ireland before they leave but also on their earnings abroad during the remainder of the tax year while also paying tax in their new home. They might, of course, be able to get some relief under a double taxation agreement between Ireland and their new host country. But that's complicated to say the least. What's known as "The Split Year Rule" allows you to ignore that.

If you leave Ireland to work abroad and you stay abroad for at least the following tax year, then you are only liable to pay Irish tax on income earned in Ireland before you left. There can be no disputing your claim if you have already stayed abroad for the full tax year. But you can make the claim even before you emigrate. The Revenue Commissioners may accept that you intend staying abroad if you have sold your house, for instance, or if you have evidence of taking a long-term job abroad. So, how does the rebate arise?

> **A tax rebate may be due both in the year you leave and in the year you return**

Under the PAYE system your tax allowances are spread out equally over the full year. You are allowed a proportion of them for each week or month, depending on how you're paid. So if you leave a job and emigrate after say six months you will only have got the benefit of half of your tax allowances for the year. It's the other half that entitles you to the rebate. Suppose, for instance, that you're single earning €40,000 a year. Your basic tax credits for the year amount to €3,660 just counting personal and employee allowances. Your allowances could be more if you include medical insurance and mortgage interest or rent. Six months into the tax year — by June 30 — you'll have earned €20,000 and have got the benefit of half of those tax credits or about €1,830. If you leave the job and emigrate at that stage you can claim the benefit of the other €1,830. Don't forget, of course, that there is the overriding condition that you are going to work outside the country for the whole of the following tax year.

Even if you left Ireland four years ago you may still be due a rebate and it's not too late to claim

The claim should be made to whatever tax office you dealt with prior to leaving Ireland. You will need to fill out a tax return for the year you left the country. Ideally you would have a copy of the P45 form you got from your Irish employer on leaving which would show your earnings up to the date you left and details of the tax stopped.

But the tax office should have that information if your previous employer has been making his returns. Remember that the Revenue Commissioners will normally allow a back-claim for up to at least four years. The size of a possible tax rebate is obviously not the only thing to be considered when planning a date for either emigrating from or returning to Ireland. But it's a factor to be taken into account.

The point to remember is that you can earn up to your annual tax free allowance level without any liability for income tax. Since the basic annual tax credits for a single individual who is paying PAYE amount to €3,660 it follows that if a single person earns less than about €18,300 in Ireland from the beginning of the tax year before he or she emigrates there is an entitlement to a full rebate of all the tax paid in that tax year i.e since January 1. The tax on €18,300 at 20% would be €3,660 but the credit offsets that, so no tax is actually payable although the PAYE system will have collected some.

A single person returning to Ireland can earn up to about €18,300 between the date they return and the following December 31 and pay no tax on it. For example, if you return in September, get a job and decide to stay, you can earn up to €18,300 between then and December 31 without incurring any tax liability. Remember though, that this only applies to those who have spent at least a full tax year abroad. Otherwise income that you earned abroad may be taken into account.

Capital Gains Tax

If you acquire an asset at one price and sell it at a higher price or even give it away, you have made a capital gain and may be liable for tax. Some gains are exempt and gains made during any period up to January 1, 2003 are adjusted downwards to take account of inflation. For that period, you are assumed to have made a taxable gain only if the value of the asset has gone up by more than the rate of inflation. This indexation relief does not apply to periods after January 1, 2003. Gains are liable for tax at the flat rate of 20 cent in the euro on transactions concluded prior to midnight on October 14, 2008 and 22% between then and April 7, 2009. The rate of 25% applies to gains on for disposals made on or after April 8, 2009. The following are some of the more important exemptions:

- The first €1,270 made in each tax year.

- Gains from the sale of your principal residence including up to one acre of land. If the price you get is based on the development value of the land then you are liable for tax on the gain attributed to that development value.

- Gains on the sale of a residence, also including up to an acre of land, which you have been providing for the sole occupation of a dependant relative as his or her sole residence. Dependant relative, in this regard, includes any relative who because of incapacity or infirmity is not able to maintain him or herself. Also included is the widowed mother of either spouse who need not be incapacitated.

- The notional gain on the gift of a house site worth less than €500,000 to a child who builds his or her principal private residence on it. The limit was €254,000 in 2007. There is a claw-back of the tax due if the child subsequently disposes of the site to anyone other than a spouse without having built a dwelling and lived in it for three years. If the site is very valuable or if there have been previous substantial gifts the child may be liable for Capital Acquisitions Tax on the gift — see page 273. But where a liability to both Capital Gains and Capital Acquisitions Tax arise on the same transaction, one is offset against the other.

- Bonuses on Post Office or State savings schemes and gains from the disposal of Government stocks.

- Gains from life assurance policies or deferred annuities.

- Gains from the disposal of a movable tangible asset worth €2,540 or less when sold.

- Gains on assets with a predictable life of under 50 years — a car, livestock etc.

- Gains from the disposal on retirement of a farm or business to a member of one's family — see below.

- Winnings from lotteries, betting etc.

Business assets

There are also special concessions for business assets passing to a child on the retirement of a parent. Business assets which have been held for 10 years by an individual aged over 55 may be passed to a natural or adopted child without any liability for Capital Gains Tax. Child, in this case, includes not only sons and daughters but also nephews or nieces who have worked full-time in the business for at least the previous five years. The child has to retain ownership of the assets for at least six years. Shares in a family business may also qualify for this concession if the person selling them or passing them on was a full-time director of the company for at least 10 years including five years as a full-time working director.

Capital Gains Tax is payable on a self-assessment basis. From 2009 the payment dates will be October 31 and mid-December

Where the transfer is to someone other than a child the concessions are less generous. The seller has to be over 55 and no tax is payable provided the consideration is less than €750,000 (€500,000 in 2006). Where the sale is for more than €750,000, the maximum tax payable is set at half the proceeds from the sale minus €750,000.

There is no Capital Gains Tax payable on transfers between spouses. The transfer of assets on the death of the owner is

■ The following is based on an asset acquired for €4,000 during the tax year 1979/80 and sold in July, 2009 for €30,000. There were selling expenses of €600. Indexation relief applies only up until December 31, 2002. The purchase price is adjusted upwards to take account of inflation between 1979 and that date. The relevant Revenue index number is 3.742. If the value of the asset simply rose in line with inflation it would have risen in value by 3.742 times. There is a list of index numbers on page 271. It is assumed that no other capital gains were made in the year.

Selling price	**€30,000**	
Value on 31/12/2002	€24,000	
Gain since 31/12/2002		**€6,000**
Adjusted purchase price (€4,000 x 3.742)	€14,968	
Capital gain from 1979 to 31/12/2002 (€24,000-€14,968)		**€9,032**
Total capital gain		**€15,032**
Less selling expenses		€600
Less annual exemption		€1,270
Taxable gain		**€13,162**
Tax payable (at 25 per cent)	**€3,290**	

not a disposal for tax purposes so no Capital Gains Tax liability arises. The person inheriting the assets is deemed to have acquired them at their market value on the date of the inheritance.

Payment of Capital Gains Tax is made on a self assessment basis. Up to, and including 2008, the tax due on any gains made between January 1 and September 30 each year was due by October 31 in the same year. The tax on gains made between October 1 and December 31 were due by the following January 31.

From 2009 onwards, tax on gains made between January 1 and November 30 will be paid in mid-December while tax on gains made during December will be paid by October 31, the following year.

Leaving the country

An anti avoidance measure applies, in respect of disposals after December 4, 2002, to the sale of business assets where the individual owns at least a 5% stake in the company. If, in those circumstances, the individual leaves Ireland but becomes resident here again within five years, the disposal of the assets is deemed to have taken place before he or she left the country and the proceeds are liable for tax in Ireland.

Inheritance and gift taxes

Capital Acquisitions Tax is charged on the value of gifts and inheritances but only if the value goes above certain thresholds. It is the recipient who is liable for the tax and the threshold applied depends on his or her relationship with the donor. There are three thresholds. All gifts and inheritances taken after December 5, 1991 are added together to decide whether one or other of the threshold levels has been reached. The thresholds were reduced with effect from November 20, 2009 and the rate increased from 20% to 22%. It was subsequently increased to 25% in respect of gifts or inheritances taken on or after April 8, 2009.

A foster child is entitled to the benefit of the same tax-free threshold as natural or adopted children provided he or she has been cared for, maintained by and resided with the foster parent for a successive period of five years while under the age of 18. The thresholds move up each year in line with inflation.

For details of earlier thresholds and rates see page 334. In deciding whether or not a threshold has been reached, only those gifts and inheritance from the relevant class of donor are taken into account. So a person can receive €521,208 from a parent, a total of €52,121 from uncles and aunts and a further €26,060 from more distant relatives before becoming liable for tax. As outlined above all gifts and inheritances taken after December 5, 1991 are taken into account. Gifts of up to €3,000 a year from any single donor are ignored for tax purposes.

CAT on family businesses

Concessions on the transfer of agricultural and business assets, by way of gift or inheritance, have been greatly extended in recent years and since January 23, 1997 the value of such assets is reduced by 90% for tax purposes subject to certain conditions.

It's a very valuable concession. The main condition with regard to business assets is that they are held by the recipient for at least 10 years after the transfer. If this requirement is breached within six years all of the tax concession is clawed back. If it is breached between six and 10 years the relief is reduced and the difference clawed back. But the clawback is limited to the additional relief granted under the 2007 and 2008 budgets.

The business concerned must be carried on wholly or mainly within the State but the definition of business assets is quite wide ranging. It includes property consisting of a business or an interest in a business; unquoted shares or securities of an Irish company subject to some restrictions; quoted shares or securities in an Irish company which were owned by the disponer before they became quoted; buildings, land and machinery owned by the disponer but used by a company controlled by him or her, or else used by a partnership in which he or she was a partner. Businesses whose sole or main business is dealing in land, shares, securities etc. are not covered by the concession.

Capital Acquisition Tax thresholds

■ Capital Acquisition Tax is charged on inheritances and gifts at a standard rate of 25%. The threshold below which no tax is payable depends on the relationship of the donor to the recipient. Gifts and inheritance received after December 5, 1991 are combined in calculating if a threshold has been breached. The rate was 22% between November 11, 2008 and April 7, 2009 and 20% before November 2008

RELATIONSHIP TO DONOR	From 1/1/09 to 7/4/09	From 8/4/09
Child, or the minor child of a deceased child. Also from child to parent but only for inheritance tax.	€542,544	€434,000
Brother, sister, child of brother or sister or lineal descendant other than a child, or the minor child of a deceased child.	€54,254	€43,400
If none of the above.	€27,127	€21,700

The business assets on which the concession is claimed must have been owned by the disponer or his/her spouse for at least five years prior to the transfer in the case of a gift, or for at least two years where the transfer results from the death of the disponer. So the business assets don't need to have been in the family for very long to qualify for the relief.

Agricultural assets

Concessions on the valuation of agricultural assets have been a feature of Capital Acquisitions Tax since it was first introduced. They have been greatly extended in recent years in line with similar concessions which now apply to business assets outside of farming. Subject, as always, to some conditions, agricultural assets are valued at only 10% of their true market value in calculating liability for Capital Acquisitions Tax. That 90% reduction has applied since January 23, 1997. The reduction applies to farm assets transferred to a "farmer". The definition of farmer is important as is the definition of farm assets. Another important factor may be the "valuation date" for an inheritance i.e. the date on which the transfer is deemed to take place and on which the assets are valued.

Farm assets include: farm land, buildings and woodland, machinery, livestock and bloodstock. The value of Single Farm Payment entitlements are included from 2006. Money may also qualify so long as the transfer is conditional on it being invested into qualifying agricultural property and that that condition is met within two years. That latter concession widens the availability of the relief considerably. The recipient doesn't have to have ever been a real farmer or even to have owned farm assets.

A "farmer" in this context doesn't even have to know the difference between a bull and a cow or be able to tell the difference between wheat and barley or silage and slurry. The sole requirement is that at least 80% of his or her assets are farm assets. That requirement is measured after getting the inheritance or gift, or after complying with a requirement to buy such assets. Since 2007 the value of an off-farm residence is calculated net of any outstanding borrowings on the property.

A "farmer" in this context doesn't even have to know the difference between a bull and a cow

It is not too difficult to ensure that all the necessary conditions are complied with. But it is also all too easy to fail some of the tests through a lack of adequate planning. However farmers may opt to be assessed for the tax either under the business relief rules or the agricultural relief rules whichever is more beneficial. As with business assets the agricultural assets transferred must be held for at least six years to avoid a claw back of the concessions. If the assets are disposed of, and not replaced, after six but before 10 years there is a partial clawback. After 10 years there is no clawback.

Tax can also be reduced by ensuring that the maximum possible proportion of the assets being transferred consist of farm assets at the time of the gift or on the valuation date used for inheritance tax purposes. Crops in the ground are farm assets. Crops lifted are not. In the same way livestock are farm assets. The cash from their sale is not. Other factors to consider are outlined on page 273. There are such a wide range of factors involved that careful planning is essential and professional advice is advisable.

Homes are exempt provided the recipient has lived in it for the previous three years and doesn't own any other residential property

There is a further concession in respect of business property or shares in a company left or given to the child of a brother or sister. If the nephew or niece has spent five years working in the donor's business, the tax liability is calculated as if he or she were a child of the donor. The requirement is that the nephew or niece have worked at least 24 hours a week at a place where the business is carried out, or a lower 15 hours a week where there are no employees other than the person leaving the inheritance, or making the gift (the disponer), his or her spouse, and the recipient.

Private residences have been exempt from CAT since December 1999 subject to certain conditions. It must be the principal private residence of the disponer and/or the recipient and the recipient must have been living there for the three years prior to the transfer and not have an interest in any other residential property. The recipient must continue to live in the property for six years after the transfer.

Other exemptions

The owners of heritage houses or gardens can avoid Capital Acquisitions Tax liability on a transfer by gift or inheritance by allowing limited public access. The house has to be open for 60 days a year including a minimum of 40 days during the summer. Full details of opening hours and admission prices must be notified to Fáilte Ireland before January 1 each year.

A similar exemption from CAT applies to other assets of national, scientific, historic or artistic interest. This includes works of art, scientific collections, and libraries. In all cases the tax exemption may be lost if the assets are disposed of within six years of being transferred.

Other assets which are exempt from CAT include: the first €3,000 received by way of gift from any one disponer in any tax year; charitable gifts or inheritance; pension and death benefits payable to an employee; certain compensation payments; reasonable payments received from a family member and used for support, maintenance or education; prizes and lottery winnings; and, of course, the proceeds of qualifying insurance policies taken out with a view to paying eventual CAT liabilities.

14 Some ways to reduce your tax liability

Blessed is he who expects nothing, for he shall never be disappointed
— Jonathan Swift

There is nothing that can be done to alter your basic tax credits and reliefs but it is possible to reduce your tax bill by making use of the many concessions and incentives available within our complicated tax system. It is not only the self-employed who can make use of these legal tax avoidance measures. At least some of them are available to the ordinary PAYE payer as well.

Many tax reliefs go unclaimed either because of a lack of knowledge or just plain inertia

The most obvious way to reduce your tax bill is to ensure that you are claiming all the reliefs to which you are entitled A lot of reliefs go unclaimed. Have a look at the panel on page 249. You may also be able to get some of your income tax free. Options range from subsidised canteen meals to leisure and childcare facilities provided by an employer. Those are outlined on page 243. This chapter details a number of other ways of reducing your tax liability in addition to detailing the tax position for some specific groups — such as separated couples — where good management can reduce your tax liability.

Employing your child or spouse

Self-employed people may be able to cut their family tax bills by formally paying their children and/or a spouse for work done in the business. In small family businesses it is not unusual for children and a spouse to do a significant amount of work. This is particularly true of retail businesses or farms. But the type of business does not matter.

The tax saving in the case of a child arises from the fact that any individual can earn up to €18,300 a year free of tax. The annual figure takes account of only the personal and employee tax credits. In the case of a spouse the saving can arise from the fact that a two income couple benefits from an extra €27,400 standard rate tax band – €72,800 instead of the €45,400 that applies to a single income couple. So a self-employed couple with an income of over €45,400 can benefit from having two earnings. More about that later but first the potential tax saving from employing a child.

Employing your child

A child can be paid up to €18,300 a year from the family business and not be liable for tax. If that payment reduces the parent's taxable income by that amount, the family's overall position has improved. The child can get the money free of tax while the parent would have had to pay tax at his or her highest marginal rate.

That is how the tax advantage arises, but remember that the child must be genuinely doing the work for which he or she is paid. And there are other factors to be considered. It is necessary for the proprietor of the business — the father or mother in this case — to register as an employer for PAYE and PRSI purposes. And it may be necessary to pay PRSI on the wages paid to the child — even though the income is too small to be liable for tax. These requirements need not be as onerous as they might seem. In most cases, there will be very little paperwork after the initial registration.

There is no clear cut guideline on liability for PRSI payments. In some cases, PRSI may be payable on the money

> A child who works in a family firm is entitled to get a wage from it and can earn up to €18,300 tax free

paid to the child but, if it is, there could be an eventual benefit in the form of unemployment and pay related payments if you cease employing the child. The final decision rests with the Department of Social Welfare but it does not spell out in detail just who is liable for PRSI at the various rates. The following, however, is an outline of the factors it takes into account in making its decisions.

If the work is full time and there is a written or implied contract of employment, then the employee is liable for PRSI at the full rate. In deciding whether an implied contract exists, the Department will take account of whether there are fixed hours involved and whether there is a fixed wage or salary.

A son living on a farm and helping his father is unlikely to be considered to have a contract of employment for instance. In this case the son would be classified as a Class K contributor and might be liable to pay the health levy. But it is not payable if the weekly income is less than €500. Anyone earning less than tha is exempt from the health levy. The income levy would be payable on the income whether it was kept by the parent or paid to the child. Indeed, depending on the level of income, the parent might be paying it at a higher rate.

Where a child is employed in a family business, the work is likely to be part-time and the question of whether there is a contract of employment or not may not be relevant. There are two classes of PRSI which may apply. Class M applies to employees under 16 years of age — they pay no PRSI. Close relatives working in a family business or farm are exempt from the requirements of the Protection of Young Persons (Employment) Act 1996 provided the health and safety of the young person is not put at risk.

That exception apart, the general minimum age for a regular job is 16 but a 14-year-old may be employed on light work outside of school term-time subject to a maximum of 35 hours a week on holiday work or 40 hours on work experience. A 15-year-old may be employed for eight hours a week during school-term. Class J may apply to children over 16 earning less than €38 a week. In this case, the employer pays 0.5 per cent on all income.

Anyone intending to employ someone at more than €8 a week or €36 a month must register as an employer. You write to your local tax office for a form CC151. Once completed, the taxman will take it from there. It is not too complicated and the savings can be worthwhile.

Employing a spouse

There is no tax advantage in a PAYE taxpayer employing a spouse, as a housekeeper for instance, since the wages paid would have to come out of the after-tax income of the taxpayer. The couple could end up paying more tax. But a self-employed taxpayer may be able to reduce their combined income tax liability by formally employing his or her spouse. This wasn't the case before the part-individualisation of tax bands so that while many spouses did do some work in their partner's businesses there was no tax advantage in formally adding them to the payroll. That is no longer the case.

The spouse must, of course, be actually working in the business and, to get any tax benefit if he or she has an existing income, it must be less than €27,400. The joint income of the couple needs to be at least €45,400. The maximum tax saving is €5,754.

This potential saving arises from the fact that a two income family can benefit from a €72,800 standard rate band as opposed to the €45,400 band available to a single income family. To benefit from the full €72,800 band each spouse needs to have an income of at least €27,400 since no one spouse can benefit from a standard rate band in excess of €45,400.

Let's have a look at an example. Tom is a self-employed businessman earning €80,000 a year. His wife is not formally employed but she does a fair amount of office work, keeping books, answering phones etc. If Tom doesn't employ his wife, his income tax liability works out as follows:

Taxable Income	€80,000
€45,400 at 20c in €	€9,080
€34,600 at 41c in €	€14,186
Total Tax	**€23,266**

That liability will be reduced as a result of personal tax credits etc. but they are the same in each case so they can be ignored for the sake of the example.

If Tom formally employs his wife and pays her €25,000 the tax works out as follows:

Tom		Mary	
Taxable income	€55,000	Taxable income	€25,000
€45,400 at 20c	€9,080	€25,000 at 20c	€5,000
€9,600 at 41c	€3,936		
Total Tax	**€13,016**		**€5,000**

That's a grand total of €18,016 – a saving of €5,250 on the situation that would apply if Mary wasn't formally employed. That saving would be partially eroded – to the tune of €900 – if Tom and Mary were entitled to the home working spouse's allowance. They can't claim that as a two-income couple.

There is possibly no additional PRSI implication. Employed spouses come under Class K where the only payment is the Health Levy and anyone on less than €500 a week is exempt. There could be a small saving there since Tom would be paying the 2% levy on the top slice of his income. So if he kept the €25,000 he'd be paying the levy whereas in Mary's hands it is likely to be exempt. The 1% levy applies equally in either case.

Tax and marriage

Married couples can opt to be taxed as two single people, but unfortunately there is seldom, if ever, any monetary advantage in so doing unless they are legally separated. There are, in fact, three options facing two income married couples. If they do nothing, they will be automatically taken to have opted for Joint Assessment. They are treated as a single unit for income tax. The second alternative, Separate Assessment, is a variant of that. The couple is still treated as a single taxable unit but is able to arrange a more equal sharing of their joint tax burden. The third alternative, Single Assessment, is to opt to be treated as two single individuals.

Let's look at each of the options in more detail.

Joint assessment

This is how most married couples are taxed. The highest earner will automatically get the benefit of the bulk of the couple's joint tax free allowances. The lower earning spouse will normally only get his or her own PAYE credit - €1,830. That only applies, of course, if the lower earning spouse is wage earning and not working in the family company.

Under joint assessment, the couple is still legally taxed as one unit. And indeed either spouse can be nominated as the accountable person for tax purposes. The important point is that concessions not used by one spouse can be transferred to the other. This is the important point. The true legal liability for tax is worked out at the end of a tax year by way of a balancing statement which combines the two incomes.

If there is a wide difference between the two incomes it is possible that the PAYE system will result in too much tax being collected during the year. But it will be refunded at the end of the year, when the balancing statement is made out. The refunds are allocated between the spouses in proportion to the tax paid by each.

Balancing statements are not prepared automatically so two income families, in particular, should do a rough calculation each year to see that they are not being overtaxed. If they are, tax returns should be speedily prepared and a balancing statement asked for.

Separate assessment

This is only a variation on the joint assessment option. Either spouse can opt for it provided they notify the tax office before April 1, in the year of assessment. Separate assessment then continues until the tax office is told otherwise by the spouse who first opted for it.

The total tax liability of the couple is not reduced in any way by separate assessment but most credits are evenly split between them. Personal, age and blind persons' credits are evenly divided while other credits may be granted to the individual bearing the cost.

The important point is that any credits unused by one person can be passed back to the other. And the same is true for unused tax bands. So if the husband has moved into the 41c tax band while the wife still has not used up all of her 20c band, there is no loss. It will be sorted out when a balancing statement is prepared at the end of the year and a refund given. But it should be possible to avoid being overtaxed during the year by dividing the credits up broadly in proportion to each person's income.

This transferability does not apply to the income levy thresholds. A couple's liability is the same no matter what form of income tax assessment they opt for.

Separate assessment is the ideal option for couples on dissimilar incomes since it allows them to split their tax credits fairly between them. Under ordinary joint assessment, a low earner can very often find his or her income very heavily taxed since the higher earning spouse is getting the benefit of most of the tax credits. Separate assessment will not reduce their joint tax bill but it can ensure that the tax burden is more proportional to the couple's individual income levels during the year.

This is where the couple decide to be treated exactly as if they were two single people for tax purposes. Their tax liabilities are kept entirely separate. In general, there is no financial advantage to be gained by opting for single assessment. If their incomes are about equal, the joint tax bill of a couple opting for single assessment may be no higher than if they opted for joint or separate assessment. But if one of their incomes is considerably higher than the other, they could end up with a higher tax bill because one spouse cannot pass on the benefit of unused credits or standard rate band to the other. Either spouse can serve notice on the taxman for single assessment at any time during the tax year. Once served, the notice is applied to that year and all subsequent years until it is withdrawn. Only the person who served the notice can withdraw it.

Separated couples ▌

Undoubtedly reflecting the growing number of couples who are separating or getting divorced, the Revenue Commissioners recently published an explanatory booklet on "What to do about tax when you separate". It's a complicated area and there are plenty of choices to make. Agreeing on the right one can leave the couple jointly better off. It can be well worthwhile doing the sums, getting advice if necessary and then reaching agreement with your estranged spouse.

The Revenue have adopted a broad definition of separation. A couple is deemed to have separated if they are divorced, legally separated or even if they have separated in what the Revenue describe as "such circumstances that the separation is likely to be permanent." Exactly what that means is not clear but presumably decisions are made on a case-by-case basis.

Also described as separated are couples who have obtained a civil annulment but, unlike other separated couples, they cannot opt to continue being treated as a married couple for tax purposes. Legally separated and even divorced couples can. Indeed the option is available to any separated couple who are both resident in the country provided neither has remarried or has to make legally binding maintenance payments. There can be an advantage in being taxed as a married couple but both spouses must agree to adopt that option. There are other options and unfortunately there can be no hard and fast rule as to which is best. What is best for one couple may not be for another. It depends on individual circumstances. It can also depend on the couple jointly opting for the best alternative. It's not good enough for one to make the choice. They both have to.

Even divorced couples can opt to be treated as married for tax purposes

Continuing to be taxed as a married couple may be as good an option as any if one spouse has no earnings. The earning spouse gets the benefit of all the tax allowances and rate bands available to a married couple and simply makes maintenance payments out of net income. The non-earning spouse has no tax liability on those maintenance payments.

A separated couple can, in some circumstances, qualify for more tax reliefs than a couple living together.

If both spouses are earning, the situation is a bit more complicated. Normally in such a case the spouse earning the most money enjoys the bulk of the tax allowances so the lower earning spouse can lose out if nothing is done. The ideal first step would be to split the tax allowances and bands in a more equitable manner between the two. Provided that they are both resident in the State they can agree to opt for separate assessment. They are still considered to be a married couple for tax purposes but the tax allowances and low rate tax band are split more equitably between them.

Separated couples may both be able to claim one-parent family tax credits

Any couple can have that done. It's generally a good idea since it means that the lower earning spouse isn't left paying an unequal share of the couple's tax burden. Since they are still a married couple, for tax purposes, there are no tax implications for any payments such as maintenance from one to the other. More commonly, a separated couple will opt to be treated as two single individuals for tax purposes. This is also an option for any married couple but there is no benefit for a couple living together and there may, indeed, be extra tax to pay because a low-earning spouse cannot then pass unused allowances or tax bands over to a higher earning spouse.

For a separated couple, however, it can make sense and be financially beneficial to be treated as two single individuals i.e. opting for single tax assessment. Their tax affairs become completely separated in line with the reality of their situation and legally enforceable maintenance payments become taxable in the hands of the recipient.

Let's suppose that under a court settlement a husband has to pay his wife €5,000 a year. He is allowed to deduct that €5,000 from his income for tax purposes. If he is paying tax at 41c in the euro that could save him €2,050 (5,000 times 41c). The money becomes taxable in the hands of the wife but depending on circumstances she may not be liable for tax. This doesn't apply to payments in respect of children.

A husband making maintenance payments may calculate that he would be better off foregoing the tax relief on the maintenance payments and getting the full married allowances instead. On single assessment he is only getting the benefit of a single person's tax allowances and bands. So he can gain but there are potential gains and losses for his wife. She would no longer be taxed on the maintenance payment but if she is getting a single parent's allowance she would lose it. Whether the gains outweigh the losses depend on each individual case.

Separated individuals may both be entitled to claim a one-parent family tax credit in respect of dependant children. The child must reside with the claimant for at least part of the tax year. But that could be as short as one night. To be eligible, the couple cannot be living together as man and wife.

There are extra tax benefits to be claimed in the year of separation provided the couple had not previously opted to be taxed as two single individuals. Once they meet that condition one spouse can claim the full married tax credit and tax band for the year while the other spouse gets the benefit of a single person's tax credit and tax band.

Share incentives

PAYE workers have few opportunities of getting tax-free income. Wages are automatically taxed and the tax definition of wages is wide. It includes practically all monies paid by an employer to an employee. Most non-cash benefits are taxable too. They are treated as benefits-in-kind and their cash value is liable to income tax. Examples are company cars and loans at preferential interest rates.

Tax-free profit sharing

But there are some benefits that can be provided tax-free by an employer. Some of these, including subsidised canteen meals and sporting and childcare facilities, are outlined in details on page 243 But the possibilities also include certain bonus payments paid under an approved profits sharing scheme. Companies have long believed in giving top managers an incentive to perform better by linking at least some of their pay to the profitability of the enterprise. The granting of share options is one of the ways of making the link, particularly for companies whose shares are quoted on the stock exchange. A share option is simply a right to buy shares at some time in the future at a price that's fixed when the option is granted. So if the shares go up in value the option holder is on to a winner.

Given the performance of stock markets in recent years, share options may not appear like a very valuable concession. But this may be the very time to look for them, perhaps in return for accepting pay restraint or more onerous working practices. Getting share options for such concessions is certainly better than getting nothing.

Getting share options in return for pay concessions is better than getting nothing

Such options need not be the preserve of top executives. There are special tax concessions available on share option schemes that are open to all employees in a firm subject to certain conditions. If the conditions are not met share options are taxed much the same as any other benefit in kind. If someone has a right to buy shares at €1 each and they are worth €1.50 each when the option was exercised the 50c gain is taxed as income, in most cases at the top rate since beneficiaries tend to be top earners. That tax is payable whether or not the shares are actually sold. If they are subsequently sold for a higher price then there may be an additional liability for Capital Gains Tax.

Those tax rules apply to share options granted under schemes that don't comply with the inclusive rules. But if the scheme does comply, no tax is payable when the options are exercised but when the shares are eventually sold capital gains tax of 20c in the euro is payable on the difference between the purchase price and the subsequent sale price. The shares must be held for at least three years after the option is exercised.

In order to benefit from this tax concession, at least 70% of the share options issued must be granted on similar terms to all employees. That doesn't mean that all workers have to get an equal number of options. The number can be linked to length of service or pay levels or some other criterion. Employees with less than three years service may be excluded. The other 30% of the options can be granted to "key" employees under whatever rules the company likes. So a small number of managers can still enjoy far greater benefits than the bulk of workers.

Apart altogether from granting share options, companies can simply give bonuses in the form of shares. They can be tax free up to an annual value of €12,700 provided certain other conditions are met. This is a benefit-in-kind which is not taxable. To be attractive, of course, the company should be quoted on the stock exchange so that the shares can be readily sold at some stage in the future. But they do have to be held for three years and for at least two years of that they must be held by trustees. After the two years, they can be passed on to individual workers and may be sold although there is some clawback of the tax concession.

It is possible to get up to €12,700 of your income tax free each year through an approved profit sharing scheme

The rules of the scheme must apply equally to all workers. The level of bonuses may be related to salary or years of service or both but those are the only criteria which can be used. Blue-eyed boys or green-eyed girls cannot get special treatment.

Whatever benefit employers get from operating profit sharing schemes must be doubled when the bonus comes in the form of shares. The total amount to be given out in shares may be linked in some way to profitability or productivity in the same way as any other bonus scheme. A worker may prefer to take the bonus in the form of cash. But in that case it is taxable. Those who take it in the form of shares get it tax free so long as they hold the shares for three years.

This profit sharing tax concession really requires the company's shares to be marketable

During those three years, and subsequently if they hold onto the shares, the workers have a direct interest in the performance of those shares on the stock exchange. So the employer has built in an initial incentive of a bonus scheme and an ongoing incentive in the form of share ownership. Obviously this type of profit-sharing scheme is of particular interest in companies whose shares are listed on the stock exchange, although many of those schemes are, in fact, operated by firms whose shares are quoted abroad rather than in Ireland.

SAYE

Save As You Earn (SAYE) schemes have been operated in Ireland for some years. A tax concession applies where workers are given options to buy shares at a discounted price and the money required, to eventually exercise the options is saved over a three or five year period. That may sound a bit complicated but it isn't. It works like this. The workers are given options to buy shares in the company at a fixed price. That price can be up to 25% below the current value of the shares. Those options can be exercised in three, five, or seven years time when, hopefully, the shares will be worth a lot more than the price fixed at the time that the option was given. If the shares haven't risen in price, then there is no need to exercise the option. So there is no chance of incurring a loss.

If the shares don't rise in price the options don't have to be exercised

As an adjunct to the share options, the workers involved agree to save a fixed amount each week or month out of their pay packages. That money comes out of their net pay i.e. after tax, and goes into a special fund. The only tax concession on the savings part of the deal is that the money in the fund grows tax-free – any interest or bonus earned is free of income tax and DIRT. SAYE schemes are obviously less attractive to workers than the bonus type scheme where up to €12,700 worth of shares a year can be given tax-free. Under the SAYE scheme, the shares have to be paid for albeit at what may be a bargain basement price. But they are likely to be more favoured by employers for the very reason that the shares aren't entirely free. The company should also benefit from a more motivated and involved workforce. To get Revenue approval, schemes must comply with a number of requirements.

- All workers with more than a minimum service must be invited to participate. Workers with more than three years service can't be excluded.

- The same rules must apply to all but they may provide for the level of share option granted to vary according to pay levels and/or length of service.

- The workers must contract to save at least €12.70 and at most €317 a month over a three or five-year period. The actual amount saved should be geared to provide about the right amount to pay for the shares when the options are exercised.

No income tax is payable either when the option is granted or when the shares are actually purchased. That might not seem like a concession at all, but remember that the worker will be getting shares worth more than the price paid. That's a benefit he's getting from his employer. Normally the difference between the price paid for the shares and their actual value would be treated as a benefit-in-kind and taxed as such. Suppose the worker has an option to buy 1,000 shares at €2 each. That was the price fixed at the time the options were granted. It is now three or five years later and the shares have trebled in value to €6. In exercising his option the worker will be paying €2,000 for the 1,000 shares that are now worth €6,000 on the stock market. He'll be making €4,000 on the deal. And that's tax free since it is not considered to be a benefit-in-kind.

But although there is no income tax liability, the worker may be liable for Capital Gains Tax when the shares are sold. The gain is calculated as the difference between the price the shares are sold for and the price actually paid. The first €1,270 of gain in any tax year is exempt. For details of Capital Gains Tax, see page 269.

If this worker sold his shares immediately after buying them he would be liable for tax on €2,730 (€4,000 minus the exemption of €1,270. The standard rate of Capital Gains Tax is 22% so the tax payable would be €600. Of course if the sale was spread over a number of years the tax could be avoided entirely. But tax or no tax, SAYE schemes effectively allow workers to share in any growth in their company's fortunes without taking any risk themselves. They have to save a regular amount but the savings are kept in a risk-free account and the option to buy the shares doesn't have to be exercised if the share price has gone down. The Revenue has prepared specimen rules and forms for use in these schemes. Copies can be obtained from your local tax office.

Relief on loans to buy shares

There are other ways of getting tax relief on buying shares. Tax relief can be claimed on the interest on loans raised to fund the purchase of shares in the company you work for. You need to be a full time director or employee. In the case of a private company you need only be a part-time director or employee.

Tax relief can be obtained on the interest on loans used to buy shares in the company you work for

But the company cannot be quoted on the stock exchange so the shares cannot be very marketable and that reduces the attractions somewhat. There are also restrictions relating to non-trading companies. But in the case of a private trading company there is no upper limit on the relief which may be obtained on loans used to buy shares in it. In the case of a non-private company, there is an upper limit of €3,809 in tax relief per individual. This limit is in addition to any tax relief on mortgage interest.

Business Expansion Scheme

There is another share incentive scheme — the Business Expansion Scheme — which allows tax relief on up to €150,000 used to buy shares in certain qualified companies. The concession is aimed at encouraging risk investment in small to medium sized ventures in manufacturing, traded services, and certain tourism and music projects. Traded services are ventures which have to compete in the international market place. The concession is also available on money invested in certain tourism ventures aimed at

■ Did you ever get that urge to quit your secure job and go out on your own, be your own boss, build your own business. It's a big step, not to be lightly taken, but there's a little extra incentive to help tip the decision. Leave the job, set up the business and the State will give you an income tax rebate of up to €246,000 to help finance your new venture. But you do have to take up full time work with the new company and you would need to have been paying a lot of tax to qualify for the maximum rebate. You can only reclaim tax that you have actually paid. The incentive is known as the Seed Capital Scheme. How does it work? Let's look at an example.

Tim is in his mid-30s, a production manager with a multinational company. He's on a very good income and his future is secure enough. Indeed one of the problems is that it's a bit too secure, predictable and certain. Tim's need for achievement is not being fully satisfied. He has identified a business opportunity in manufacturing and is confident that he has the skills to make it work. He has access to some capital but could do with a bit more. So how can the Seed Capital Scheme help him?.

Basically it can provide him with some capital. The more he can put up himself, the easier it is to borrow the rest. He can make a back-claim for tax relief extending over the past six years on up to a maximum of €600,000 invested in the new business. In essence that means that he can get back all of the tax he paid on up to €100,000 of income in each of those years. He has been paying tax at the top rate of 41% on the top slice of his income and that top slice has been bigger than €100,000 a year. So his claim is for a rebate of €41,000 for each year, indeed slightly higher in the earlier years in which he paid tax at the old top rate of 42%.

Had he been earning less, his rebate might be less. But he's entitled to the maximum provided he invests €600,000 in the business. The income tax rebate doesn't exclude him from benefiting from other State incentives such as grants and employment incentives. Tim's venture is in manufacturing but it could equally well be in a service open to international competition; tourism; a trading operation selling Irish goods abroad; certain shipping ventures; some research and development activities; and even the cultivation of crops in greenhouses.

The basic requirement is that the would-be entrepreneur is setting up a new business having been employed. The incentive isn't available to an existing businessman moving into a new venture. To ensure that this requirement is met, the condition is that no more than half of the claimant's income subject to a maximum of €19,050 should have come from non-employment sources during the three years prior to the first investment being made. Each claimant must own at least 15% of the venture.

bringing tourists from abroad. While investments in hotels, guest-houses, and self-catering accommodation are excluded, that still leaves a wide range of possibilities. In the music sector, the concession covers projects involving the production, marketing and promotion of new artist's studio recordings and associated videos.

Subject to a cap of €2 million on the total investment in a project and no more than €1.5 million in any one year, an individual can get tax relief on up to €150,000 a year used to buy shares under the scheme. The investor buys shares in the venture and gets full tax relief on that investment. So for every €1 put in, a top rate tax payer gets a tax rebate of 41c. But the shares have to be held for at least five years. Normally, there is an exit mechanism put in place to guarantee that there is someone there to buy the shares at the end of the five years. There should also be some agreed process for valuing the shares at that stage. Guarantees are not allowed. Investors have to accept a risk. But provided the shares are really worth whatever is paid for them initially, the tax relief provides a sizeable cushion against loss.

The concession is confined to businesses that meet the EU's definition of small and medium sized enterprises (SMEs). No more than 25% of the voting shares in the enterprise can be held either solely or jointly by enterprises that are not themselves SMEs. Enterprises with turnover of up to €40 million and balance sheet totals of up to €43 million may be defined as SMEs for the purposes of this concession.

Investors do need to take care. If you want to make use of them you have three options.

- Invest in a fund that will in turn invest your money in a number of BES projects thereby spreading the risk.

- Invest in a single project run by someone else.

- Invest in your own project.

The second option is obviously the most risky. The shares you buy, either directly or through an investment fund, cannot be quoted on any stock exchange. So you have no easy way of judging exactly what they are worth. There is no market price. Neither will you have any great idea of future prospects. And, most importantly, there may be no guarantee that you will be able to dispose of the shares in the future.

You may get some basic accounts, or you may not. Either way you will not be able to do the type of detailed analysis necessary to really value the shares or to evaluate the prospects of the venture during the five years for which you have to hold the shares if the tax relief is not to be clawed back. The trick is to reduce the risk as much as possible. One way is to opt for option one above and have your investment spread over a number of different ventures and relying on reliable fund managers to value the initial shares that they buy.

But remember that promoters usually charge a 3% fee up front and may have a conflict of interest since they collect fees from the companies in which they invest. Also not all funds have guaranteed exit mechanisms. Be wary of any fund that doesn't. The tax relief works like this: Someone buying shares worth €10,000 at a real cost, after tax relief, of €5,900 will be doing alright if he or she can sell those shares at the initial €10,000 at the end of the five years. A real initial investment of €5,900 will have grown to €10,000. That is a compound return of 10% a year after allowing for an initial set-up commission of 3%.

> **Using BES you can get tax relief on money invested in producing and marketing the recordings of new artists**

As well as the commission there is another initial cost in that it may take up to a year to get the tax rebate. The investor, in our example, has to put up the €10,000 and has to wait to get the €4,100 rebate or reduction in his or her tax bill. So there is a loss of interest on that money. Investing in a fund rather than a single project helps to spread the risk. The shares bought have, by the nature of the scheme, to be in relatively small enterprises. While they have the potential to grow rapidly, they also have the potential to fail miserably.

If things go well, and the return is big enough, there may be a liability for Capital Gains Tax but it is the full investment, before tax relief, which is taken into account as the purchase price of the shares. So, in our example, the purchase price is €10,000 not the actual post tax relief cost of €5,900. The first €1,270 of capital gains realised by an individual in any one year is tax free so providing the net return on the investment does not exceed €11,270 on the initial real investment of €5,900, there would be no liability for Capital Gains Tax on present rules. Indeed a larger tax free gain would be possible given that the initial purchase price is adjusted upwards in line with inflation.

A wide range of tourism projects can qualify for BES tax relief

There is an even better use for the BES concession. That is to start your own venture. This is possibly easier in the tourism area than any other. The investment cannot just be in accommodation — that loophole which allowed people to set up tourism ventures comprising houses in Dublin 4 has been closed off. But it still leaves a lot of opportunities, particularly for people in rural areas. Remember an investment of €100,000 in a venture will only cost €59,000 after tax relief at the top rate. Spread that over say four investors and the sums involved need not be prohibitive. It is possible to start with a relatively small project. The possibilities are legion. They include the following:

- Caravan and camping sites

- Holiday hostels

- Holiday camps

- Pleasure boat hire

- Horse-drawn caravan hire

- Equestrian centre services

- Sailing, yachting, marina services

- Sub-aqua centre services

- Heritage houses, castles, gardens

- Game fishing services

- Chauffeur drive for tourists

- Outdoor activity centres

- Tourism guide agencies

- Tour coach services

The project must be aimed at attracting tourists from abroad and must have a three year marketing plan approved by Fáilte Ireland. There are upper limits on the amount of the total investment which goes on land and buildings. It is up to 75% in the case of hostels, holiday camps etc; 70% in the case of caravan and camping sites and equestrian centres; 65% in the case of marina services; and 50% for most other projects. Further information can be obtained from Fáilte Ireland, Baggot Street Bridge, Dublin 4. The scheme is ideally suited to individuals or groups who are already paying high amounts of income tax. They can get the project up and running while retaining their jobs but reducing their tax bills.

A variant of the BES scheme, known as the Seed Capital Scheme, allows for tax relief on up to €600,000 invested in a new project. Under this scheme the relief comes by way of a refund of tax previously paid. Someone who has left a job and takes up full-time employment with the new company can claim back the tax they paid over the previous six years against their investment in the venture. See page 293 for details.

The best use of the BES tax incentive is to set up your own venture

Tax breaks for relatives and carers

Many elderly people are not liable for tax simply because their incomes are too small. Tax exemption limits apply to the over 65s. In 2009 a couple, either of whom is over 65, can have an income of up to €40,000 before coming into the tax net. That remains the same in 2010. While in general it is good to be exempt from tax, there are drawbacks such as not being able to claim any tax reliefs such as those on medical expenses.

Those over 70 are no longer automatically entitled to a medical card since January 1, 2009 but even if they have medical cards they can be faced with nursing care expenses that are not covered and anyone can incur very heavy medical expenses. If the pensioners involved are not liable for tax, they obviously can't claim back the tax relief and even if they can, the relief is only available from January 2010, at the standard rate of tax. But there are other ways in which tax relief, at the top rate, can be effectively transferred to children or other relatives who provide some financial help to the elderly people. There are three possible options, one of which is being closed off.

- Making use of special carer's tax allowance.

- Making payments under a deed of covenant.

The Special Carer's Allowance provides tax relief on the cost of employing a carer to look after a person who is permanently incapacitated by old age or infirmity. The tax allowance, subject to a maximum of €50,000 a year, can be claimed by the taxpayer, his or her spouse or by other family members who contribute to the cost. The maximum claim is €50,000 but it can be spread among a number of claimants. The relief is allowed at the claimant's top rate of tax so it can be worth up to €20,500 (41% of €50,000) a year in saved tax. It can be claimed in respect of wages and other costs such as expenses and employer's PRSI. It may not be necessary to register as an employer but, if it is, the Revenue will let you know. It's an easy enough process.

Tax relief is, of course, allowed on medical expenses including nursing home costs but since January 1, 2009 the relief is only available at the standard rate. It continued to be allowed at the top-rate during 2009 on nursing home costs but the standard rating applies to all medical expenses from Januatu 1, 2010. The relief can be claimed by the person availing of the care or by any relative who is paying or contributing to the cost. See page 234.

Another way for children to get tax relief on contributions made to a parent's healthcare, is by making the payments under covenant. In this way, it may be possible to get tax relief at the top rate. These can be used irrespective of what the money is finally used for. And can provide some tax relief where anyone makes a regular payment to a person over 65 or to an incapacitated person of any age provided the recipient has unused tax credits. A covenant is simply a legal undertaking to make payments to someone else. In order to qualify for tax relief, the payments must be capable of lasting for at least six years.

> **A child can give a parent €1,000 at an cost of only €590**

Let's assume, for example, that a son wants to give €1,000 a year to a parent. Other brothers and sisters could, of course, do the same thing providing the total transfer doesn't push the parent into the tax net. The son makes out a covenant and pays €800 to the parent. The parent gets the other €200 by way of a tax rebate while the son also gets an additional tax relief of €210. The cost to the son is only €590 while his parent gets the benefit of €1,000. The logic behind this is relatively simple although you do not have to understand it to benefit from it. Because the son has entered into a legal undertaking to pass the money to the parent, the taxman considers the €1,000 to be the parent's rather than his. But he has already paid €410 tax on the €1,000. That tax is returned. The mechanics of the process dictate that €210 goes back to the son and €200 to the parent.

There are some points to watch. Covenants may provide no saving if a parent is in receipt of some means-tested benefit since the covenanted income will be treated as means. The covenant should include a clause allowing it to be ended on the say so of a third party e.g. a trusted friend. This is just a precaution. A covenant can always be ended by the mutual consent of the parties but circumstances could arise where it is desirable to end it for one reason or another and the mutual consent cannot be obtained. For instance, the covenant could, in some circumstances, prevent the parent from

■ There is no need to get a solicitor to draw up a covenant. Simply copy the wording below and adjust it as appropriate with the relevant details

I ....(name) of

....(address)

covenant to pay my father/mother ....(name)

of ....(address)

an amount which after the deduction of standard rate tax amounts to € ....(sum)

each year for seven years or during our joint lives or until (name of third party) says the covenant should end the first payment to be made during December 2010.

Signed, sealed and delivered by ....(name)

in the present of ....(witness's name, address and occupation)

....(Date)

claiming some means-tested benefit. There is nothing to stop the parent making gifts of money to his or her children, even returning the covenanted money provided that there is no prior understanding that that would be done.

Making a covenant

The covenant can be drawn up using the wording above. You don't need a solicitor. You can get the wording typed out or even write it out filling in the blanks as appropriate. The person making the covenant should also get a tax form R185 from his or her local tax office. It is a single page requiring very little information such as PPS number and place of employment or source of income. That completed form together with the signed covenant and, of course, the money is given to the parent. The parent can get a tax reclaim form from a local tax office or by phoning the special Revenue Commissioner's 24 hour phone number at LoCall 1890 306706. That form together with a copy of the covenant, form R185 and some evidence of the payment (a photocopy of the cheque or a bank statement showing the deposit) is then returned to the tax office.

Your shortcut to a quick & easy money makeover

This isn't a book designed to be read from cover to cover. It's for dipping into for information and advice on personal finance matters that can save, or make, you money. This section is an exception. It is designed to be read from start to finish to help you undertake a money makeover, reviewing past financial decisions, setting goals and mapping out the path towards achieving them. Financial decisions, once made, are all too seldom reviewed, yet the financial environment is constantly evolving while personal circumstances change. Ideally you should be constantly evaluating the appropriateness of past decisions in the light of these changes. But an occasional review is better than nothing. Remember that even if you initially picked the right bank, mortgage lender, insurance company or investment outlets, they may no longer be the best choice.

There's money to be made, or saved, by sitting down and reading this section on your own or with a partner. It suggests the questions that you should be asking yourself and the courses of action you should be taking. You'll find more information on the various topics in the main body of the book.

In this section you'll find advice on

- **Quick fixes if your budget has become unbalanced**
- **Planning for the future**

    Identifying your goals,

    assessing where you are, and

    mapping a route to where you want to be.

℘ Getting started

Financial planning has become an essential part of modern living and it shouldn't be a daunting prospect. It's simply a matter of ensuring that you make the best use of your resources to achieve your personal goals. It's an on-going process that needs to take into account, not only changing personal circumstances, but also the ever-evolving financial environment. The need for such a review is not confined to those facing some financial difficulty. Everyone is likely to benefit from a money makeover.

It's basically a matter of evaluating past decisions in light of current circumstances and future prospects and then taking fresh decisions taking account of where you are and where you want to be.

℘ The first steps

- ☐ **Identify your goals.**
- ☐ **Assess your current financial position.**
- ☐ **Map a route from where you are to where you want to be.**

Set your own objectives depending on your personal circumstances and make-up.

There's a list of suggestions on the next page. The choice is yours. Take your pick but be as specific as possible.

Once you have set your goals you need to assess how realistic they are and how best to achieve them. Your objectives don't exist in isolation. Their achievement depends partly on the resources you can muster and partly on the decisions you make. In all cases, of course, you have to start from where you are now.

ଛଠ Setting out your goals

When setting objectives, it's important to be as specific as possible. It's not enough to simply decide that you should put some money aside for retirement. That's not a bad objective but it's likely to remain just that unless you put some flesh on the bones by outlining the sort of pension you would like to have and how much you are prepared to put aside. You need to go beyond drawing up a simple wish list.

The following are some possible goals that you might consider setting for yourself.

Short-term

- ☐ **Manage your day-to-day finances to better effect. You must start by drawing up a budget. When are you going to do it?**

- ☐ **Pay off short-term debt. How much and when?**

- ☐ **Save for a holiday or a special occasion. Set a target amount, for instance how much on each pay day?**

- ☐ **Provide adequate insurance cover for the family. Preview your existing cover and detail your requirements.**

- ☐ **Build up an emergency fund. Outline exactly how much and how you intend doing it.**

- ☐ **Make a will. Set a firm date for doing it.**

Medium-term

- ☐ **Buy a house. Save how much by when?**

- ☐ **Build up an investment fund. For what purpose? What's your target?**

- ☐ **Save for future needs, children's education etc. Set a target amount and a time scale.**

Long-term

- ☐ **Provide for retirement. Set a pension target and detail any shortcomings in your existing entitlements.**

✂ Where are you now?

Informed decisions can only be made on the basis of adequate information. So there is no alternative to drawing up a personal statement of affairs. That statement of affairs should include a balance sheet of assets and liabilities and also as detailed an income and expenditure budget as you can prepare. That may seem like a chore but it is one that can yield high dividends. The worksheets, starting on page 318 can be used as a guide.

Your balance sheet

List all your assets itemising the value of each and the income it is generating. Include items such as your house which could yield an income if you decided, for instance, to trade down to a smaller home.

It's nice listing your assets but it's just as important to list your liabilities. Include details of all outstanding loans, the repayments, interest rates and any early repayment penalties that may be applicable. Just gathering that information will help you pinpoint those loans that should get first priority, if and when you have any spare cash.

Planning is about making choices which should only be made on the basis of good information

Your income and expenditure budget

Detailing your income is easy enough. It's harder to itemise your spending. But you do really need to get an idea of where the money goes. You can adjust the worksheets to suit your own circumstances. The more detail you include, the easier it is to pinpoint those areas where spending patterns can be changed to best suit your goals. Once you have gathered the data, you can carry out your own financial audit covering:

- ☐ Savings and investments
- ☐ Borrowings
- ☐ Family protection
- ☐ Retirement planning
- ☐ Wills and inheritance planning

So let's look at the questions you need to ask yourself in each of these areas and the actions you may need to take.

Savings and investments

Saving is an essential element in achieving many financial goals. At its simplest, it only involves holding onto some money to meet the occasional expense that arises less regularly than pay days – a holiday, car insurance, even ESB or gas bills. That type of saving has more to do with the day-to-day management of money. The money is normally not at any risk and since the amounts are small, the rate of return doesn't really matter.

That's not the case, of course, with savings aimed at some longer-term objective such as providing a pension in retirement, saving the deposit for a house or paying for a child's education. Rates of return and risk are important considerations and there is a wide range of options from basic deposit accounts to investment funds. There is no definitive correct choice. It depends on individual circumstances, attitudes to risk and personal goals.

Saving is an essential element in achieving many financial goals including the ability to borrow

Whatever the goals, there is a need to consider:

Questions you should be asking yourself

- ☐ the provision of emergency funds,
- ☐ the scope for saving, and
- ☐ whether existing investments are yielding the best possible returns.

ᔓ Savings and investments 2

Ensuring that you have speedy access to financial resources is a reasonable first goal to have in the area of saving and investment. The need is to provide flexibility to take advantage of opportunities that may arise and it also provides security against running into financial difficulties in an emergency. Emergencies come in all shapes and sizes. There are the joyful ones like being invited to a wedding abroad or having your favourite team qualify for international competition. But there can be less happy events such as unexpected medical expenses, a cut in income or an unforeseen bill for major car repairs. This goal of having access to money when needed can be satisfied, to some extent, by having the ability to borrow by way of overdraft, term loan or by having a sufficiently flexible credit card limit.

☐ **Have you got an overdraft permission?**

☐ **Have you a good enough relationship with a bank to get one?**

☐ **Is your credit card limit adequate?**

Actions to take

✔ Save to build up an emergency fund.

✔ Ensure that some of your savings can be accessed reasonably quickly without penalty.

✔ Develop a good relationship with a bank to ensure speedy access to overdrafts and/or term loans.

✔ Get an increase in your credit card limit if you can be sure of using it only for short-term needs and not for getting into long-term debt.

&) Savings and investments 3

You can think of saving as the actual act of accumulating money. In the short term you may simply be building up a surplus in your bank account when your income exceeds your spending needs. Or you may be putting regular amounts into a formal savings plan such as an investment fund. There is a wide range of options and the boundary between saving and investment is far from clear cut.

? **Questions you should be asking yourself**

☐ What are you saving for?

☐ How much can you afford to save?

☐ Do you need access to your money?

☐ Are you getting the best rate of return consistent with your need for access?

☐ Have you too much, or not enough money, in relatively low yielding short-term savings?

Actions to take

✔ Specify targets for your savings in terms of amounts and timescales.

✔ Undertake regular reviews to ensure that you are getting the best rate of return.

ℰ Savings and investments 4

Your current mix of investments reflects a series of past decisions. They may have been the right decisions at the time but they need to be assessed in the light of your present circumstances, your future needs and changes in the financial environment. There is a need to regularly review your investments to ensure that you are getting the best possible return. If you have completed the worksheets starting on page 318 you have a list of investments, rates of return and some measure of the degree of risk involved in each.

Part of your assessment involves balancing your attitude to risk with the riskiness of your investments. It's important to consider both when making a decision on any investment option. It is very much an individual decision but it's a decision that should be taken in a considered way and not just left to a gut feeling.

In assessing each investment, the starting point has to be the present, not sometime in the past. In the case of a share, all that counts is the current price and future prospects. The price you bought at should have no place in the decision making. The share is currently worth a certain amount of money. If that money can yield a better return elsewhere then it should be switched. The loss has already been incurred even if it hasn't been realised.

If one of your objectives is saving for retirement then investing in a pension fund offers very distinct advantages, in particular the tax relief on contributions. So investing in a pension fund must be considered as one of your options. The restrictions on what can be done with the money built up in a personal pension fund or through additional voluntary contributions (AVCs) to a pension scheme have been greatly eased in recent years, adding to the attractions of such investments.

Questions you should be asking yourself

☐ **Examine each investment in the light of**

— **what you want from it,**

— **when you might have to cash it in,**

— **the prospects over that timeframe,**

— **its riskiness in the light of your current attitude to risk, and**

— **the alternatives.**

☐ Is your mix of personal use assets (house, holiday home, boat, caravan etc.) appropriate to your needs? Should you be thinking of converting them into investment assets by, for instance, selling or renting them?

☐ Are you making the best possible use of investment tax incentives such as those on pensions and some property investments?

Actions to take

✔ List all your investments.

✔ Assess each one as outlined above.

✔ Make the appropriate adjustments. If in doubt, take professional advice.

✔ Read Chapter 3, Page 40.

❧ Borrowing

Sensible borrowing can play a beneficial role in your financial planning. It's not a case of saving being good and borrowing being bad. Both have a part to play in managing your finances over time. There is a cost involved in borrowing, of course, but that can often be justified. The benefits can outweigh those costs. Borrowing can enable you to buy something now rather than having to wait until you have saved up the money. Whether or not that benefit offsets the interest paid on the loan is a matter of personal judgement. In some cases such as borrowing to buy a home, tax relief can reduce the real rate of interest payable.

Interest is not the only cost, of course. There is a reduction in financial flexibility if only because of the need to meet the repayments on the loan. But also if you have borrowed for one purpose, it reduces your ability to borrow for something else. There is a tendency not to review financial decisions once made. This can be particularly true of borrowing. Yet personal circumstances change, interest rates vary and the need for debt may diminish as other assets become available. So it is worthwhile doing an occasional check of outstanding loans.

The following are some of the factors you should consider

Questions you should be asking yourself

□ Are you paying over the odds on any of your loans? Are there savings to be made by switching lenders?

□ Have you got the optimum mix of loans in terms of interest payable and risk? Could you increase your mortgage, for instance, and pay off some more expensive loans. That's not a decision to be taken lightly since you are increasing the risk of losing your home in the event of default.

□ Are you relying too much on expensive credit card debt?

□ Have you spare cash that would be better used in reducing your debt?

□ What capacity have you got to borrow more? Could you use extra money to finance projects that would yield benefits more than enough to offset the cost?

Actions to take

✔ List details of all your loans.

✔ Check out the interest rates being charged by the competition.

✔ Work out the savings that could be achieved by switching, taking into account any penalties for early repayment. The bigger the loan the greater the potential. Switch if the savings justify it.

✔ If you are constantly in debt on your credit card get a term loan to pay it off. If you go into long-term credit card debt again take the scissors to your card.

✔ Work out the cost/benefits of borrowing to finance new projects where you think the benefits may outweigh the costs.

✔ Read Chapter 5 page 93.

℘ Family protection

Every financial plan should contain some provision for insurance against the unexpected and the unpredictable. That includes protection against the financial loss that you and/or your dependants would suffer as a result of serious illness, disability or untimely death. It should also include some general insurance against other losses, house insurance, for instance.

With life insurance policies, it is important not to confuse saving for the future with actual life insurance which only pays a benefit in the event of death. Many policies include elements of both although that is not the case with what is known as term insurance which simply provides a guaranteed benefit, either a lump sum or an income, if death occurs within a fixed term of years. If the insured person is still alive at the end of the term, then no benefit is paid and it may seem like a waste of money. But the premiums have provided a very real benefit by way of peace of mind in much the same way as house or car insurance. People are generally pleased if they never have to make a claim on their house or car policies. They certainly have no reason to believe that the policies represented bad value just because they didn't have to claim. The same principle applies to term life insurance.

If the aim is to provide the maximum financial cushion for dependants in the event of your untimely death, then term insurance is the cheapest option. For the same death cover the premiums are significantly lower than for policies that do include a savings element. There is a trade off between the ideal level of protection and the premiums payable. But meaningful decisions on the balance to be taken must be based on a consideration of all the information. Having decided what you need, it can be well worthwhile shopping around for the best deal.

? Questions you should be asking yourself

- ☐ What events, over which I have no control, could cause me or my family to suffer significant financial loss? Which of them can I reasonably insure against?

- ☐ What financial loss would I or my family suffer in the event of my partner or I suffering illness, disability or death?

- ☐ How much of that potential loss should I insure against?

- ☐ What cover have I already got, including cover through company schemes?

☐ If my partner or I were to lose our jobs, would the impact be sufficiently severe to justify taking out some insurance protection for the repayment of loans?

☐ Have I sufficient cover on my house and other assets?

Actions to take

✔ Gather the information on the work sheet on page 326. Compare the cover you have with what you think you need.

✔ If you need additional cover, shop around for the cheapest option. Term insurance rates differ greatly from company to company for exactly the same cover. Take advice.

✔ Check out your general insurance policies. Shop around when they come up for renewal.

✔ Read chapter 4, page 74.

℅ Planning for retirement

There's a lot more to planning for retirement than simply ensuring an adequate income. But it's a good place to start. People are living longer and hoping to retire earlier. The income you'll have in retirement will generally depend on how much you have saved during your working life, either in a pension scheme or otherwise.

Saving through a pension fund makes good sense if only because of the generous tax relief available on contributions. The tax concession is available on up to 40% of income put into a pension fund and effectively means a State top-up of 41c for every 59c contributed by a top income tax payer. There can also be savings in PRSI and health levy payments. The top-up is less for those paying tax at the standard rate but it is still better than the one-for-four top-up which encouraged so many people to open SSIA accounts. The main drawback is that the fund cannot be accessed until retirement but that can be seen as a benefit if you are really saving for retirement.

Pension entitlements can be enhanced if you take action early enough. It's too late to start planning when you reach retirement age. Some pension schemes are better than others. If your scheme is not one of the best or if you are not going to have enough service to qualify for the maximum pension, there's undoubtedly scope for improving your entitlements and getting some tax relief in the process.

With many newer occupational pension schemes, the pension is determined by the amount of contributions made and the investment return on the fund. The same is true, of course, of personal pension plans taken out by the self-employed and by those not in occupational pension schemes.

It is particularly important with such schemes to regularly assess the likely future benefits since the outlook can change significantly with changing interest rates and stock market trends. You may want to increase your contributions if investment returns are not coming up to expectations.

? Questions you should be asking yourself

- ☐ **How adequate will my income be in retirement?**

- ☐ **What income will I need, or like to have?**

- ☐ **What pension can I currently look forward to?**

- ☐ **Are some of my existing savings and investments really earmarked for retirement?**

Actions to take

✔ Calculate how much it costs you to live now and how much you would ideally like to be able to spend in the future.

✔ Detail the income you can expect to have in retirement from existing entitlements.

✔ Do the calculations as accurately as you can. If you are in a company scheme, find out in detail how your pension is calculated. If it is based on "final pay" how is that defined? Is there provision for post-retirement increases? Will some pension continue to be paid to your spouse should you die?

✔ If you have your own personal pension plan or if you are in a defined contribution scheme that doesn't guarantee a pension based on final salary, what pension can you expect on current projections? How confident are you that those projections can be achieved?

✔ Check your entitlement to a State pension.

✔ If there is a shortfall between your potential income and your lifestyle aspirations then you should take advice on increasing your pension entitlement.

✔ If you are in an occupational scheme, examine the possibility of making additional voluntary contributions (AVCs) or opening an additional personal pension plan of your own.

✔ Look at the possibility of speeding up contribution, if you are a top-rate tax payer, or postponing them, if you are a standard rate payer, in anticipation of the expected standardisation of tax relief.

✔ If you are self-employed, you need to look at improving your personal pension scheme or starting one if you haven't already done so.

✔ Read chapter 10, page 171.

‰ Wills, inheritances

Everyone over 18 years of age, or younger if married, should have a will drawn up. It's particularly important, of course, where there are dependants. A will ensures that your estate is distributed in accordance with your plans. Once drawn up, wills should not just be put away and forgotten. They need to be reviewed from time to time. Personal circumstances change and so too does the tax code.

Inheritance tax isn't going to be a problem for most people inheriting from parents. But there are situations where a little advance planning can significantly reduce the tax payable. Wills must be in writing. While a simple will can be drawn up at home, it is well worthwhile getting a solicitor to oversee the task. The few euro it costs can save a lot of trouble in the long run. Tax advice is also advisable where the estate is large or some of it is going to people other than a spouse or children. Conferring an enduring power of attorney on a person of your choice allows him or her to look after your affairs in the event of you becoming unable to because of illness or disability. The role can be shared. It can also be limited and there is a range of legal protections. A living will, while of no legal import, can provide family and friends with an insight into your wishes should you lose the ability to make them known yourself.

Questions you should be asking yourself

☐ **Have I drawn up a will and, if so, does it still reflect my wishes?**

☐ **Do I need to change the executor?**

☐ **Have I considered the inheritance tax implications? If one person is to inherit the family home will he or she be able to benefit from the tax exemption on homes?**

☐ **Have I drawn up an enduring power of attorney? Should I draw up a living will?**

Actions to take

✔ Consider all the questions above and take the appropriate actions as soon as possible, seeking professional advice if you have any doubts over the impact of what you are doing.

✔ Read chapter 7 page 133.

Colm Rapple

Read my column every week, only in

Gathering information for your financial makeover

The first step in any financial review is to marshal the facts. You don't necessarily have to put them down in writing but it helps if you do. A little time spent filling in the worksheets on the following pages can help to concentrate the mind and aid the decision-making process. The worksheets provide only a suggested format. You may find it simpler to jot down the information on a separate sheet of paper.

But whether you do it in your mind or on paper, any financial review entails much the same approach. It involves a consideration of all your assets itemising the current value and the income it is currently generating and/or may generate in the future. You should include items like your house that could yield an income if you decided, for instance to trade down to a smaller home. Everything that could yield an income is relevant. It is worth ranking each investment according to risk.

These worksheets can be useful in assessing how best to achieve your financial goals

You could allocate a score between one and five – the higher the score the greater the risk that the value of your investment could go down. You might allocate a score of one to bank deposits, three to a broadly based managed fund and five to speculative shares. Liabilities, mainly borrowings, are the other side of the balance sheet. They need to be listed and assessed too. It can often make financial sense to borrow, while, at other times, it may make sense to use spare resources to pay off borrowings. Keeping an eye on income and expenditure trends can also be useful particularly if they start getting out of balance. Preparing a list of your insurance policies, such as suggested on the next page, may encourage you to review your needs and your existing cover from time to time. That can save you money so it's well worthwhile.

Safe, Strong, Secure.

Today 2.9 million members enjoy the benefits of credit union membership. Credit unions are based in communities and built on trust. Each individual credit union is owned and independently managed by its members. It's people just like you, who save with their credit union and borrow from it, who control it and share in its success.

So it's a good time to be part of your local credit union.

Credit unions are regulated by the Financial Regulator.

CU AT YOUR PLACE

creditunion.ie

Assets	Current value	Income	Rate of return	Risk rating
Savings accounts				
Investment funds				
Shares				
Business assets				
Family home				
Holiday home				
Boat, caravan				
Other				
Pension entitlements				
Total				

Liabilities	Amount due	Interest rate	Repayments
Mortgage			
Car loan			
Credit card debt			
Term loans			
Other loans			
Total			

Income		Notes
Salaries – net		
Child benefit		
Interest, dividends from savings and investments		
Other, self-employed income, asset sales etc.		
Occupational pension		
Social welfare pension		
Other		
Total income		

One of the golden rules of finance is that the demands on a family budget tend to exceed the amount of money available. The solutions fall into two categories. You can reduce spending demands or you can increase the supply of money. Neither option is easy.

If the money supply is fixed, then budgeting is going to involve economising and there are two approaches to that. You can zone in on the big items of spending and try to save on those or you can try to penny-pinch right across the board. Your personal make-up has a lot to do with which approach you adopt. But, in every case, it makes some sense to put a little structure on your budget.

Don't let the word "budget" put you off. Drawing up a budget can be as simple, or as complicated, as you like. The amount of detail is up to yourself. But even the simplest budget will help you to get the most from your spending.

For Home Insurance we tick **All** ✔ the right boxes...

- ✔ **24 Hour** Home Assist Emergency Service
- ✔ **Monthly** Payment Option
- ✔ **Audio & Visual** Equipment Cover
- ✔ **Home** Office Equipment Cover

- ✔ **Increased** Christmas & Wedding Time Cover
- ✔ **Optional** All Risks Cover

Plus... the backing and financial strength of Allianz

When you simply want it **All**

Allianz ⑪

Online Discounts Available

For a quote call: **1890 48 48 48** or visit **www.allianz.ie**
Freetext Quote to 50048

Expenditure		Notes
Mortgage/rent		
Loan repayments		
Electricity/gas		
Fuel/heating oil		
Telephone		
Life/medical insurance		
Car insurance/tax		
Household insurance		
TV – cable and licence		
Housekeeping		
Newspapers		
Petrol/public transport		
Meals out		
Entertainment/sport/hobbies		
Personal grooming		
Alcohol and tobacco		
Books, stationery etc.		
Medical expenses		
Clothing		
House maintenance		
Car maintenance		
Garden		
Donations etc.		
Holidays/Christmas		
Total expenditure		
Total income		From previous page
Surplus or shortfall		

CARRY ALL YOUR CASH IN A CARD

LASER

FAST · HANDY · SAFE

Life insurance Company	Policy number	Person insured	Purpose, cover and maturity date

General insurance		Policy number	Amount insured Notes
Type	Company		
House			
Car			
All risks			
Medical			
Disability			
Travel			

Other

Will – date
        when last reviewed
        where it can be found	

PPS Number	
Employer's tax number	
Credit card numbers	

STANDARD LIFE

Helping you feel confident about your financial *future*

Standard Life is one of Ireland's leading pension and investment providers. This year we're delighted to celebrate 175 years in Ireland, having set up our first business here in 1834.

Did you know that if you take out a Standard Life pension or investment policy in Ireland, your policy is protected by the Financial Services Compensation Scheme in the UK. It covers

- 100% of the value of their policy up to £2,000, plus
- 90% of the balance, **without limit**

in the event that Standard Life is in default.

There is no equivalent Irish compensation scheme.

Speak to your financial adviser about our range of pension and investments.

175 years in Ireland 1834 - 2009

Standard Life 90 St Stephen's Green Dublin 2
Telephone (01) 639 7000 Email customerservice@standardlife.ie Website www.standardlife.ie

Standard Life Assurance Limited adheres to codes of conduct issued by the Financial Regulator in Ireland and is authorised and regulated by the Financial Services Authority in the UK.

Income tax rate bands

2007

SINGLE
First €34,000 20%
Balance   41%

MARRIED (one income)
First €43,000 20%
Balance   41%

SINGLE PARENT
First €38,000 20%
Balance   41%

MARRIED (two income)
Up to €68,000 20%
Balance   41%

2008

SINGLE
First €35,400 20%
Balance   41%

MARRIED (one income)
First €44,440 20%
Balance   41%

SINGLE PARENT
First €39,400 20%
Balance   41%

MARRIED (two income)
Up to €70,800 20%
Balance   41%

2009

SINGLE
First €36,400 20%
Balance   41%

MARRIED (one income)
First €45,400 20%
Balance   41%

SINGLE PARENT
First €40,400 20%
Balance   41%

MARRIED (two income)
Up to €72,800 20%
Balance   41%

2010

SINGLE
First €36,400 20%
Balance   41%

MARRIED (one income)
First €45,400 20%
Balance   41%

SINGLE PARENT
First €40,400 20%
Balance   41%

MARRIED (two income)
Up to €72,800 20%
Balance   41%

QUINN'life

"Watch Your Investment Grow"
Investments, Savings, Pensions, ARFs & AMRFs

Start a QUINN-*life* policy today for:
- ✓ The EASY, LOW COST way to invest
- ✓ Low Annual Charges of 1% - 1.5% across Global Equity Funds
- ✓ View your policy details and performance online with the "My QUINN-*life*" online interactive web service

For further information call us on
1850 77 1851

QUINN-*life* direct Limited is regulated by the Financial Regulator. Terms & Conditions apply.

Warning: The value of your investment may go down as well as up. This product may be affected by changes in currency exchange rates.

www.**quinn-life**.com

Basic tax credits

	2006	2007	2008	2009	2010
Single	€1,630	€1,760	€1,830	€1,830	€1,830
Married	€3,260	€3,520	€3,660	€3,660	€3,660
Widowed	€1,630	€1,760	€1,830	€1,830	€1,830
– without dependent children	€2,130	€2,310	€2,430	€2,430	€2,430
Additional one-parent family	€1,630	€1,760	€1,830	€1,830	€1,830
Widowed parent – bereaved in					
2009	—	—	—	—	€4,000
2008	—	—	—	€4,000	€3,500
2007	—	—	€4,000	€3,500	€3,000
2006	€3,750	€3,500	€3,250	€3,000	€2,500
2005	€3,100	€3,250	€3,000	€2,500	€2,000
2004	€2,600	€2,750	€2,500	€2,000	—
Home carers	€770	€770	€900	€900	€900
Employee credit	€1,490	€1,760	€1,830	€1,830	€1,830
Age – single/widowed	€250	€275	€325	€325	€325
– married	€500	€550	€650	€650	€650
Blind – one spouse blind	€1,500	€1,760	€1,830	€1,830	€1,830
– both spouses blind	€3,000	€3,520	€3,660	€3,660	€3,660
Incapacitated child	€1,500	€3,000	€3,660	€3,660	€3,660
Dependant relative	€80	€80	€80	€80	€80
Carer for incapacitated person[1]	€10,000	€10,000	€10,000	€10,000	€10,000
Rent credit for under 55s (maximum)					
– single	€330	€360	€400	€400	€400
– married/widowed	€660	€720	€800	€800	€800
Rent credit for over 55s (maximum)					
– single	€660	€720	€800	€800	€800
– married/widowed	€1,320	€1,440	€1,600	€1,600	€1,600
Trade union subs		€60	€70	€70	€70

(1) These allowances are allowed at the taxpayer's top rate of tax. The tax credits shown, only reflect the relief at the standard rate. Those paying tax at the top rate get additional relief.

postbank

Your bank at the Post Office

Now you have a choice

Great value in banking and insurance

- Current Account
- Overdraft
- Savings and Investments
- Credit Card

- Car Insurance
- Home Insurance
- Life Assurance

Ask at your local Post Office

LoCall 1890 30 30 40 or log on to www.postbank.ie today!

Exemption limits

Persons whose income is below these limits are exempt from income tax.

	2005	2006	2008	2009	2010
Single/w'ed over 65	€17,000	€19,000	€20,000	€20,000	€20,000
Married over 65	€34,000	€38,000	€40,000	€40,000	€40,000

The limits increase by €571 for the first and second child and €825 for each subsequent child. Persons earning more than these exemption limits are entitled to marginal relief. Their total tax liability can be no more than 40% of the income above the threshold.

PRSI and health levy

PRSI rates (including the health levy) for 2007 to 2009 applicable to most private sector and State employees, are as follows.
See page 240 for full details of the PRSI and income levies for 2010.

		Private Sector	State Sector	Self Employed
2007	First €48,800	6%	3.15%	5%
	Next €51,300	2%	2%	5%
	Remainder	2.5%	2.5%	5%
2008	First €50,700	6%	3.15%	5%
	Next €49.400	2%	2%	5%
	Remainder	2.5%	2.5%	5%
2009				
to April30	First €52,000	6%	3.15%	5%
	Next €48,100	2%	2%	5%
	Remainder	2.5%	2.5%	5.5%
From May 1	First €75,036	8%	5.15%	7%
	Next €48,100	2%	2%	5%
	Remainder	2.5%	2.5%	5%

No PRSI is payable on the first €127 weekly earned by those paying the 6% rate. For those paying the lower rate the first €26 is exempt. Those earning less than €500 in any week are exempt from the 2% health levy and those earning less than €352 are exempt from PRSI.

Family Protection from AIB

How would your family cope without your income?
Take steps to secure your family financially
whatever the future holds.

Call into any AIB branch today to make
an appointment with one of our financial advisers.

be with AIB

Capital Acquisitions Tax

Threshold Levels

Relationship to donor	2007	2008	2009	From 20/11/2009
Child, or the minor child of a deceased child. Also from child to parent but only for inheritance tax. Since December 6, 2000 foster children enjoy the same tax threshold as natural and adopted children.	€496,824	€521,208	542,544	434,000
Brother, sister, child of brother or sister or lineal descendant other than a child, or the minor child of a deceased child	€49,682	€52,121	54,254	43,400
If none of the above	€24,843	€26,060	27,127	21,700

For gifts and inheritances received between December 1, 1999 and November 20, 2009 the tax was charged at a rate of 20%. It was increased to 22% from November 20, 2008 and to 25% in respect of gifts and inheritancs received on or after April 8, 2009

There are major concessions for agricultural land passing to a farmer; for business assets, and for businesses or farms passing to a nephew or niece who has worked on the farm or in the business for at least five years. Since December 1999, a house left to someone who has been living in it for at least three years is exempt from the tax, subject to certain conditions— **see page 273**.

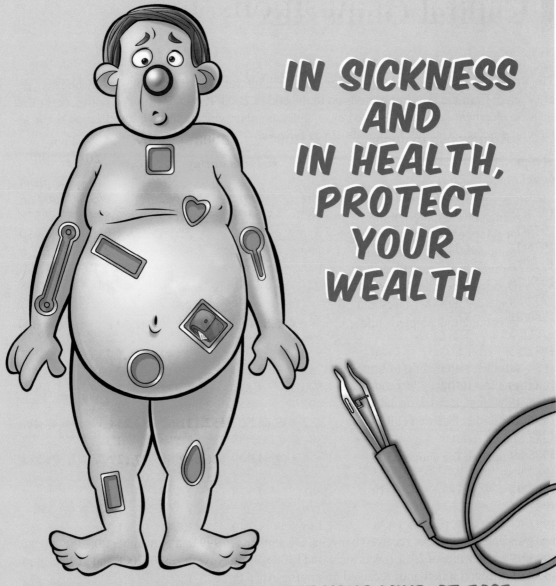

IN SICKNESS AND IN HEALTH, PROTECT YOUR WEALTH

INCOME PROTECTOR COULD PUT YOUR MIND AT EASE

You work hard to keep your family happy and secure. But what would happen if you became ill and had to stop working? There is a very simple solution to remove this worry. With **'Income Protector'** from Irish Life, you will receive a monthly income which can significantly help if you're unable to work due to illness or injury.

Irish Life

Irish Life is Ireland's largest provider of Income Protection. We provide cover during prolonged illness or injury for over 200,000 people. To find out more about the benefits of **'Income Protector'** and how it could help you, contact your Financial Adviser, visit **www.irishlife.ie** or call **1850 356 200** today.

Capital Gains Tax

The first €1,270 of gains made by an individual (€2,540 for a married couple) in any one tax year are exempt from the tax. For periods up to the end of 2003, the acquisition price of assets other than development land, is multiplied by an index number which adjusts it for inflation in the intervening period. The index numbers are as follows:-

Assets bought in				And sold during			from
	1998/99	1999/00	2000/01	2001*	2002	2003	2004 on
1974/75	6.215	6.313	6.582	6.930	7.180	7.528	7.528
1975/76	5.020	5.099	5.316	5.597	5.799	6.080	6.080
1976/77	4.325	4.393	4.580	4.822	4.996	5.238	5.238
1977/78	3.707	3.766	3.926	4.133	4.283	4.490	4.490
1978/79	3.425	3.479	3.627	3.819	3.956	4.148	4.148
1979/80	3.090	3.139	3.272	3.445	3.570	3.742	3.742
1980/81	2.675	2.718	2.833	2.983	3.091	3.240	3.240
1981/82	2.211	2.246	2.342	2.465	2.554	2.678	2.678
1982/83	1.860	1.890	1.970	2.074	2.149	2.253	2.253
1983/84	1.654	1.680	1.752	1.844	1.911	2.003	2.003
1984/85	1.502	1.525	1.590	1.674	1.735	1.819	1.819
1985/86	1.414	1.436	1.497	1.577	1.633	1.713	1.713
1986/87	1.352	1.373	1.432	1.507	1.562	1.637	1.637
1987/88	1.307	1.328	1.384	1.457	1.510	1.583	1.583
1988/89	1.282	1.303	1.358	1.430	1.481	1.553	1.553
1989/90	1.241	1.261	1.314	1.384	1.434	1.503	1.503
1990/91	1.191	1.210	1.261	1.328	1.376	1.442	1.442
1991/92	1.161	1.179	1.229	1.294	1.341	1.406	1.406
1992/93	1.120	1.138	1.186	1.249	1.294	1.356	1.356
1993/94	1.099	1.117	1.164	1.226	1.270	1.331	1.331
1994/95	1.081	1.098	1.144	1.205	1.248	1.309	1.309
1995/96	1.054	1.071	1.116	1.175	1.218	1.277	1.277
1996/97	1.033	1.050	1.094	1.152	1.194	1.251	1.251
1997/98	1.017	1.033	1.077	1.134	1.175	1.232	1.232
1998/99	—	1.016	1.059	1.115	1.156	1.212	1.212
1999/00	—	—	1.043	1.098	1.138	1.193	1.193
2000/01	—	—	—	1.053	1.091	1.144	1.144
2001	—	—	—	—	1.037	1.087	1.087
2002	—	—	—	—	—	1.049	1.049
from 2003 on	—	—	—	—	—	—	1.000

* period from 6/4/2001 to 31/12/2001

ENGAGE WITH YOUR

PENSION

www.pensionsboard.ie

Pension
Calculator

Information
Booklets

Pension
Checklist

An Bord Pinsean -
The Pensions Board
Authority for Pensions

Civil Service Mileage

Per mile

Official travel in a calendar year	Under 1200cc	1,201cc to 1,500cc	1,501cc and over
Up to 4,000 miles	62.94c	74.42c	95.05c
4,001 miles and over	34.13c	38.00c	45.79c
Reduced rate	23.55c	26.76c	31.36c

Per kilometre

Official travel in a calendar year	Under 1200cc	1,201cc to 1,500cc	1,501cc and over
Up to 6,437km	39.12c	46.25c	59.07c
6,438km and over	21.22c	23.62c	28.46c
Reduced rate	14.65c	16.64c	19.49c

The reduced rate applies where the journey is connected with official business but not actually in the discharge of that business. These rates apply from March 5, 2009.

Motoring benefit-in-kind

The use of a company car is assessed for tax as a benefit-in-kind. The assessment is based on a percentage of the original market value of the car, depending on the business mileage done during the year.

Business miles	CO_2 emissions up to 155g/km	156g/km 190g/km	over 191g/km
Under 24,000	30%	35%	40%
24,001 to 32,000	24%	28%	32%
32,001 to 40,000	18%	21%	24%
40,001 to 48,000	12%	14%	16%
Above 48,000	6%	7%	8%

You know what?
Our pension matured and wasn't
affected by the stock market dip.

The Zurich Eagle Star Pension
delivers when it matters.

By choosing the Lifestyle Option, your money is directed
into lower risk funds as retirement age approaches to
safeguard the return on your investment.

There are pensions and there are
Zurich Eagle Star Pensions.

For more information, talk to your financial advisor,
call 1850 202 102 or visit www.zurichlife.ie

**Warning: The value of your investment
may go down as well as up.**

Social Insurance

Maximum rates of benefit	2009	2010[1]
State pension (contributory)/(transition)		
Under 80		
— Personal rate	€230.30	€230.30
— Person with qualified adult under 66	€383.80	€383.80
— Person with qualified adult over 66	€436.60	€436.60
80 or over		
— Personal rate	€240.30	€240.30
— Person with qualified adult under 66	€393.80	€393.80
— Person with qualified adult over 66	€446.60	€446.60
Widow's/Widower's Contributory Pension		
— Under 66	€209.80	€201.50
— 66 and under 80	€230.30	€230.30
— 80 or over	€240.30	€240.30
Invalidity Pension		
Personal rate under 65	€209.80	€201.50
Personal rate 65 to 80	€230.30	€230.30
Personal rate 80 or over	€240.30	€240.30
Person under 65 with qualified adult	€359.50	€345.30
Person 65 to 80 with qualified adult [2]	€436.60	€436.60
Person over 80 with qualified adult [2]	€446.60	€446.60
Jobseeker's/Illness Benefit[3]		
Personal rate	€204.30	€196.00
Person with qualified adult	€339.90	€326.10
Guardian's payment (contributory)	€176.50	€169.00
Payments for child dependants		
All schemes — Each qualified child	€26.00	€29.80

Note: 1. *From January 1, 2010.* **2.** *Over 66.* **3.** *Lower rates apply to new claimants under 25 after December 30, 2009.*

Social Assistance

Maximum weekly rates of social assistance	*2009*	*2010*[1]
State pension (non-contributory)		
Under 80		
— Personal rate	€219.00	€219.00
— Person with qualified adult	€363.70	€363.70
80 or over		
— Personal rate	€229.00	€229.00
— Person with qualified adult	€373.70	€373.70
Widow's/Widower's non-contributory pension		
— Under 66	€204.30	€196.00
— 66 and under 80	€219.00	€219
— 80 or over	€229.00	€229.00
Disability allowance		
— Personal rate	€204.30	€196.00
— Person with qualified adult	€339.90	€326.10
Jobseeker's allowance [2]		
— Personal rate	€204.30	€196.00
— Person with qualified adult	€339.90	€326.10
Supplementary welfare allowance		
— Personal rate	€204.30	€196.00
— Person with qualified adult	€339.90	€326.10
One-parent family payment *(including one child)*		
— Under 66	€230.30	€225.80
Carer's allowance		
— Under 66	€220.50	€212.00
— 66 years and over	€239.00	€239.00
Increases for child dependants		
— All schemes	€26	€29.80
Child benefit		
For first and second child	€166.00	€150.00
For third child onwards	€203.00	€187.00

Note: *1. From January 1, 2010. 2. Lower rates apply to new claimants under 25 after December 30, 2009.*

Index

A

Annuities   52 - 55
APR   95
Assurance
    see life insurance   74

B

Bank deposit guarantees   49
Benefits in kind
    taxed and tax free   243
Borrowing   93
    APR   95
    Finance houses   99
    Pawnbrokers   107
    Term loans   98
    Top-up mortgages   100
Budget accounts   98
Building societies
    Personal loans   99
Business Expansion Scheme   292

C

Capital allowances   262
    Motor cars   265
Capital Gains Tax   269
Charge cards   20, 26 - 27
Consumer protection   188
    Deposit guarantees   49
    European union   201
    Financial advisers   193
    Financial Services Ombudsman   192
    Goods and services   202 - 203
    Insurance   88
    Life insurance   87
    Pensions ombudsman   177
    Solicitors   193
    Unfair contracts   204 - 205
    Using your rights   206
Consumer Protection Act   188
Credit Cards   20
    Borrowing   107
    Insurance   166
    The rules   28
Credit ratings   198
Credit Unions   48, 106

D

Data Protection Act   194
Debit cards   20, 27
Debt, tackling problems   108
Deposit accounts   47
DIRT
    Rate of tax   50
    Reclaiming   50
    Tax free accounts for over 65s   50
Divorce   138

E

Employment legislation   142
    Emergency time off   156
    Equality rights   153
    Holiday entitlements   148 - 149
    Maternity leave   156 - 157
    Minimum notice   153
    Minimum wage   150 - 151
    Parental leave   156
    Redundancy entitlements   144 - 146
    Unfair dismissal   152
Equality rights   153
Executors   139

F

Fair deal nursing home payment   219
Family home
    rights to   138
Farmers
    Budget changes   226
    Capital acquisitions tax   275
Freedom of Information Act   197

G

Guaranteed bonds   52

H

Health insurance   90 - 92
Hire purchase   106
Holiday Money   32
House insurance
    All risks   170
    Buildings   164 - 165
    Contents   167
    Switching   201

House purchase   111
   Affordable housing scheme   126
   Costs   119
   Grants   126
   Mortgage tax relief   130

I

Impaired life annuities   53
Inheritance
   Capital Acquisition Tax   273
   Joint bank accounts   16
Interest rates
   APR   95
Investment funds   57
   Switching   62

J

Judicial separation   138

L

Laser cards   20
Life insurance   74
   Borrowing against   106 - 107
   Buying   84, 86
   Critical illness   82
   Disability   81
   Endowment   79
   Income protection   81
   Term   76
   Whole of life   79

M

Marital breakdown
   Pension rights   187
Medical expenses
   Tax relief   234
Medical insurance   90
Minimum notice   153
Minimum wage   150 - 151
Mobile phone insurance   166
Money makeover
   Worksheets   318
   Your guide   301
Mortgages
   Endowment versus annuity   117
   Home Choice Loan   118
   Local Authority loans   118
   Options list   116
   Tax relief   130
   Top-up mortgages   100

N

National Consumer Agency   188
Nursing home 'fair deal' payment 219
Nursing home fair deal   219

P

Part-time workers
   Social welfare   209
Pensions   171
   AVCs   147
   Defined benefit   176
   Defined contribution   178
   Last minute AVCs   174
   Legal rights of members   177
   Marital breakdown   187
   Maximum contributions   238
   Occupational schemes   176 - 179
   Options on retirement   184
   Social welfare   210
Personal liability insurance   169
Post Office Investment Schemes   50
   Instalment Saving   51
   Saving Certificates   51
   Savings Bonds   50
Postbank   50
Power of attorney   135
Probate, taking out   140
PRSI
   Rates   240

Q

Quinn Health Care   91

R

Redundancy entitlements
   Tax   145
Rental income
   payable to non-residents   266
   Rent a room tax relief   121, 132
   Tax treatment   263
Revenue online service ROS   260

S

Same-sex couples
   Emergency time off work   156
Saving
   Regular Saving Accounts   48
Small Claims Court   196
Social welfare
   Budget changes 2010   208

Contributory pension 210, 214
Family Income Supplement 215
Free telephone rental 224
Free travel 222
Free TV licence 224
Medical cards 216 - 218
Part-time workers 209
Rates of payment 340
Transitional State Pension 214
Stock Exchange
Shares and stocks 54
Store budget accounts 105
Store Cards 29
Sunday work
Entitlement to pay 151

T
Tax
Benefits in kind 243
Calculating liability 252
Company cars 247
eWorkers 250
Income tax certs 231
Income tax credits 232

On inheritances and gifts 273
On investment funds 58
On rental income 263
PAYE 229
Personal allowances 232
Reducing your bill 227
Rent a room tax relief 132
Summary of rates 328
Tracker bonds 51
Travel insurance 35

U
Unfair dismissal 152 - 153
Unit funds 58 - 59
Unit trusts 58

V
VHI 90

W
Wills 133
Duties of executors 139
Living will 137
Taking out probate 140
Working hours 149